GUIDE TO THE ACACIAS

ACACIAS
OF SOUTH AFRICA

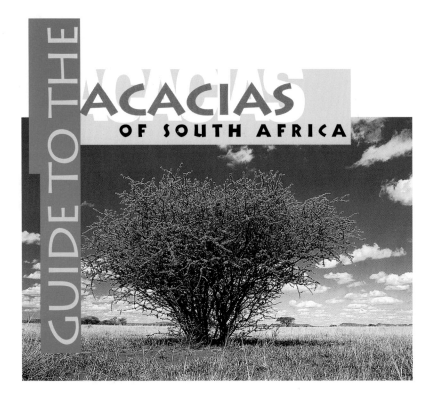

GUIDE TO THE

ACACIAS
OF SOUTH AFRICA

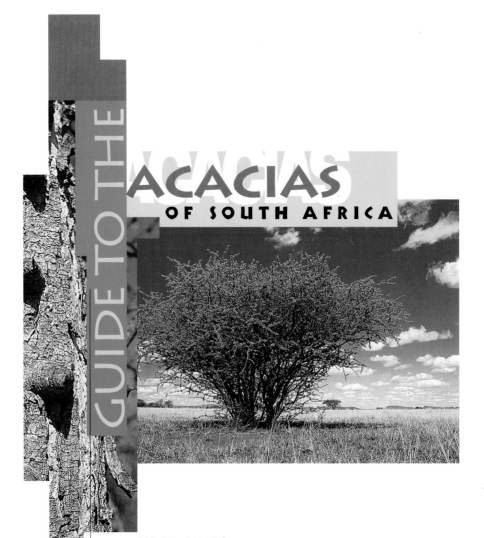

NICO SMIT

BRIZA

Published by Briza Publications

CK 90/11690/23

P.O. Box 56569
Arcadia
0007
Pretoria
South Africa

First Edition 1999

Text and photographs © Nico Smit
Cover design by Andrew Breebaart
Language edited by Debbie Schroeder
Book design & layout by Suzanne Enslin, Antworks
Reproduction by Unifoto, Cape Town, South Africa
Printed and bound by Tien Wah Press, Singapore

ISBN 1 875093 15 X

CONTENTS

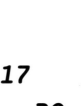

ACKNOWLEDGEMENTS

Compiling a book of this kind is impossible without the support and assistance of a host of people. While it is impossible to name every person who has made a contribution, I would like to thank the following people in particular:

Nic Zambatis of the Kruger National Park for collecting material and arranging accommodation and permission to photograph in the Kruger National Park. Errol Pieterson, also of the Kruger National Park, for providing an accompanying game ranger during field work. The following people are also thanked for collecting material and assisting in fieldwork: Dr. Hugo Bezuidenhout of the South African National Parks in Kimberley, Arnaud le Roux of Ecoguard, Brian Robinson and Johan Swart of the Towoomba Agricultural Development Centre, Chris Richter of the Glen Agricultural Development Institute, Theunis Meyer of the Department of Agriculture, North West Province and Marc Stalmans of the Mpumalanga Parks Board in Nelspruit. Fanie Venter for providing valuable information and encouragement, and Prof. Johan Venter of the University of the Orange Free State for providing the meanings of the botanical (Latin) names of some of the species. Marthinus Steyn is thanked for permission to use his illustration of the flowers of *Acacia goetzei*. My colleagues at the Department of Grassland Science of the University of the Orange Free State are thanked for their support and encouragement.

I would like to thank Deon Marais (Department of Environmental Affairs and Tourism, Pretoria) for permission to use their biome map and for preparing this particular map for publishing.

My sincere thanks also go to Briza Publications, and in particular to Frits and Ilse Van Oudtshoorn for their patience, support and encouragement.

Lastly I want to thank my wife Lizette, not only for her support and encouragement during my many long journeys in search of illustrations and study material, but also for her invaluable assistance in reading the manuscript, offering advice and corrections.

Nico Smit

INTRODUCTION

The vegetation of South Africa is extremely diverse and includes some of the richest floral areas in the world. Broadly speaking, South Africa comprises of 7 different vegetation biomes (Savanna, Grassland, Nama Karoo, Succulent Karoo, Fynbos, Forest and Thicket). While some of the South African *Acacia* species, like *A. karroo*, have an extensive distribution range that includes several biomes, the savanna biome (bushveld) is clearly distinct with the highest concentration of *Acacia* species. The Spanish term savanna, once restricted to describe central South American grasslands, is now widely accepted as describing vegetation with a herbaceous layer, dominated by graminoids (grasses), with an upper layer of woody plants which can vary from widely spaced to a 75 % canopy cover occurring in a seasonal summer rainfall environment. The savanna biome is the largest South African biome and covers an area of 408 876 km^2, which is 33.49 % of the country. Within the savanna biome, the *Acacia* species, of which 40 species, subspecies and varieties are represented in South Africa, is a well-known and distinctive feature. They belong to the Family Mimosaceae, which is the third-largest woody plant family in southern Africa. Though woody plants are not such a prominent feature of other biomes like the Grassveld and Nama Karoo, *Acacia* trees may often form local dominant stands. The ecological, economical, socio-economical and aesthetical importance of the *Acacia* group of woody plants cannot be underestimated and some of these are highlighted in the discussion on the following pages:

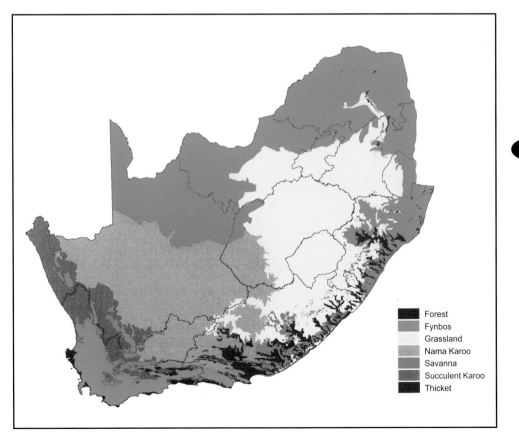

Biomes of South Africa (Low, A.B. and Rebelo, A.G. (eds) 1996. Department of Environmental Affairs and Tourism, Pretoria)

Legend:
- Forest
- Fynbos
- Grassland
- Nama Karoo
- Savanna
- Succulent Karoo
- Thicket

GROWTH AND REPRODUCTION

Growth refers to the vegetative growth of established plants, while reproduction refers to the ability of mature trees to flower and produce viable seeds, the dispersal and germination of these seeds and the survival of the newly-established seedlings.

Some determinants of vegetative growth of woody plants, and thus also the *Acacia* species, include tree age, competition, defoliation and shoot pruning, carbohydrate reserves and plant hormones, soil water availability and water stress, soil nutrient availability and various other soil and climatic conditions.

In most savanna tree species, including the *Acacia* species, young trees display a faster growth rate than older trees. Competition from neighbouring trees will also affect the growth rate of the trees. It was shown that *A. nilotica* trees, whose neighbours within a five metre radius were removed, showed a significant increase in both stem diameter increment and shoot extension when compared with control trees. In an *Acacia* community at Nylsvley, dominated by *A. tortilis* and *A. nilotica*, the growth of mature trees was reduced by competition from the grass-dominated herbaceous layer. This was ascribed to the grasses taking up topsoil water (0–30 cm) at a rate sufficient to reduce drainage into the subsoil (30–130 cm), thus lowering the volume of subsoil water available to the trees.

Browsing by herbivores may stimulate growth, provided that the browsing is not too intense. One theory for the observed rapid regrowth of shoots of some *Acacia* species like *A. nigrescens* and *A. tortilis*, pruned by browsers, is reduced intershoot competition for nutrients. Interestingly, it was found that *A. karroo* trees reacted differently to defoliation of the upper canopy than to defoliation of the lower canopy. It was shown that a 100 % defoliation of the upper canopy only, resulted in the same amount of growth as when trees were completely defoliated, while a 100 % defoliation of the lower canopy only, stimulated growth to the same degree as defoliation of the whole canopy at 25–50 %.

It has been shown that carbohydrate reserves are important in the regrowth of *A. karroo*, but growth is inhibited under certain circumstances where carbohydrate supplies appear to be adequate. This was ascribed to a deficiency of plant hormones. *A. karroo* trees are very sensitive to defoliation in the early-flush phenophase when carbohydrate reserves are at their lowest, and are very tolerant of defoliation when reserves are high.

Increased atmospheric CO_2 concentrations may also have an effect on the different floristic components of ecosystems. Increases in atmospheric CO_2 improve water-use efficiency and increase carbon uptake in C_3 plants. All the South African *Acacia* species are C_3 plants. However, there is as yet no conclusive evidence that elevated CO_2 levels in the atmosphere are contributing to the encroachment of *Acacia* species into C_4 grasslands.

Another form of vegetative growth, especially important in dry deciduous savannas, is leaf emergence and leaf senescence. Species differ in these respects. At Nylsvley leaf fall is initiated much earlier in *A. mellifera* than in *A. burkei* and *A. caffra*. In the Kruger National Park, young *A. nigrescens* trees tended to retain some leaves over the dry season, whereas the mature trees generally lost most of their leaves. The same phenomenon was recorded for *A. burkei* at Nylsvley. Leaf retention by saplings of winter-deciduous species may, in part, be attributed to late summer shoot growth in response to damage by browsing herbivores. Data from pruning trials on *A. tortilis* showed that shoots of pruned trees were significantly more leafy in winter than shoots of control trees at the same site. Regarding shoot growth, a prolonged growth in young *A. nigrescens* trees in comparison with adult trees was also recorded.

Rainfall also affects leaf drop in general. Leaf fall as a result of water stress is often used as a drought avoidance strategy. Water stress may also inhibit shoot growth as demonstrated by the shoot production and basal increment of *A. tortilis* that were found to be positively correlated with rainfall and indicators of soil water.

Dieback, either partial or complete, may be a concurrent event, directly opposed to vegetative growth. Causes of partial or complete dieback of woody plants include drought, fire, pathogens, cold damage and severe impact from herbivores, especially mega-herbivores. Related to the dieback of even-aged populations of *A. xanthophloea*, it was suggested that individuals in an even-age stand may survive a number of occasional stressful events when young and more vigorous, but may succumb to an event in itself no worse than the others, but which occurs after the trees have begun to senesce. Biotic agents may act as tertiary or dieback-hastening causes. Such biotic agents are the fungi *Phoma glomorata*, *P. cava*, *P. eupyrena* and *Cytospora chrysosperma* which cause a dieback disease that has already killed thousands of hectares of *A. mellifera* subsp. *detinens* trees in Namibia.

The most common effect of a hot fire on woody vegetation is "top kill" whereby the above-ground parts of the tree are destroyed or damaged. These trees are seldom killed by the fire and coppice re-growth from the collar region of the stem usually occurs, resulting in structural changes. Some *Acacia* species are more resistant to fire than others, and most *Acacia* species become more resistant to fire as their height increases. Some species differences do occur as in the case of *A. erioloba* where there are indications that older trees may be more fire sensitive.

The occurrence of dwarf growth forms of some *Acacia* species under certain conditions is an example of impairment of vegetative growth or dieback. These dwarf growth forms are often due to limitations in the

Elephants favour many *Acacia* species as fodder plants and they have the ability to drastically alter the structure of the vegetation as demonstrated by the damage done to this *A. tortilis* tree.

soil or severe impact from browsing herbivores. African savannas have an evolutionary history of high levels of browsing ungulate herbivory, capable of significantly modifying the structure and composition of woody plants. Browsing herbivores may include small herbivores and mega-herbivores, notably elephants.

Seeds of many tree species have a seasonal dormancy, which prevents the seed from germinating under unfavourable environmental conditions. Dormancy can be due to the seed coat preventing or interfering with water uptake, mechanical restraint or prevention of leaching of inhibitors. The *Acacia* species are noted for their hard-seededness that varies from 18 % in *A. caffra* to 96 % in *A. sieberiana*.

The pericarp of seeds of some woody species contains allelochemicals, which inhibit seed germination and seedling growth of that species. The presence of these substances in the seeds of *Acacia* species is largely unknown.

Pods and seeds of various *Acacia* species are often ingested by a variety of herbivores. In passing through the gut of herbivores, seeds of some species may be digested and killed, while others with hard impermeable seed coats, survive. Germination of these seeds is often improved by scarification by digestive fluids, while being dispersed when defecated. Small seeds may escape mastication, but larger seeds often do not escape mastication and are destroyed or suffer extensive structural damage. In one experiment the percentage of seeds that survived through the gut of elephant, giraffe, kudu and impala ranged from as low as 2.1 % in the case of *A. caffra* ingested by giraffe to as high as 50.4 % of *A. karroo* ingested by elephant. *Acacia* seeds that have been chewed and discarded by rodents may also germinate better than unchewed seeds. This was found to be the case in *A. tortilis* and *A. nilotica* where chewed seeds exhibited a greater germination than unchewed seeds. Burial of seeds by rodents may also contribute to the spread of some woody species.

The influence of a diverse range of other environmental conditions on the germination of the seeds of many species has been demonstrated by various laboratory experiments, illustrating the influence of varying temperature, light regimes, substrate salinity, pH, soaking in water, seed age, soil type and depth of sowing on the germination of seeds.

Because of hard-seededness, species like *A. nilotica* and *A. tortilis* may form persistent soil seed banks that can remain viable for a period of at least 1–5 years. Such seed banks may number several hundred to several thousand seeds per m^2.

Seeds of some Australian *Acacia* species have been shown to be viable after 50 years. Seeds that are buried in the soil exhibit greater persistence than those exposed on the soil surface. Larger seeds may also have greater longevity in the soil than smaller seeds, while more spherical seeds would be buried more deeply than larger, less spherical seeds. Germination may be impaired when seeds have been heavily parasitized and invertebrates may damage seedlings. It was shown that predation of *A. erioloba* seeds in the Kuiseb River valley by bruchid beetles was significantly lower in canopy-held pods than pods on the ground. Infestation of seeds by bruchid beetles may affect species differently. As an example the germination of *A. gerrardii* seeds were negatively influenced by bruchid beetle infestation, while infestation promoted early germination and establishment in *A. sieberiana*. Some seeds may escape predation, and the large number of seeds produced in some instances increase the possibility of escape. It is estimated that a single mature *A. tortilis* tree can produce up to 50 000 seeds.

An example of a heavy infestation of the seeds of *A. hebeclada* by bruchid beetles.

Young seedlings that are highly palatable are also damaged by mammalian herbivores. Fire may destroy seeds of some *Acacia* species, but incidents of enhanced germination of seeds have been reported. As an example a high emergence of *A. sieberiana* seedlings (172 seedlings per m²) were observed after a fire of high intensity compared with unburned areas (6 seedlings per m²). Fire might not prevent seedling establishment, but may retard the development of seedlings.

An important determinant of the establishment of *Acacia* seedlings is competition from other plants, either from other woody plants or herbaceous plants. As an example it was demonstrated that trees of communities dominated by *A. senegal – A. tortilis* and *Euclea divinorum – A. nilotica* have characteristic dispersal strategies. These were manifested through intra- and inter-

specific competition among the dominant tree species. *Acacia senegal* became dominant in areas previously dominated by *A. tortilis*, while *E. divinorum* was replacing previous dominance by *A. nilotica*.

Tree-on-tree competition appears to be species specific or related to the shade tolerance of the seedlings. In some, seedling establishment is unaffected by a tree canopy while in others, establishment is limited to between-canopy environments. In the eastern Cape, shading increased the density of surviving *A. karroo* seedlings, while at Nylsvley in the Northern Province shading decreased the density of surviving *A. tortilis* seedlings. In another study it was established that, for example, *Euclea divinorum* does have the ability to establish under canopies, while seedlings of several *Acacia* species are distinctive as they fail to establish under the canopy of any established individual, regardless of species. Significant positive correlations between the size of a tree and the distance to its nearest neighbour were reported for some *Acacia* species.

Overgrazing of grasses is often the main cause of woody plant increase. Under conditions of prolonged overgrazing the exclusion of competition from a vigorous grass layer can benefit the establishment of *Acacia* seedlings. *Acacia* species notorious for encroachment into grasslands include *A. mellifera*, *A. erubescens*, *A. karroo* and several others.

The importance of competition from grasses as a determinant of woody seedling establishment is reflected in several studies. On a site dominated by *A. tortilis* and *A. nilotica* it was observed that large numbers of seedlings germinated and survived in a plot cleared of herbaceous vegetation, while few were found in a control plot. However, it is important to note that a well-established grass layer may limit the number of *Acacia* seedlings that survived, but will not completely prevent the establishment of seedlings. For example, an experiment in the Eastern Cape showed that a well-established grass cover did not prevent the establishment of *A. karroo* seedlings after eradication of the mature trees.

VALUE AS FODDER

The presence of trees, in addition to grasses, provides for an additional food source, which is utilised by a variety of game species as well as domestic stock. Depending on the tree species, tree density and height structure, unique habitats are created, often with great aesthetical appeal. These habitats are often of considerable importance in ensuring genetic diversity since they are able to support a large number of grazer and browser herbivore species within the same area. They also support numerous smaller creatures like insects, which are of critical importance in the complex food chains that exist in these habitats. The potential of these areas in terms of eco-tourism and game farming is immense.

The potentially edible material of woody plants is often referred to as browse, and browse is most commonly regarded as the current season's growth of both leaves and shoots. Available browse is usually a more restricted quantity than browse, and in most studies available browse is determined simply on the basis of maximum height above ground to which a specified animal can utilise browse. The availability of browse below a specified browse height may be

Acacia species form an important part of the diet of a wide range of herbivore species like the giraffe feeding on *A. nigrescens* in the Mkuzi Game Reserve and these springbok browsing on *A. haematoxylon* in the Kalahari Gemsbok National Park.

reduced by obstruction of browse material towards the centre of the plant by dense branch entanglements, while leaf senescence of winter deciduous species will lower available browse during certain periods.

Browser herbivore species select among plant species as markedly as grazers do. The actual intake of available browse may be influenced by chemical defences of woody plants, as well as nutritional characteristics of leaves in different phenological stages. Chemical defences of plants may include chemical substances which may be poisonous or reduce palatability. A diverse array of secondary metabolites deters feeding by mammals on woody plants. Condensed tannins are especially important as a defence mechanism in woody plants. Tannins are a diverse group of compounds, widespread among dicotyledonous forbs and trees, which precipitate protein and sometimes act as a toxin rather than as a digestion inhibitor. Plants known to have chemical defences against vertebrate herbivory are prominent on nutrient-deficient soils, while those with structural defences like spines and prickles are predominant on fertile soils.

The effectiveness of these defences may vary between browser and woody species. In one study it was found that the leaves of *A. nigrescens* trees displayed a 70 % increase in tannin concentration 2 minutes after disturbance, followed by a further, delayed, response after 30 to 100 minutes after the disturbance. Giraffes subsequently select leaves with a low tannin content.

11

Regarding structural defences, it was found that the presence of straight spines on *Acacia* trees has little effect on the feeding of goats and impalas, while hooked spines and prickles are more effective deterrents. In some species the physical defences of juvenile and mature trees differ. For example it was found that juvenile *A. nilotica* trees were physically more heavily defended than mature plants.

Many *Acacia* species flower profusely, as in *A. tortilis* with up to 400 inflorescences per metre of twig, but only a small percentage develop into pods. These flowers form an important food supplement for many game species and livestock. Many insects are also utilising this food source. The pods of several *Acacia* species, especially those with indehiscent pods in which the seeds are retained, are highly palatable with a high crude protein content and play an important role in the nutrition of many herbivore species. The value of the pods and seeds as a feed supplement during the dry season has long been realized by pastoralists who actively collect pods to feed to their livestock. The pods of *A. erioloba* and *A. tortilis* are particularly favoured. The pods of *A. erioloba* can contain up to 6 % crude protein and the seeds up to 33 % crude protein and 3.5 % fat. The leaves of *A. erioloba* may contain up to 17 % crude protein with a digestibility of 35 %. However, the pods and young leaves of *A. erioloba* contain prussic acid and may cause poisoning in livestock. Similarly, the wilted leaves of *A. sieberiana* may also cause poisoning. The bark of a number of species is also stripped off by game, notably by elephant.

SOIL ENRICHMENT

Nutrients, such as nitrates, phosphorus, a series of anions and cations and various trace elements are essential to the nutrition of plants, and act as determinants of the composition, structure and productivity of vegetation. While the base-richness of the parent material is initially important in determining soil fertility, biological activities are important in the creation and maintenance of localised areas of enhanced soil fertility, often on base-poor substrates. Trees, and more specifically leguminous trees like the *Acacia* species, are important in establishing areas of enhanced soil fertility.

Ample evidence to support soil enrichment under tree canopies exists, and while soil enrichment was reported for a large variety of tree species, most comparative studies which have involved *Acacia* species (leguminous species) have shown that soil enrichment under their canopies was higher than under non-leguminous tree species. Studies have shown that soil under tree canopies has higher concentrations of Nitrogen, soil organic matter, Phosphate and exchangeable cations like Potassium, Magnesium and Calcium compared to soil from the open areas. In addition, soil under tree canopies often exhibits a higher pH and lower electrical resistance (high concentration of soluble salts) than soil between tree canopies. A higher pH under canopies of savanna trees will enhance the availability of exchangeable cations due to the positive association between increases in exchangeable cations and soil-pH (higher base saturation). The physical properties of soil under tree canopies may also differ from that in the open, the most notable the soil bulk density which may be lower (more porous) under tree canopies.

The influence of the tree canopy on the pattern of soil enrichment is clearly demonstrated by the gradient of soil nutrients found away from the trunk. The highest concentrations are often found adjacent to the trunks, and decline away from the trunk. However, evidence exists that soil enrichment under tree canopies is a slow process. This is demonstrated by correlations between total C and Nitrogen in soil under tree canopies and tree girth, an index of age.

The question of source and mechanism of soil enrichment under tree canopies remains largely unexplained. Many theories have been presented. Leaf litter from leaf fall has been mentioned as a possible source. In one experiment it was estimated that an *A. tortilis* community produced an amount of 2.32 ton litter per hectare annually. This litter consisted of 29 % leaves, 14 % flowers, 26 % pods and 31 % shoots. Structural differences in leaves of microphyllous (like *Acacia* species) and broad-leafed trees present a possible source of difference in the number of leaves reaching the soil under tree canopies, the latter being more subject to further dispersion by wind.

Stemflow and throughfall represent another source of mineral input to soil. Experiments have shown that throughfall and stemflow chemistry differed significantly from that of precipitation above the tree canopy. The occurrence of Nitrogen fixation due to microbial activities under leguminous trees is a possible source of N enrichment, and legume-*Rhizobium* symbiotic systems proof to be the most important. It was also shown that Nitrogen concentrations in leaves were substantially higher in potentially N_2-fixing tree species than in non-N_2-fixing tree species.

Droppings of birds and dung of large mammals spending loafing time under trees have also been mentioned as a source of soil enrichment.

INTERACTION WITH THE GRASS LAYER

In savanna, negative competition interaction between woody plants and grasses has been demonstrated by several studies. This negative competition interaction is mainly for available soil water, and high tree densities, especially in the more arid savannas, will suppress the grass layer. The increase in tree density is commonly referred to as bush encroachment and it is considered by farmers to be a serious problem in large areas of the savanna. Several *Acacia* species contribute to the problem of bush encroachment. The reasons for woody plants increasing in density are complex, the most notable being long term overgrazing of the grass layer, the exclusion of sporadic hot fires and the exclusion of browser herbivore

An increase in tree density at the cost of grasses is commonly referred to as bush encroachment. This phenomenon is clearly illustrated by this dense stand of mainly *A. erubescens* trees.

species. In areas with high tree densities a reduction in tree density, either mechanically or chemically (arboricides), will usually result in an increase in grass production. For example, in the Kalahari Thornveld increases of between 220 % to 740 % in grass production was measured after aerial applications of an arboricide to dense stands of *A. mellifera* and *A. luederitzii*.

The reduction in grass production (and grazing capacity) attributed to an increase in woody plant density, appears to differ between savanna types. The grazing capacity of veld is defined as the productivity of the grazeable portion of the vegetation expressed as the area of land required to maintain a single animal unit over an extended number of years without deterioration to the vegetation or soil. It is normally expressed as the number of hectare (ha) required per animal unit. An animal unit in turn is defined as an animal with a mass of 450 kg which gains 0.5 kg per day on forage with a digestible energy percentage of 55 %.

Clearing woody plants in mixed savanna dominated by *Combretum apiculatum* and *A. tortilis* resulted in an improvement in the grazing capacity from 9.1 ha per animal unit to only 7.3 ha per animal unit, while a reduction in tree density in the Kalahari Thornveld improved the grazing capacity from 45.8 ha per animal unit (230 kg grass dry matter per ha) to 8.7 ha per animal unit (1200 kg grass grass dry matter per ha). These differences may be ascribed to differences in soil type and soil fertility, which are considered important determinants of the magnitude of increased grass production after tree thinning. In years of high rainfall, higher grass yields are attained in thornveld on relatively fertile clay soils than in sandveld on nutrient-poor soils. On an *A. nigrescens* dominated site in the lowveld areas of the Northern Province, cleared of all woody plants, the increase in herbaceous production ranged from 300–2 500 kg per ha. During a period of prolonged water stress an increase in dead grass tufts was also recorded in the uncleared plots.

The reaction of the herbaceous layer to tree removal largely depends on rainfall. The roots of woody plants are fundamental in their competitive interaction with the grasses. Roots determine the spatial distribution of water and nutrient uptake and can cause an increase or a decrease in resource availability. The roots of savanna woody plants normally extend far beyond their projected crown radius (horizontal distribution) and lesser distances for herbaceous plants. In some *Acacia* species, like *A. mellifera*, the lateral roots can extend linearly up to seven times or more the extent of the canopy-spread.

When considering the vertical distribution of roots, ample evidence exists to suggest that the roots of savanna trees are often concentrated at a very shallow depth. However, roots of some species may penetrate to a considerable depth. The root distribution of *A. nigrescens* and that of grasses was found to be significantly deeper under tree canopies compared to that between tree canopies. However, no significant differences between root types under *A. nigrescens* canopies and in the open were found. Testing for differences between tree species, it was established that *A. nigrescens* had a significantly lower proportion of roots in the topsoil (< 350 mm) under tree canopies in comparison to species like *Combretum apiculatum* (Red bushwillow) and *Hardwickia mopane* (Mopane).

Species differences exist in the vertical distribution of woody plant roots in relation to those of herbaceous plants. In a comparison of the root biomass of herbaceous and woody vegetation in the Nylsvley Nature Reserve, it was found that in *Acacia*-savanna the density of the herbaceous roots is considerably higher than that of woody plant roots. The herbaceous roots form a dense mat in the top 30 cm and some penetrate down to 100 cm, while the woody plant root distribution, on the whole, is even over the profile. In the Eastern Cape it was found that *A. karroo* trees are able to influence the vertical distribution of soil water up to a distance of 2.5 m from their stems.

The effect of trees on grasses may not always be negative and the net effect of favourable or unfavourable influences of woody plants on grass production depends on tree density. Establishing trees create subhabitats which differ from those in the open, with subsequent influences on the grasses. In the false thornveld of the Eastern Cape, a consistent pattern of grass production

around isolated *A. karroo* was found to exist. This pattern was characterized by high grass yields under and immediately south of the tree canopy, and low yields immediately to the north of the canopy. The former was attributed to favourable influences by the tree (e.g. shade and tree leaf litter), whereas the latter was attributed to reduced water input associated with physical redistribution of rainfall by the tree and competition from the tree for soil water. This led to the conclusion that grass production was greater where there were a few *A. karroo* trees than where there were no trees, but that grass production declined as the tree density increased beyond a critical level.

The shallow root system of *A. mellifera* with an extensive horizontal spread enables it to survive in areas with a low rainfall and also allows it to compete successfully with other plants for water and nutrients.

The higher levels of soil nutrients in the soil under tree canopies may also be reflected in the herbaceous plants growing under the tree canopies. Differences between the total nutrient content under tree canopies compared to that in the open may often be ascribed to differences in the species composition and total dry matter yield between the various subhabitats. A well documented tree-grass association in southern African savannas is that of *Panicum maximum* (Guinea Grass) with tree canopies, especially those of several *Acacia* species. *P. maximum* is highly palatable to cattle and other grazers and it has a high production potential. Accordingly, it is considered to be one of the most important fodder grass species in many savanna areas. It has been suggested that possible contributing factors to this association are enhancement of the nutrient supply under tree canopies, especially in respect of N and P, and enhanced germination of *P. maximum* seeds due to the relative abundance of litter and low temperatures under tree canopies. Results of an investigation into the relation between tree height of *A. karroo* and *A. tortilis* and the associated occurrence of *P. maximum* in the Northern Province showed that *P. maximum* was mainly associated with larger trees. *P. maximum* attained pure stands under *A. tortilis* and *A. karroo* trees of >2.0 m and >4.0 m respectively.

OTHER USES

For many rural communities, wood is still the only source of fuel for cooking and heating. The wood of most tree species is used as firewood and for charcoal. The wood of several *Acacia* species is known for their excellent fuel properties, especially species with dense heartwood. These species also yield excellent charcoal. Many *Acacia* species grow relatively fast and their ability to coppice is important where they are managed for fuelwood. However, directly opposed to the problem of bush encroachment, many rural areas suffered from serious over-exploitation of the fuelwood resource.

A well documented tree-grass association in southern African savannas is that of *Panicum maximum* (Guinea Grass) with tree canopies. In this case *P. maximum* has formed a dominant stand under an *A. tortilis* tree.

Some of the larger *Acacia* species like *A. erioloba*, *A. galpinii*, *A. xanthophloea* and even smaller species like *A. nilotica* have been used locally for the construction of furniture. The wood of *A. nigrescens* is very hard and in the past it proved durable for mining timbers and railway sleepers. It has also been made into furniture. The wood of a number of other *Acacia* species like *A. caffra*, *A. burkei* and *A. tortilis* is used for durable poles and fence-posts. In many rural areas the wood of sev-

The wood of several *Acacia* species is known for their excellent fuel properties, escpecially species with dense heartwood. These species also yield excellent charcoal.

eral tree species, including *Acacia* species, is used as rough construction material in the building of traditional huts and fences. The inner bark of *A. gerrardii* and *A. robusta* is used to make twine. The stems of species like *A. ataxacantha* are split and used to make woven baskets. Branches from spiny species like *A. tortilis* and *A. erubescens* are used

extensively for the construction of fencing kraals to protect livestock from predators.

With the expansion of the tourism industry the market for wooden carvings from indigenous tree species has become very popular. Subsequently, wood carving has developed into a major industry in many southern African countries and the wood of a wide range of tree species, including *Acacia* species, is being used. Of some concern though is the threat of non-sustainable harvesting of trees, brought about by increasing numbers of entrepreneurs who resort to this practice as an only source of income. This is especially true where larger trees are being cut down indiscriminately in the quest for larger and more spectacular carvings.

The bark and fruit of several *Acacia* species, notably *A. karroo* (bark) and *A. nilotica* (bark and pods) contain tannins, which is widely used in the tanning of leather. In South Africa commercial extraction of tannin is mainly from Black Wattle (*Acacia mearnsii*), an introduced Australian species of which the bark yields 36–44 % tannin.

Parts of some *Acacia* species, including the fruit, flowers, bark, leaves and roots have traditionally been used as food for humans and as medicines. For example the leaves of *A. caffra* are chewed for stomach ache, the bark of *A. erioloba* is burnt, crushed and used in treating headaches and the bark of *A. xanthophloea* is used for fevers and eye complaints.

Acacia species can produce large quantities of seeds and in times of need the seed of a number of species has been eaten by pastoral people. *Acacia* trees may also indirectly provide food like the edible cerambycid wood borer larvae found in the dead wood of *A. robusta*. The flowers of species like *A. mellifera*, *A. karroo*, *A. caffra*, *A. robusta*, *A. ataxacantha* and several others are important sources of nectar for bees and the production of honey.

Gum is a very important product from *Acacia* trees. Several species like *A. karroo* and *A. nilotica* yield an edible gum of good quality and is also used as glue. Gum arabic, originally from *A. senegal*, is used to thicken many convenience foods, pharmaceuticals and cosmetics. It is also used as a component of water-colour paints and printing inks. The bark of *A. burkei* (yellow) and the pods of *A. nilotica* (yellow, red or black) are sometimes used for making dye.

It is possible to propagate most of the Acacia species and some species like *A. xanthoploea*, *A. galpinii*, *A. karroo*, *A. sieberiana*, *A. robusta* and *A. burkei* are popular as garden trees. Propagation can be done by seed or from cuttings.

Several *Acacia* species, like *A. karroo* yield an edible gum of good quality.

Wood carving has developed into a major industry in many southern African countries.

ABOUT THIS BOOK

This book attempts to give a complete account of all 40 recognized species, subspecies and varieties of the genus *Acacia* that occur within the borders of South Africa. One recognised hybrid is also included. Four pages are devoted to each form, which include numerous colour photographs, a distribution map, a graphic illustration of the species' phenology and a comprehensive text. The main components of the information are discussed below:

Scientific name (genus, species, subspecies and varieties)

The scientific name of a species is made up of two parts. The first part is the genus name (*Acacia* in this case) and in writing always starts with a capital letter. The second part is the species name (e.g. *nilotica*) and is always written in lower case. The name of subspecies or varieties (which are variants within a species) consists of the name of the species in which it is classified, followed by a word indicating its rank (subsp. or var.) then the subspecific or varietal epithet. For reference purposes and as a source of historical information, scientific names are often followed by one or more personal names, which are sometimes abbreviated. These so-called authority citations refer to the person(s) who originally described the particular species, subspecies or variety. The "type" refers to the material from which the plant was first described and which is now housed in a herbarium, locally or abroad. The geographic area from which the type material originates is also indicated.

Synonyms

The names by which a plant was previously known, or is alternatively referred to, are its synonyms. Plants often have to be reclassified following the discovery of new information. As a result, a species may be transferred from one genus to another, or a single species may be split into two or more species. Similarly, two or more species may be combined into a single one, or what has previously been considered a subspecies or variety may be given specific rank. In certain circumstances a name may also change if an older published name is found. An example of a recent taxonomic change that involved a member of the genus *Acacia* is the reclassification *A. albida* to *Faidherbia albida*. Synonyms may facilitate cross-referencing between this book and other publications, particularly older ones. Synonyms are given in accordance with Ross (1979) and Arnold & De Wet (1993).

Common Names

Common names can be confusing since the same name may apply to two or more different species, or the same species may have more than one common name. Common names, including both English and Afrikaans names, used in this book are given in accordance with the *National List of Indigenous Trees* (Von Breitenbach 1990). Occasionally other, less frequently used names are also provided.

National Tree Number

These have been proposed as a handy means of marking trees along highways and hiking trails, in nature reserves and recreation resorts, and also as a general quick-reference guide. The National Tree Number of each form is given in accordance with the *National List of Indigenous Trees* (Von Breitenbach 1990).

17

Outstanding features

This entails a short summary of the general growth form, main stem, shoots, thorns (spines and prickles), leaves, inflorescences, pods and seeds of each form with emphasis on the most notable features.

Phenology

The phenology of a plant refers to the seasonal pattern of leaf emergence and leaf fall (winter deciduous species), flowering and fruit-bearing. Each species, genetically, follows a specific pattern. In some it takes place within fairly narrow limits, while in others it may vary considerably. External determinants of the beginning and end of each phenological stage include soil water availability, daylight length (photoperiodism) and temperature. The graphical illustration of leaf bearing, flowering and fruit-bearing reflects the most likely time of the year that any of the particular phenological stages can be expected, provided that conditions are favourable. Extraordinary climatic conditions, like early or late seasonal rains, may stimulate species to flower outside their normal routine or cause the plant to retain its leaves and pods for longer than usual. An important aspect of the phenology of each species, subspecies or variety is the flowering time in relation to leaf emergence. In some species flowering takes place before the emergence of the leaves, in others the flowers appear with the new leaves, while in others flowering takes place long after leaf emergence. This trend of each species can easily be assessed from the graphic illustrations. Where there is a considerable overlap in the flowering and fruit-bearing period, it likely means that more than one flowering during the season is possible. A tree may already bear some well developed pods from the first flowering during a subsequent flowering.

Distribution maps

The distribution of any particular species under natural conditions is determined by limitations in its habitat requirements. Species with a wide habitat tolerance will normally exhibit a wider geographical distribution than species with more specialised habitat requirements. Geographical barriers like mountains may also restrict the natural spread of a species to other suitable habitats. The shaded areas on the distribution maps are presented as a guide to the known geographical distribution of a particular species. The distribution perimeter of any particular species is approximate and it does not indicate specific localities, nor does it give any indication whether a species is evenly spread over the area or occurs only in isolated localities. The distribution maps should always be interpreted with the information given on the specific habitat preferences of that particular species. Since many of the *Acacia* species are suitable for cultivation as garden trees, it is likely that individuals of many species may be encountered in gardens and on farms outside their normal distribution range.

Habitat

A brief description of the known habitat preferences of each form is given. Some of the most important habitat features which may be included in each description are: association with a specific topographical terrain, height above sea level,

soil preferences (e.g. type, depth, texture, structure, chemical properties) and other relevant information like tolerance to drought and cold.

General description

The general appearance of each form is described. Emphasis is placed on the typical growth form (e.g. single-stemmed tree or multi-stemmed shrub), size, crown characteristics and other notable features that may be relevant.

Main stem

A description of the main stem(s) of each form is given. Some can be smooth and others rough and deeply fissured. The bark may be thick and corky or thin, papery and peeling. The colour of the bark is also described. The differences between the main stems of young plants and older, more mature plants are given, where applicable.

Shoots

The shoots are described based on their age. A description of young, new season's shoots as well as older, previous seasons' shoots is given. Emphasis is placed on diagnostic features like their colour, hairiness, presence of glands and lenticels, as well as the presence and characteristics of bark.

Thorns

A description of the thorns of each form is given. Emphasis is placed on their shape, size, position, colour and hairiness. The definition of a "thorn" is a "stiff, sharp-pointed process on plants", and our indigenous *Acacia* species are well known for this feature, hence the common name "thorn trees". However, the term "thorns" is rather a general term used to describe the armour of the South African *Acacia* species, which taxonomically consists of either spines or prickles. A spine is a hardened, modified stipule with a sharp point (spinescent), while a prickle is a hardened epidermal outgrowth, also with a sharp point. A stipule, in turn, can be described as a basal appendage of a leaf stalk (petiole). All the South African *Acacia* species have stipules. Those species that have prickles also have stipules, but the latter are unmodified and they are not persistent. Prickles are invariably short and recurved, while spines may either be short or long, straight or recurved. The unmodified stipules vary in shape. The heavily inflated bases of spines found on some *Acacia* species is often referred to as "ant-galls". However, there is, as yet, no evidence in any South African species that ants cause the inflation of these spines, though ants often do inhabit these inflated hollow spines. The species are divided into five groups according to the shape and position of the thorns (spines and prickles) (page 20).

Leaves

The leaves of all the *Acacia* species are bipinately compound consisting of a petiole (leaf stalk), rachis (the axis of a compound leaf), pinnae (the secondary divisions of a compound leaf) and leaflets (the individual divisions of a compound leaf, which is usually leaf-like and has a stalk of its own). Some aspects of the leaves that are described include their size, colour, hairiness, number of pinnae and leaflets and the presence of glands on the petiole and rachis.

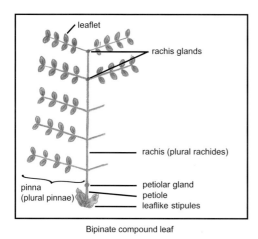

Bipinate compound leaf

Inflorescence

An inflorescens is defined as any arrangement of more than one flower. The flowers of the *Acacia* species are arranged in either a globose flowering head or a flowering spike with a central rachis. A flowering head or spike is borne on a peduncle (the common stalk of a flower) on which may be located the involucel (a whorl of bracts).

Other features that are described include the colour of the developing buds, colour of open, fully developed flowering heads or spikes, their size (diameter and length) and a description of the peduncles (length, colour, hairiness and position of the involucel).

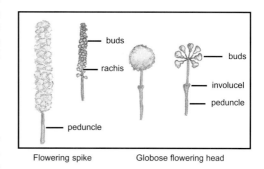

Flowering spike   Globose flowering head

Pods and seeds

A pod is a general term applied to any dry and many-seeded fruit which usually splits open along one or both the two opposite seams to release the enclosed seeds (dehiscent pods). The two separable walls of a pod are called the valves. In some of the *Acacia* species the pods do not split and they are called indehiscent pods. In the description of the pods features like the size, shape, colour, covering (e.g. hairy, leathery) and venation are described. The enclosed seeds are also described.

19

Similar species

A short listing of closely related species and their diagnostic characters is provided, as well as the diagnostic characters of species with similar characters with which it can be confused. It would not be possible to account for all possible similarities between species and only the most notable ones are given.

General

Some additional information, relevant to each species, subspecies or variety, includes an explanation of the meaning of its scientific name, its distribution outside South Africa and a short description of the wood.

SUMMARY OF GROUPS

Based on the shape and position of the thorns (spines and prickles)

For the sake of simplification the shape and position of the thorns (whether they are spines or prickles) are divided into five main groups. The order in which the species are presented in the book is according to these groups:

Group One
page   22 - 105

Straight, paired, located at the nodes

- stipules that are modified into hardened, spinescent spines
- bases may be inflated or not.

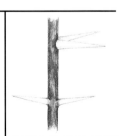

Group Two
page 106 - 123

Straight and recurved, paired, located at nodes

- stipules that are modified into hardened, spinescent spines
- recurved and straight spines usually occur seperately in pairs at the nodes, but mixed pairs do also occur
- bases of straight spines may be inflated or not
- tips of straight spines may be recurved.

Group Three
page 124 - 169

Recurved, paired, located at the nodes

- prickles
- stipules not spinescent and they do not persist.

Group Four
page 170 - 187

Recurved, scattered irregularly along the internodes

- prickles
- stipules not spinescent and they do not persist.

Group Five
page 188 - 197

Recurved, in threes at the nodes

- prickles
- stipules not spinescent and they do not persist.

DESCRIPTION
OF THE
SOUTH AFRICAN SPECIES

Group One

Straight thorns, paired, located at the nodes

Additional characteristics and variations
- stipules that are modified into hardened, spinescent spines
- bases may be inflated or not

Acacia tenuispina
Acacia nebrownii
Acacia permixta
Acacia swazica
Acacia exuvialis
Acacia borleae
Acacia stuhlmannii
Acacia davyi
Acacia nilotica subsp. *kraussiana*
Acacia grandicornuta
Acacia karroo
Acacia gerrardii var. *gerrardii*
Acacia rehmanniana
Acacia sieberiana var. *woodii*
Acacia haematoxylon
Acacia erioloba
Acacia erioloba x *Acacia haematoxylon*
Acacia robusta subsp. *robusta*
Acacia robusta subsp. *clavigera*
Acacia xanthophloea

Acacia tenuispina

Fyndoring

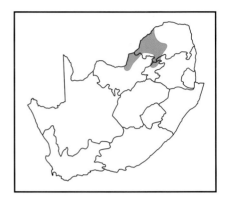

Name with author
Acacia tenuispina Verdoorn –
Type from Northern Province, South Africa

Synonyms
A. permixta Burt Davy var. *glabra* Burtt Davy

National Tree Number Not numbered

Outstanding features

- Low growing multi-stemmed shrub, associated with black turf soil,
- The bark surface is rough to the touch, dark grey to brownish, occasionally revealing a reddish-brown base colour,
- Young shoots are covered with numerous protruding glands and are very sticky,
- Paired, spinescent spines are slender and hairless,
- Leaves with 1–6 pinna pairs and sticky when young, leaflets comparatively large and hairless,
- Globose flowering heads are bright yellow with long, sticky peduncles covered with glands,
- The pods are small, dehiscent with numerous, protruding black glands, sticky to the touch.

24

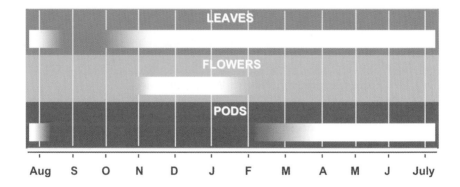

Habitat
Confined to black turf soil, typically in flat savanna areas.

General description
A multi-stemmed stoloniferous shrub, 0.5–3 m high. It may, in relation to its height, attain a substantial basal ground coverage (up to 10 m in diameter) due to a large number of stems that emerge from the ground some distance apart. It occurs individually or may form localised thickets.

Main stem
The main stems do not attain a large diameter. The colour of the bark varies from dark grey to brownish, occasionally revealing a reddish-brown base colour. Elongated, buff-coloured lenticels are often visible. The bark surface is rough to the touch, though it appears smooth, occasionally peeling longitudinally.

Shoots
Very young new season's shoots are green, hairless and covered with numerous protruding glands. They are very sticky and may appear shiny due to the sticky substance. With maturation, these young shoots turn to a reddish-brown

colour with small, inconspicuous, circular lenticels. They gradually lose their stickiness. Older, previous seasons' shoots are smooth, non-sticky with a greyish colour.

Thorns
The stipules are modified into hardened, spinescent spines and occur in pairs at the nodes. The spines are straight or slightly curved and hairless. They are slender (base diameter averaging 1.5 mm) and may attain a length of 55 mm. The spines are usually oriented at right angles to the stem, but can be raked either back or, occasionally, forward up to 10° from the normal. Within pairs the spines are set at an angle of approximately 80°–120°. Young spines on new season's growth are greenish, changing to white with reddish tips with maturity.

Leaves
The leaves are borne at the nodes, as many as 10 leaves or more per node. Young leaves are sticky. The leaflets are hairless with inconspicuous venation. The petiole and rachis are grooved on top with numerous protruding glands. The petiole length may vary from 2–11 mm, while the petiole and rachis, combined, may attain a length of 38 mm

(14–20 mm typical). The number of pinna pairs range from 1–6 (2–4 typical), and the number of leaflet pairs per pinna from 4–9. Leaflets are comparatively large in comparison to the size of the leaves. They have a mean length of 4.2 mm (range: 3–5 mm) and mean width of 1.6 mm (range: 0.8–2 mm). Infrequently a yellowish domed, or cupped, petiolar gland is present near the junction of the first pinna pair. Similar glands occur on the rachis at each of the pinna junctions.

Inflorescence
Globose flowering heads are borne at the nodes, usually single but occasionally up to four per node on both new season's and previous seasons' shoots. The colour of the developing buds are green initially, turning to a yellowish colour prior to full bloom. The open, fully developed flowering heads have a mean diameter of 10.5 mm. They are scented and have a bright deep yellow colour. Peduncles are hairless, covered with numerous protruding glands and are very sticky. They are long with a mean length of 20 mm (range: 8–30 mm). The involucel is distinct, light brown in colour and located at or above the middle of the peduncle.

Pods and seeds
The pods are borne in bunches, occasionally single. They are slightly curved, with minor constrictions between seeds, tapering at the base but less at the tip. They are dehiscent with some indistinct longitudinal venation and may attain a length of 35–65 mm and a width of 6–9 mm. The young developing pods are green with numerous, protruding black glands and are sticky to the touch. With age the colour changes to brown. The number of seeds vary from 4 to 8. The seeds are slightly flattened, elliptic with a mean size of 6 x 4.5 mm and vary in colour from brown to olive green or a light khaki colour. The central areole, 2.5–3.5 mm in diameter, is visible as a light-coloured outline surrounding a slight depression which is darker in colour.

Similar species
In some areas, notably the Springbok flats, a small, multi-stemmed form of *A. karroo* may be confused with *A. tenuispina*. The leaflets of *A. tenuispina*, however, differ in having short, sharp points and the pods are characteristically glandular, while young shoots, peduncles and pods are very sticky. Intermediates suggest possible hybridisation. It can also be confused with *A. nebrownii* and *A. borlea*. *A. nebrownii* usually has only 1 or 2 pairs of pinnae and the leaflets are more rounded and their size increases to the tips of the pinnae. The absence of glands on the surfaces and margins of the leaflets distinguish it from *A. borlea*. Also, its distribution range doesn't overlap with that of *A. borlea*.

General
Name derivation: *tenuispina* = slender spine. Elsewhere in Africa, *A. tenuispina* is only recorded from south-eastern Botswana.

26

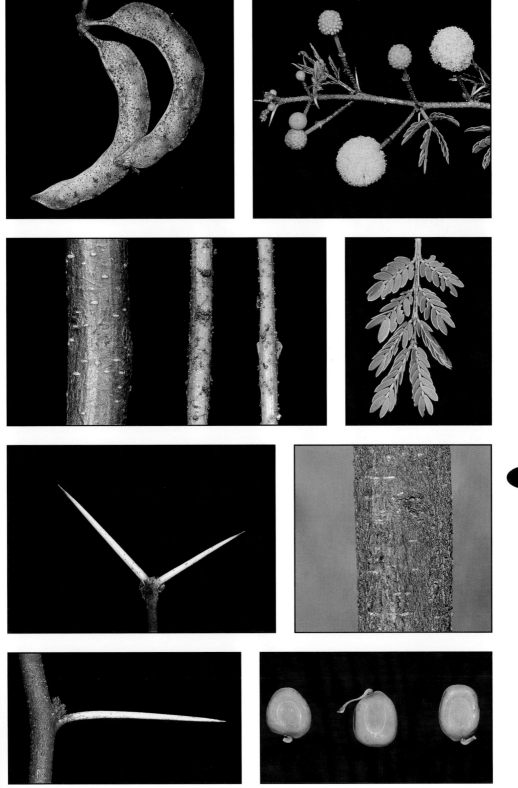

Acacia nebrownii

Water Thorn • Waterdoring

Name with authors
Acacia nebrownii Burtt Davy – Types from Botswana

Synonyms
• *A. glandulifera* Schinz • *A. rogersii* Burtt Davy
• *A. walteri* Süsseng.

National Tree Number 177.1

Other common names
Gomdoring, Taaidoring

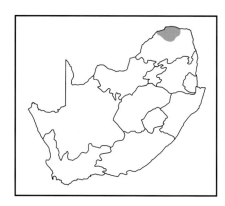

Outstanding features

• Erect multi-stemmed shrub or slender tree, often associated with banks of dry water courses,

• The bark is smooth, bluish-grey in colour with some reddish tinges,

• Shoots, when very young, are covered with protruding glands and are moderately sticky,

• Paired, spinescent spines are slender and hairless,

• There is usually only a single pinna pair, occasionally two,

• Globose flowering heads are golden-yellow, peduncles glandular and basal involucel inconspicuous,

28

• The pods are small, dehiscent with numerous, protruding black glands, sticky to the touch.

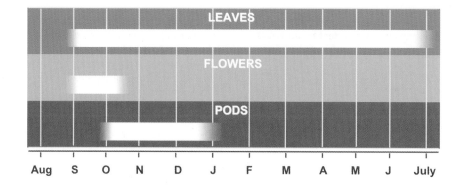

Habitat

Prefer low lying areas, particularly along banks of dry water courses, hence the name "Water Thorn", though tolerant to hot, arid conditions prevalent within its geographical distribution range. Considered to be an indication of underground water, probably due to its association with water-bearing calcrete.

General description

Typically an erect, multi-stemmed shrub, 2–4 m high, but occasionally a slender tree up to 5–7 m. It often occur in pure stands, forming thickets.

Main stem

The main stems do not attain a large diameter. The bark is smooth, bluish-grey in colour with some reddish tinges and occasional black spots. Persisting spines are common on young stems.

Shoots

Young new season's shoots are green, hairless and covered with minute glands. These young shoots are moderately sticky and may appear shiny due to the sticky substance. Within the same season they become yellowish-brown or reddish-brown, smooth and non-sticky. With maturation, these shoots take on a homogenous grey colour with some reddish tinges still discernible. Light-coloured, transversely-elongated lenticels are also present.

Thorns

The stipules are modified into hardened, spinescent spines and occur in pairs at the nodes. The spines are straight or slightly curved and hairless. They are slender (base diameter averaging 1.6 mm) and may attain a length of 70 mm, but on average are less than 40 mm long. Spines are either oriented at right angles to the stem or raked back up to 10° from the normal. Within pairs the spines are set at an angle of approximately 110°. The spines are white with dark tips.

Leaves

The leaves are borne at the nodes, as many as 5 leaves per node. There is usually only a single pinna pair, occasionally two, and the number of leaflet pairs per pinna vary from 3–5. The petiole are hairless, grooved on top and dotted with small, black glands. Its length may vary from 6–11 mm. The oval-shaped leaflets are comparatively large in comparison to the size of the leaves and their size increase to the tips of the pinnae. They have a mean length of 4.7 mm (range: 2–8 mm) and mean width of 3.4 mm (range: 0.9–5 mm). The lateral vein is inconspicuous on the underside. A small brown cupped petiolar gland is present near the junction of the first (often the only) pinna pair.

Inflorescence

Globose flowering heads are borne at the nodes, usually singly but occasionally up to four per node on both new season's and previous seasons' shoots. The colour of the developing buds is green to yellowish-green. The open, fully-developed flowering heads have a mean diameter of 11 mm (range: 9–15 mm). They are scented and have a golden-yellow colour. Peduncles are hairless, covered with small glands and vary in colour from green to dark red. They are relatively short with a mean length of 10 mm (range: 6–24 mm). The basal involucel is inconspicuous.

Pods and seeds

The pods are borne at the nodes, singly or occasionally in small bunches. They are slightly curved, linear with occasional minor constrictions between seeds, tapered at the base but less at the tip. They are dehiscent, papery when dry and may attain a length of 20–56 mm and a width of 6–13 mm. Young developing pods are green with numerous, protruding black glands and are sticky to the touch. With age the colour changes to light brown. The number of seeds vary from 2 to 6. The seeds are flattened, elliptic or roughly circular with a mean size of 6–10 x 5–7 mm and vary in colour from light brown to olive green. The central areole with a mean size of 2–4 x 1.5–2.5 mm is visible as a light-coloured outline surrounding a slight depression which is darker in colour.

Similar species

Can be confused with *A. tenuispina* (see the comments under the latter species). The basal involucel is an identifying character that distinguishes it from the other glandular podded *Acacia* species like *A. borlea*.

General

Name derivation: *nebrownii* = named after N. E. Brown, a botanist who did much plant collecting in Botswana. Elsewhere in Africa, *A. nebrownii* is common in some parts of Namibia (especially the Etosha National Park) and also occurs in Botswana and south-western Zimbabwe.

Acacia permixta

Slender Thorn • Slapdoring

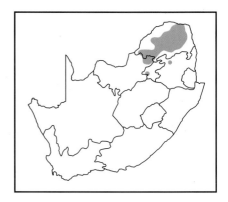

Name with author
Acacia permixta Burtt Davy –
Type from Northern Province, South Africa

Synonyms None

National Tree Number 179.1

Other common names
Hairy Thorn

Outstanding features

- Slender shrub or small tree with sparse, straggling branches, often bending downwards,
- The main stems are covered with thin layers of peeling papery bark,
- Young shoots are densely covered with whitish hairs and dotted with small, black glands,
- Paired, spinescent spines are slender and hairy when young,
- Pinna pairs range from 1–6 and the leaf petiole and rachis are hairy and dotted with small, black glands,
- Globose flowering heads are bright yellow, peduncles glandular and hairy, involucel conspicuous,
- The pods are small, with numerous reddish-brown to black glands and are moderately sticky.

32

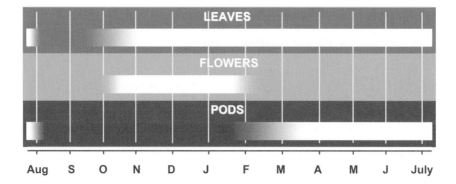

| | LEAVES | | | | | | | | | | |
| Aug | S | O | N | D | J | F | M | A | M | J | July |

FLOWERS

PODS

Habitat

Prefer sandy or shallow coarse gravelly soil, often derived from granite formations. Tend to increase locally on disturbed areas such as on overgrazed veld.

General description

A slender shrub or small tree, often single-stemmed, but multi-stemmed plants not uncommon. It has a characteristically open appearance with sparse, straggling branches, often bending downwards. Grows to a height of 1–2.5 m, occasionally up to 5 m.

Main stem

The main stems usually do not attain a large diameter. The main stem is predominantly reddish-brown or yellowish-brown and covered with thin layers of peeling papery bark that vary in colour from grey to greyish-yellow. Underneath the peeling bark the stem is smooth with grey, transversely elongated lenticels. Persisting spines are common on young stems. The bark on old stems is rough, longitudinally fissured with some transverse splitting, thus forming rectangular shaped flakes.

Shoots

The base colour of young new season's shoots is green, often dotted with small, black glands. These young shoots appear whitish or silvery due to long, densely packed whitish hairs, which disappear with maturation, and they have a velvety feel to the touch. Older, previous seasons' shoots have a reddish-brown colour, while still older shoots are covered with thin layers of reddish-brown flaking bark. They are smooth underneath and are covered with grey, transversely-elongated lenticels.

Thorns

The stipules are modified into hardened, spinescent spines. They are straight to slightly curved, and occur in pairs at nodes. They are slender (base diameter averaging less than 2 mm) and may attain a length of 65 mm or more, though usually less than 40 mm long. They are either born at right angles to the stem or raked backwards up to 20° from the normal, occasionally slightly forward. When young, they are covered with whitish hairs which disappear with maturation. Young spines on new season's growth are greenish, while older spines are white with reddened tips.

Leaves

The leaves are borne at the nodes, as many as 8 leaves per node, appearing dense due to the short distances between nodes. A cluster of leaves may consist of a primary leaf and several smaller secondary leaves. The number of pinna pairs range from 1–6 (2–4 typical), and the number of leaflet pairs per pinna from 3–9. The petiole and rachis are hairy, grooved on top and dotted with small, black glands. The petiole length may vary from 3–17 mm (6–12 mm typical), while the petiole and rachis, combined, may attain a length of 48 mm (14–20 mm typical). The leaflets are sharp-pointed with a mean length of 4.8 mm (range: 2–7 mm) and mean width of 1.8 mm (range: 0.9–2.6 mm). The colour is the same above and below, with the main vein faintly distinguishable on both surfaces. Leaflet margins are fringed with hairs. Infrequently a raised green gland is present immediately above the moderately swollen petiole base. Elongated, somewhat pointed, yellow glands occur on the rachis at from 2 to 5 of the distal pinna junctions.

Inflorescence

Globose flowering heads are borne at the nodes, either single or two per node on both new season's and previous seasons' shoots. The colour of the developing buds are green. The open, fully-developed flowering heads have a mean diameter of 11.5 mm (range: 10–12 mm). They are scented and have a bright yellow colour. The peduncles are long with a mean length of 28 mm (range: 25–35 mm). They are covered with hairs and small glands, notably the section below the distinct involucel which is located at or above the middle of the peduncle. The colour of the peducles vary from green to purple-red.

Pods and seeds

Pods are borne in bunches. They are slightly curved, linear, tapering sharply at the base but less at the tip. They are dehiscent, papery when dry and may attain a length of 20–58 mm and a width of 6–14 mm. The colour of the developing pods varies from reddish to green. Pods are hairless with numerous conspicuous, protruding glands which vary in colour from reddish-brown to black. Green pods are moderately sticky to the touch. With age the colour of the pods change to brown. The number of seeds vary from 5 to 7. The seeds are flattened, elliptic or roughly circular with a mean diameter of 5–6 mm and vary in colour from olive to light brown or light brown at the edges with the inner area a darker brown. The central areole is visible as a light-coloured elliptic outline with a mean size of 2–4 x 1.5–2.5 mm, surrounding a darker central area.

Similar species

Can be distinguished from other glandular podded *Acacia* species by the spreading hairs on young shoots, rachides and peduncles.

General

Elsewhere in Africa, *A. permixta* also occur in southern Zimbabwe and south-eastern Botswana.

Acacia swazica

Swazi Thorn • Swazidoring

Name with authors
Acacia swazica Burtt Davy –
Type from Swaziland

Synonyms
None

National Tree Number 187.2

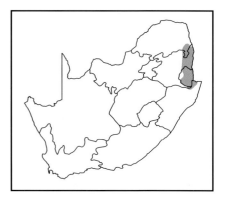

Outstanding features

- A slender shrub or small tree that prefers rocky habitats,
- Main stem is characteristically transversely wrinkled and covered with thin segments of peeling papery bark,
- Young shoots are hairless and less sticky than other small glandular podded species,
- Paired, spinescent spines are hairless and exceptionally slender,
- Pinna pairs range from 1–5, leaflet size tends to increase towards the tips of pinnae, venation on the underside of the leaflets is distinct,
- Globose flowering heads are bright yellow, peduncles are long and involucel large,
- The pods are small, dehiscent with numerous black glands, moderately sticky to the touch.

36

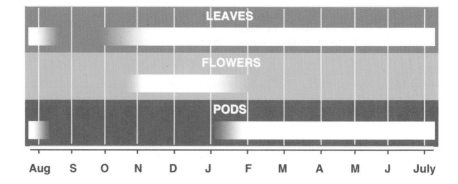

Habitat

They prefer rocky habitats in areas that range from arid to fairly high rainfall in the eastern parts of southern Africa.

General description

A slender shrub or small tree, often single-stemmed, but multi-stemmed plants not uncommon. It has an open appearance with sparse, erect branches. They grow to a height of 2–3 m, occasionally up to 4 m.

Main stem

The main stem is characteristically transversely wrinkled and covered with thin segments of peeling papery bark that varies in colour from brown to yellowish-brown. Underneath the peeling bark the stem is smooth with a predominantly green or yellowish-green base colour with pale grey, transversely elongated lenticels. Persisting spines (short and slender) are often found on young stems.

Shoots

Young new season's shoots, initially, have a light green colour, which turn to reddish-brown. They are hairless and covered with numerous projecting pale orange or dark glands. They are occasionally sticky to the touch but more often this is not an important feature. Previous seasons' shoots have a brown colour with small, inconspicuous, whitish lenticels. Older, thickened shoots have a brown or orange-green colour and are covered with a thin layer of peeling papery bark with a reddish colour.

Thorns

The stipules are modified into hardened, spinescent spines and occur in pairs at the nodes. The spines are straight and hairless. They are exceptionally slender (base diameter averaging less than 1 mm) and though they may attain a length of 74 mm, they are usually short (on average less than 20 mm long). Spines are notably raked forward, up to 20°

from the normal, though in exceptional cases slightly backwards. Within pairs the spines are set at an angle of approximately 90°–120°. The spines are white with dark tips, but on new growth they have a pink colour.

Leaves

The leaves are borne at the nodes, singly or as many as 6 leaves per node, appearing rather sparse. The number of pinna pairs ranges from 1–5 (1–3 typical), and the number of leaflet pairs per pinna from 3–7. Individual pinnae may attain a length of 18 mm. The petiole and rachis are hairless, grooved on top with scattered red to black projecting glands. The petiole length may vary from 3–19 mm, while the petiole and rachis, combined, may attain a length of 40 mm or more (12–20 mm typical). The leaflets are fairly broad but taper down to a sharp point. They tend to increase in size towards the tips of the pinnae with a mean length of 6.5 mm (range: 4–9 mm) and mean width of 2.6 mm (range: 1.5–5 mm). Venation, on the underside of the leaflets, is quite distinct. A small, unobtrusive gland may be present at the junction of each pinna pair.

Inflorescence

Globose flowering heads are borne at the nodes, either single or up to 12 per node on new season's shoots only. Peduncles are hairless, covered with numerous small glands and have a green colour. They are slender and fairly long with a mean length of 28 mm (range: 14–47 mm). The involucel is large and located at or above the middle of the peduncle. The colour of the developing buds is green to yellowish-green. The open, fully developed flowering heads have

a mean diameter of 9–10 mm. They are scented and have a bright yellow colour.

Pods and seeds

Pods are borne in bunches of up to 12, but more often less. They are curved, linear, sharply tapering at the base and bluntly pointed to rounded at the tip. They may attain a mean length of 30 mm (range: 20–66 mm) and a mean width of 9.5 mm (range: 7–12 mm). Young pods are hairless, shiny green with numerous conspicuous dark protruding glands. These young pods are moderately sticky to the touch. The dehiscent pods, when dry, are papery with a brown colour. A profusion of dangling seeds can often be seen hanging from the dry pods and the number of seeds per pod varies from 2 to 5. The seeds have an olive to brown colour. They are flattened with an elliptic shape and a mean size of 4–7 x 4–6 mm. The areole, with a mean diameter of 2.5–4 mm, has a centre darker in colour than the rest of the seed and bordered by a pale olive outline.

Similar species

Within its distribution range it can be confused with *A. borlea* and *A. exuvialis*. It can be distinguised from these species by the prominent venation on the underside of the leaflets. The main stem is also characteristically transversely wrinkled (unlike that of *A. exuvialis*) and covered with thin segments of peeling papery bark (unlike that of *A. borlea*).

General

Name derivation: *swazica* = from Swaziland. Elsewhere in Africa, *A. swazica* is only recorded in Swaziland.

Acacia exuvialis

Flaky Thorn • Skilferdoring

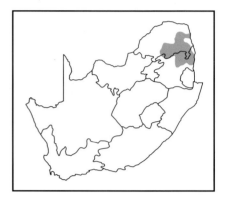

Name with author
Acacia exuvialis Verdoorn –
Type from Mpumalanga, South Africa

Synonyms
None

National Tree Number 164.1

Outstanding features

- An upright shrub or small tree, single- or multi-stemmed,
- The main stem is smooth underneath thin segments of yellowish to grey peeling papery bark,
- Young shoots are initially slightly sticky with a green colour, changing to reddish or reddish-brown,
- Paired, spinescent spines are straight to slightly recurved, often with thickened bases,
- Larger primary leaves and smaller secondary leaves occur and the leaflet size increases progressively from the base to the tip of each pinna,
- Globose flowering heads are bright yellow, peduncles long and involucel conspicuous,
- Pods are sickle-shaped, flat, tapered at both ends and have marked constrictions between seeds.

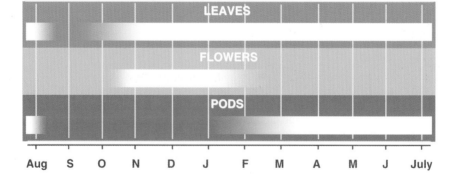

| | LEAVES | | | | | | | | | | |
| Aug | S | O | N | D | J | F | M | A | M | J | July |

Habitat

A species that occurs at low altitudes, either in localized dominant stands or as scattered individuals among other dominant plants (e.g. in mopane woodland). Also found on stony hillsides often in gravelly soils.

General description

An upright shrub or small tree, single- or multi-stemmed, that grows to a height of 1.5–3.5 m, occasionally up to 4.5 m. It has a rather open appearance with sparse, erect branches. Numerous long white spines make the plants quite conspicuous when leafless.

Main stem

The main stem is characteristically covered with thin segments of peeling papery bark, especially in the case of younger plants. The colour of the pa-pery bark varies from yellow, yellowish-brown to grey. Underneath the peeling bark the stem is smooth and shiny with a colour that varies from yellowish-green to orange or reddish-brown. Long white persisting spines are often found on young stems.

Shoots

Young new season's shoots, initially, have a homogeneous light green colour. They are hairless, slightly sticky with small, unobtrusive lenticels. Within the same season these young shoots take on a characteristic reddish or reddish-brown colour. They are shiny, smooth and no longer sticky to the touch. Previous seasons' shoots have a bright green colour underneath thin layers of peeling papery bark with a brownish or reddish colour. These older shoots are covered with indistinct, buff, transversely elongated lenticels.

Thorns

The stipules are modified into hardened, spinescent spines. They are straight to slightly curved, and occur in pairs at nodes. Their bases may be thickened. On older shoots and branches the spines can be short, while on younger shoots they may attain a length of 78 mm with a base diameter of 5 mm. They are borne at right angles to the stem or raked backwards, occasionally forward, up to 10° from the normal. On new season's growth the young spines are whitish-green with yellowish tips. Older spines are white with tips and bases that can have a reddish colour.

Leaves

The leaves are borne at the nodes and their number per node varies from 1 to 9. Each cluster of leaves consists of a larger primary leaf and smaller secondary leaves. Leaflets are hairless and their size increases progressively from the base to the tip of each pinna. They have a light green colour with inconspicuous ventral veins. The petiole and rachis are hairless and grooved. The number of pinna pairs ranges from 3–5 on primary leaves to 1–2 on secondary leaves. The petiole have a length of 3–15 mm, while the length of the petiole and rachis, combined, ranges from 5 mm (secondary leaf with only one pinna pair) to 50 mm (primary leaf with several pinna pairs). The number of leaflet pairs per pinna varies from 4–10 on primary leaves to 3–4 on secondary leaves. Leaflets are comparatively large and the leaflets located at the pinna bases have a mean length of 5.8 mm (range: 5.5–6.5 mm) and mean width of 2.1 mm (range: 1.5–2.5 mm). Those at the tips of the pinnae have a mean length of 6.5 mm (range: 5.5–10 mm) and mean width of 3.4 mm (range: 3.0–4.5 mm). A slight swelling occurs at the base of the petiole of primary leaves. A small cupped petiolar gland occurs infrequently. Small glands do occur on the rachis at the terminal pinna junctions and they are prominent on primary leaves.

Inflorescence

Globose flowering heads are borne at the nodes, either single or 2 per node. Peduncles are hairless, covered with numerous inconspicuous small glands and have a green colour. They are slender and long with a mean length of 20 mm (range: 13–40 mm). The involucel, with reddish bracts, is positioned at from 50 to 90 % of the peduncle length measured from the base. The colour of the developing buds is green. The open, fully developed flowering heads have a mean diameter of 10 mm. They are scented and have a bright yellow colour.

Pods and seeds

Pods are borne in bunches of up to 4. They are sickle-shaped, flat, tapered at both ends and have marked constrictions between seeds. They may attain a mean length of 50 mm (range: 15–70 mm) and a mean width of 7.5 mm (range: 4–9 mm). Young pods are hairless, indistinctly to markedly longitudinally venose with a green colour. Glands are not obvious but the young pods are slightly sticky. The dehiscent pods, when dry, are papery with a dark brown colour. A profusion of dangling seeds can often be seen hanging from the dry pods and the number of seeds per pod varies from 2 to 5. The seeds have an olive green colour. They are flattened with an elliptic shape and a mean size of 5–8 x 3.5–6 mm. The areole, with a mean size of 3–5 x 2.5–3 mm, takes the form of a slightly lighter-coloured, narrow, horseshoe-shaped outline, which is slightly recessed.

Similar species

Within its distribution range it can be confused with *A. borlea* and *A. swazica*. It can be distinguished from *A. borlea* by the main stems that are covered with thin segments of peeling papery bark. The bases of the spines may also be thickened opposed to the slender spines of *A. borlea*. For the differences between *A. swazica* see the comments under the latter species.

General

Elsewhere in Africa, *A. exuvialis* is confined to south-eastern Zimbabwe.

42

Acacia borleae

Sticky Thorn • Kleefdoring

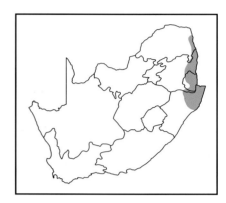

Outstanding features

- Low growing multi-stemmed shrub, normally associated with clayey soil,
- The bark on the main stems of young plants is relatively smooth and dark-coloured,
- Young shoots are covered with numerous protruding glands and are very sticky,
- Paired, spinescent spines are slender and hairless,
- The leaves, with 2–10 pinna pairs, are dark green, shiny and very sticky,
- Globose flowering heads are bright yellow with long, sticky peduncles covered with glands,
- The pods are small, dehiscent with numerous, protruding black glands, sticky to the touch.

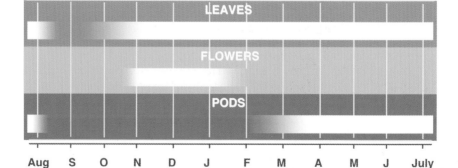

Habitat

This is a lowveld species occurring in dry savanna where they are usually associated with clayey or poorly drained soils.

General description

Growth form variable from a multi-stemmed shrub to a slender, single-stemmed tree with a rounded crown, 1.5–3 m high, occasionally up to 6–7 m. As a multi-stemmed shrub it may, in relation to its height, attain a substantial basal ground coverage due to a large number of stems that emerge from the ground some distance apart. May form localised thickets.

Main stem

The bark on the main stems of young plants are relatively smooth, dark-coloured (dark brown) and covered with light-coloured lenticels. Long, persisting spines are common on these young stems. The bark on the main stem of older plants, notably those of single-stemmed trees, is dark grey with some lighter grey patches and in some instances, with longitudinal reddish markings.

Shoots

Very young new season's shoots are hairless and covered with numerous pale to reddish glands. They are light green in colour and appear shiny due to a very sticky substance. With maturation, often within the same season, these young shoots turn to a homogeneous reddish-brown colour, but remain shiny and sticky. Previous seasons' shoots are reddish with small, inconspicuous, whitish lenticels. Older, thickened shoots are occasionally covered with a thin layer of papery bark.

Thorns

The stipules are modified into hardened, spinescent spines and occur in pairs at the nodes. The spines are straight or slightly curved and hairless. They are slender (base diameter averaging less than 2 mm) and may attain a length of 65 mm, but on average are less than 40 mm long. Spines is either oriented at right angles to the stem or raked backwards, occasionally forward, up to 10° from the normal. Within pairs the spines are set at an angle of approximately 80°–120°. Young spines on new season's growth are whitish-green with yellowish tips, changing to white with dark tips with maturity.

Leaves

The leaves are borne at the nodes, singly or as many as 8 leaves per node. They are dark green, shiny and very sticky. The number of pinna pairs range from 2–10 and the number of leaflet pairs per pinna from 5–18. The petiole and rachis are hairless and grooved on top and are spotted with numerous small dark glands. The petiole length may vary from 5–18 mm, while the petiole and rachis, combined, may attain a length of 75 mm. Leaflet size is extremely variable and they tend to be bigger on leaves with few pinna pairs than on leaves with many pinna pairs. The leaflet size varies from a mean of 6.1 x 3.1 mm on leaves with few pinna pairs to a mean of 5.2 x 1.9 mm on leaves with many pinna pairs (range – all leaflets: 1.5–6.5 x 0.8–3.2 mm). No venation is visible. There is no petiolar gland, but there are raised glands on the rachis at from 4 to 5 of the distal pinna junctions.

Inflorescence

Globose flowering heads are borne at the nodes, either single or up to 3 per node on new season's shoots only. Peduncles are hairless and sticky, covered with numerous small glands. They are slender and fairly long with a mean length of 21 mm (range: 16–34 mm). The prominent involucel is positioned at from 50 to 90 % of the peduncle length measured from the base. The colour of the developing buds is green to yellowish-green. The open, fully developed flowering heads are deep yellow in colour with a diameter of 10–16 mm.

Pods and seeds

Pods are borne in bunches. They are sickle-shaped, tapered at both ends and have marked constrictions between seeds. They may attain a length that ranges from 30–75 mm and a width that ranges from 5–8 mm, but as little as 3 mm at the constrictions between the seeds. The pods can either be hairless or covered with short, rough hairs. They are covered with numerous pustular glands, giving the pod a shiny appearance and they are sticky to the touch. The dehiscent pods, when dry, are light brown to dark brown in colour. A profusion of dangling seeds can often be seen hanging from the dry pods and the number of seeds per pod varies from 2 to 8. The seeds are olive green in colour. They are flattened with an elliptic shape and a mean size of 4.5–6 x 3.5–5 mm. The areole, with a mean size of 2.5–4 x 2.5–3.5 mm, is visible as a lighter olive green, horseshoe-shaped marking surrounding an olive brown centre, which is sometimes recessed.

Similar species

Within its distribution range it can be confused with *A. swazica* and *A. exuvialis* (see the comments under the latter species).

General

Elsewhere in Africa, *A. borleae* also occurs in south-western Zimbabwe, southern Mozambique and Swaziland.

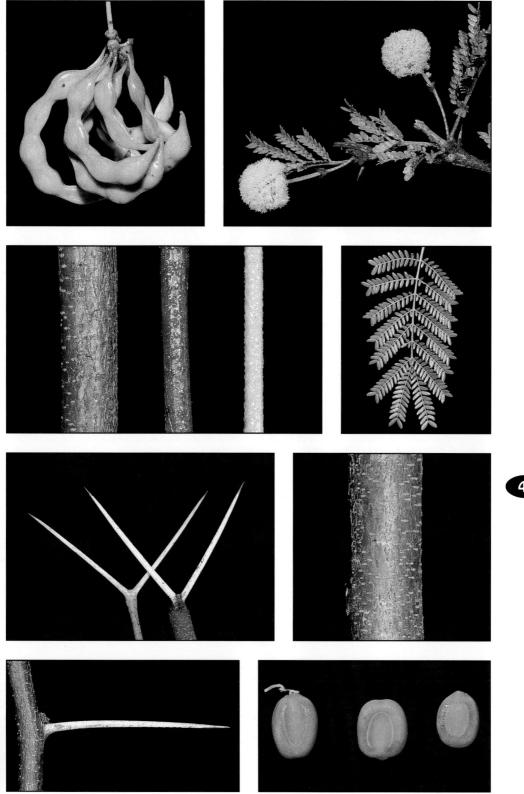

Acacia stuhlmannii

Vlei Thorn • Vleidoring

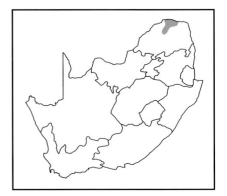

Name with authors
Acacia stuhlmannii Taub – Type from Tanzania

Synonyms
None

National Tree Number 187.1

Outstanding features

- A low, spreading bush up to 4 m with a horizontal spread that can exceed its height,
- Main stem is green, smooth and shiny,
- Young shoots are covered with long bright golden-yellow hairs,
- Paired spines are straight to slightly recurved, covered with long golden-yellow hairs when young,
- The petiole and rachis are light green in colour and are covered with numerous white hairs,
- Globose flowering heads are large and borne on short, hairy peduncles on previous seasons' shoots,
- Young pods are covered with long spreading greyish-white hairs, seeds are almost circular with little or no flattening.

48

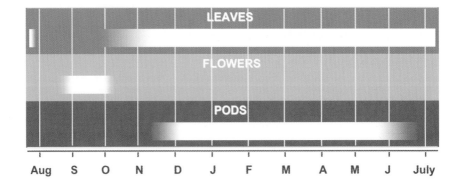

Habitat

Confined to low lying vlei areas and along dry river banks on poorly drained clayey soils as well as on alluvial soils, often in low rainfall areas.

General description

Usually a low, spreading bush up to 4 m, but with a horizontal spread that can exceed its height. It is shaped like an inverted cone with numerous, fairly straight stems radiating from the bole at ground level to form a rounded to flattened crown. Due to its sparse foliage the general appearance is not particularly dense.

Main stem

The main stem is characteristically smooth, shiny and green in colour and covered with numerous, greyish-white, transversely elongated lenticels. Thin segments of peeling papery bark, yellowish-green in colour, may sometimes be present. Long white persisting spines are commonly found on young stems. Outermost main stems on older specimens are often bent down parallel to the ground.

Shoots

Young new season's shoots are very diagnostic. They have a green ground colour but appear golden-yellow due to a cover of long (3 mm) bright golden-yellow hairs. The green ground colour becomes more visible with maturation of the shoots, but the hairiness persists for some time. Previous seasons' shoots are hairless, smooth, shiny and green and covered with large yellowish lenticels. On much older shoots a thin layer of greyish bark may be present.

Thorns

The stipules are modified into hardened, spinescent spines. They are straight to slightly curved, and occur in pairs at nodes. There is a pronounced ridging or swelling of the stem at the point of emergence. On new season's growth the young spines have a greenish yellow to whitish colour with reddened tips and they are characteristically covered with long golden-yellow hairs. These young spines are quite long – up to 65 mm. On older shoots and branches the spines are usually shorter with hairs that persist for some time at the base. They are borne at right angles to the stem but can be raked backwards or forward, up to 20° from the normal. Long spines are usually present on the main trunk of younger trees.

Leaves

The leaves are borne at the nodes and the number of leaves per node varies from 1 to 5.

The petiole and rachis are light green and are covered with numerous white hairs. The length of the petiole ranges from 3–10 mm and the mean length of the petiole and rachis, combined, is 40 mm (range: 25–90 mm). The number of pinna pairs ranges from 3–17 (8–9 typical), and the number of leaflet pairs per pinna from 6–25 (10–12 typical). The leaflets have a fresh green colour. They are relatively small with a mean length of 3 mm (range: 2–5.5 mm) and mean width of 1 mm (range: 0.8–1.5 mm). The margins of the leaflets are sparsely fringed with white hairs and the main vein is only discernible on the underside. On the petiole an inconspicuous, brown to yellow-green, cupped or stalked gland is usually evident. On the rachis there may occasionally be a small brown stalked gland at one to three of the distal pinna junctions.

Inflorescence

Globose flowering heads are borne at the nodes on previous seasons' shoots, usually single but occasionally 2 per node. The developing buds have a dull greenish colour prior to full bloom. The open, fully developed flowering heads are quite large with a mean diameter of 20 mm. They have a light cream to almost white colour and are borne on short, hairy peduncles with a mean length of 14 mm (range: 10–15 mm). The involucel is small and located at the base of the peduncle or close to it.

Pods and seeds

The pods are distinctive. They are borne at the nodes, singly or 2 per node. They are mostly straight or slightly curved on the one side, sharply tapering at the base and bluntly pointed to rounded at the tip. They may attain a mean length of 60 mm (range: 40–105 mm) and a mean width of 15 mm (range: 12–25 mm). Young pods are covered with long spreading greyish-white hairs. There are no visible venation. The base colour of the young pods is green with some reddish colouration, especially at the base. The pods are indehiscent and when dry they have a cinnamon colour. The number of seeds per pod varies from 1 to 6 (4 typical). The colour of the seeds varies from olive to brownish olive. They are almost circular to elliptic in shape with little or no flattening and with a mean diameter of 4.5–9 mm. The areole is in the form of a slightly lighter coloured, indistinct, raised ellipsoidal outline about 4–7 mm x 2.5–4.5 mm. The testa is thick and has a roughened appearance.

Similar species

Unlikely to be confused with any other *Acacia* species. Viewed from a distance its general appearance may resemble that of *A. senegal* var. *rostrata* but on closer inspection they are easily distinguished based on the hairiness of *A. stuhlmannii* as well as it having straight spines as opposed to the recurved prickles, in groups of 3, of *A. senegal* var. *rostrata*.

General

Name derivation: *stuhlmannii* = named after F.L. Stuhlman, a German zoologist and collector who collected the type specimen from Tanzania. Elsewhere in Africa, *A. stuhlmannii* is also found in Somalia, Tanzania, southern Zimbabwe and eastern Botswana.

50

Acacia davyi

Corky Thorn • Kurkdoring

Name with authors
Acacia davyi N.E. Br. – Types from the
Soutpansberg, South Africa and Swaziland

Synonyms
None

National Tree Number 163.1

Other common names
Paper Thorn, Papierdoring

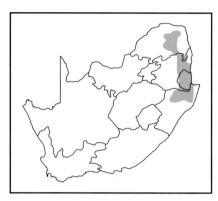

Outstanding features

- Small single-stemmed tree with a rounded crown up to 5 m high or a multi-stemmed shrub of about 2 m,
- The bark on the main stem is thick, corky and relatively soft with deep longitudinal fissures,
- Young shoots are hairless and smooth with a homogeneous bright green colour, while older shoots become covered with light-coloured corky bark,
- Paired stipular spines are slender and relatively short,
- The leaves, typically with 16–24 pinna pairs, are fairly large, bright green to yellowish-green when young,
- Deep yellow globose flowering heads are borne in large panicles at terminals of new season's shoots,
- Pods straight or slightly curved, linear with marked to minor constrictions between seeds.

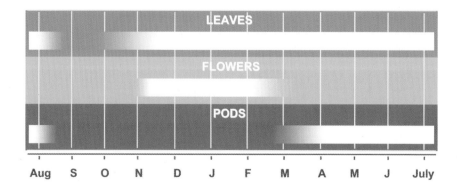

| | LEAVES | | | | | | | | | | |
| Aug | S | O | N | D | J | F | M | A | M | J | July |

Habitat

Distribution is sporadic and localised. Their typical habitat includes grassy hillsides or mountainous country where they are predominantly found on high lying areas. Here they grow scattered in open savanna or grassland which receives a fairly high rainfall.

General description

Usually a small single-stemmed tree with a rounded crown that can grow to a height of 5 m or a multi-stemmed shrub of about 2 m. The branches of the plant often bend at right angles from the main stem and then upright again, giving the plant a rather untidy appearance. Early in the season, when viewed from a distance, the tree has a character-istically yellow-green appearance due to the col-our of the foliage. Later in the season the foliage takes on a deep green colour.

Main stem

The main stem can attain quite a large diameter (up to 250 mm) in comparison to the size of the tree. The bark is thick, corky and relatively soft with deep longitudinal fissures as well as some minor transverse fissures. The thick, corky bark extends onto the side branches. The colour of

the bark on the main stem of mature trees is quite dark (dark to medium grey) and contrasts sharply with the lighter, creamy to yellowish-brown colour of the bark on the younger branches. The main stem of young trees resem-bles these younger branches.

Shoots

Young new season's shoots are hairless and smooth with a homogeneous bright green colour. With age the shoots take on a brownish colour with orange transversely-elongated lenticels. Older, previous seasons' shoots become increas-ingly covered with light coloured corky bark with longitudinal fissures that may assume a diamond pattern. A pink, yellow or orange coloration is vis-ible in the fissures.

Thorns

The stipules are modified into hardened, spinescent spines. They occur in pairs at nodes, spaced at intervals that range from 8 mm to 25 mm. The spines are straight and hairless. They are slender (base diameter averaging 1.5 mm) and relatively short (normally not exceeding 25 mm, though a length of 50 mm is attainable). Young spines are usually raked forward at an angle of approximately 80° to the stems and shoots, often less in the case of older spines. Within pairs the spines are set at an angle of approximately 80°–90°. Spines are whitish and their tips are orange (when young) or brown.

Leaves

The leaves are fairly large and usually occur singly at nodes, but occasionally in pairs. The leaflets may vary in colour from yellowish-green when young, to a bright green. The petiole and rachis are hairless to slightly hairy, grooved on the upper side and bright green in colour. The petiole is short with a mean length of 3–10 mm, while the petiole and rachis, combined, attain a mean length of 100–130 mm (range: 80–190 mm). The number of pinna pairs range from 8–27 (16–24 typical), and the number of leaflet pairs per pinna from 15–44. Leaflets have a mean length of 4.6 mm (range: 2–7 mm) and mean width of 1 mm (range: 0.6–1.2 mm). They are mostly hairless, though sometimes with minute short hairs on the margins. Venation is not visible without magnification. The petiole base is slightly swollen and a green petiolar gland may be present close to the basal pinna pair. On the rachis there are green domed glands at from 1 to 6 of the distal pinna junctions.

Inflorescence

54

Globose flowering heads are borne in quite large panicles at terminals of new season's shoots. Leaves are generally absent from the nodes at the terminals of flower-bearing shoots. Some flower-heads may also be found among leaves at axils some way down from the tip of the shoots. The colour of the developing buds is initially green, turning to a yellowish colour prior to full bloom. The open, fully developed flowering heads are relatively small with a mean diameter of 7 mm (range: 6–10 mm). They are deep yellow in colour and are borne on peduncles with a mean length of 16 mm (range: 8–30 mm). Peduncles can either be densely covered with hairs or be relatively hairless. A distinctive involucel is located close to the midpoint of the peduncles and in some instances there can be a whorl of stamens at the involucel, having the same colour as the florets on the head.

Pods and seeds

Pods are borne either singly or in bunches. They are straight or slightly curved, linear with marked to minor constrictions between seeds. They may attain a length that range from 70–170 mm and a width that range from 5–8 mm. Young pods are green, hairless, venose and have a narrow but distinct raised edge to the valves. The dehiscent pods, when dry, are sub-woody with a brown colour. There can be up to 12 seeds per pod. The seeds have an elliptic shape and a mean size of 6–7.5 x 3–5.5 mm. They are dark brown. A light olive green, horseshoe-shaped areole, with a mean size of 4–5 x 2.5–3.5 mm, is barely visible and is not impressed.

Similar species

Its thick, corky bark readily distinguishes this species from most other *Acacia* species. Its feathery leaves may resemble that of *A. caffra,* but the round yellow flowering heads in panicles at terminals of new season's shoots and straight white spines differ from the cream coloured flower spikes and hooked prickles of *A. caffra.*

General

Name derivation: *davyi* = named after the British botanist J.B. Davy. Elsewhere in Africa, *A. davyi* is restricted to southern Mozambique and Swaziland.

Acacia nilotica

(subsp. *kraussiana*)

Scented Thorn • Lekkerruikpeul

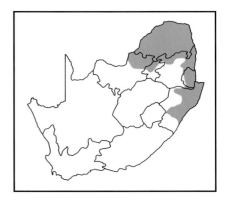

Name and authors
Acacia nilotica (L.) Willd. ex Del.
subsp. *kraussiana* (Benth.) Brenan –
Type from KwaZulu-Natal, South Africa

Synonyms
• *A. arabica (Lam.)* Willd. var. *kraussiana* Benth.
• *A. benthamii* Rochebr. • *A. nilotica* (L.) Willd. Ex Del.
var. *kraussiana* (Benth.) A.F. Hill
• *Mimosa nilotica* Thunb.

National Tree Number 179

Outstanding features

- Small to medium sized single-stemmed tree of 5–6 m with a compact rounded to flattened crown,
- The bark of mature trees is rough, blackish-grey to black, with longitudinal fissures,
- Young new season's shoots are homogeneously green and covered with a thin layer of short whitish hairs,
- The paired spines are straight to slightly recurved and are often raked backwards,
- The leaflets are small and the leaflet pairs per pinna increase distally,
- Globose flowering heads are bright yellow with moderately hairy peduncles,
- Pods, with marked constrictions between seeds, have a beaded appearance and a characteristically sweet smell.

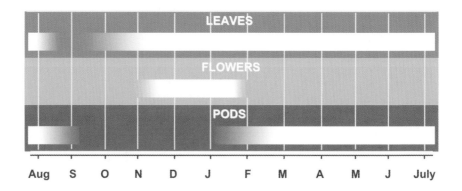

Habitat

A species with a wide habitat tolerance. In semi-arid savanna areas it is commonly found on heavy (clayey) soils as well as sodic soils, while in coastal areas it shows a preference for sandy and alluvial soils. It is generally absent from shallow gravelly soils as well as wet watercourses.

General description

A small to medium sized tree of 5–6 m in height, but under favourable conditions may grow to a height of 10 m. It is usually single-stemmed with a compact rounded to flattened crown, often branching from low down, with a horizontal spread that can equal or exceed its height.

Main stem

The bark on the main stem of mature trees is rough, blackish-grey to black, with longitudinal fissures. A light, almost orange, coloration is sometimes visible in the fissures. The rough bark of the main stem contrasts with the younger branches, which are smoother and also lighter in colour, sometimes

reddish-brown. Main stems of young trees resemble these younger branches.

Shoots

Very young new season's shoots are homogeneously green and covered with a thin layer of short whitish hairs. With maturation these hairs disappear and shoots may exhibit striations, buff to brown in colour with the spaces between them a green colour. They are also covered with light coloured lenticels. Older, previous seasons' shoots have a greyish-brown to a reddish-brown colour with a tendency to peel and with small white, transversely-elongated lenticels.

Thorns

The stipules are modified into hardened, spinescent spines. They are straight to slightly curved, and occur in pairs at nodes. On new season's growth the young spines are greenish-white to pink, with yellowish tips. They are soft and flexible and covered with whitish hairs that disappear with maturation. Older spines are white to greyish-white with darkened tips. On older shoots and branches the spines can be short, while on younger shoots they may attain a length of 175 mm. In most cases they have a mean length of 30–50 mm with a base diameter of 2–3 mm. There is usually an appreciable swelling of the stem at the thorn base. Spines are either borne at right angles to the stem or more typically raked backwards up to 10° from the normal.

Leaves

The leaves are borne at the nodes, as many as 8 leaves per node, though usually less. Where there are several leaves per node, the group usually comprises one or more large primary leaves surrounded by smaller secondary leaves. The number of pinna pairs range from 2–14 (6–7 typical). On each leaf the number of leaflet pairs per pinna increases distally, varying from 7–36 pairs per pinna. The petiole has a length of 4–12 mm, while the length of the petiole and rachis, combined, ranges from 25–65 mm (30–50 mm typical). Both the petiole and rachis are green and hairless, except on new season's growth when sparse hairs can cover them. The rachis is grooved on top. The leaflets are bright green above and somewhat lighter on the underside. They can be covered with sparse hairs and the main vein is visible on both sides. Leaflets are small with a mean length of 4 mm (range: 1.5–7 mm) and mean width of 0.8 mm (range: 0.5–1.5 mm). A small petiolar gland is usually present, but it is highly variable. There are small raised glands at the junctions of the distal pinna pairs.

Inflorescence

Globose flowering heads are borne at the nodes, singly or up to 8 per node on new season's shoots only. The colour of the developing buds is green prior to full bloom. The open, fully developed flowering heads have a mean diameter of 13.5 mm (range: 10–20 mm). They are scented and have a bright yellow colour. Peduncles are moderately hairy, quite long with a mean length of 20 mm (range: 12–45 mm). The involucel is prominent and located from near the base to just over halfway up the peduncle. Specimens from coastal areas of KwaZulu-Natal are distinctive in having a whorl of stamens at the involucel with the same colour as the florets on the head.

Pods and seeds

The characteristic pods are borne either singly or in bunches. They are mostly straight, occasionally slightly curved, linear, pointed at the base, bluntly tapered at the tip. There are marked constrictions between the seeds and the position of each seed is marked by a distinct raised bump in the valves, giving the pods a beaded appearance. They attain a length of 80–170 mm and a width of 9–22 mm. Young pods are green, fleshy and hairless, with a distinct raised edge to the valves. When ripe they have a characteristically sweet smell which gave rise to the common name "Scented Thorn". The indehiscent pods, when dry, are dark coloured, almost black, sub-woody and breaking up transversely into single-seeded segments when the pods fall to the ground. There can be up to 16 seeds per pod. The seeds are reddish-brown to purplish-black, somewhat thickened with an elliptic shape and a mean size of 6.5–9 x 5–8 mm. The areole is in the form of a narrow, olive green elliptic ring of 5–7 x 4–6 mm, which is not depressed. When removed from the pod the seeds may be fringed with adhering whitish pith.

Similar species

The pendent, beaded and sweet smelling pods, when present, readily distinguish this species from all other *Acacia* species. Other features that distinguish it from *A. karroo* are its shoots and spines, which are moderately hairy when young.

General

Name derivation: *nilotica* = from the Nile, and *kraussiana* = named after Dr Ferdinand Krauss, former Director of the Stuttgart Museum. This species has been divided into seven subspecies in tropical Africa and all the southern African material may be assigned to subsp. *kraussiana*. It is found from Tanzania southwards to Zambia, Zimbabwe, Namibia, Botswana, Mozambique, South Africa and Swaziland. The heartwood is hard and heavy (air-dry 1 100 kg/m^3) with a dark reddish-brown colour, surrounded by pale brown sapwood. It is mainly used for fence posts and firewood.

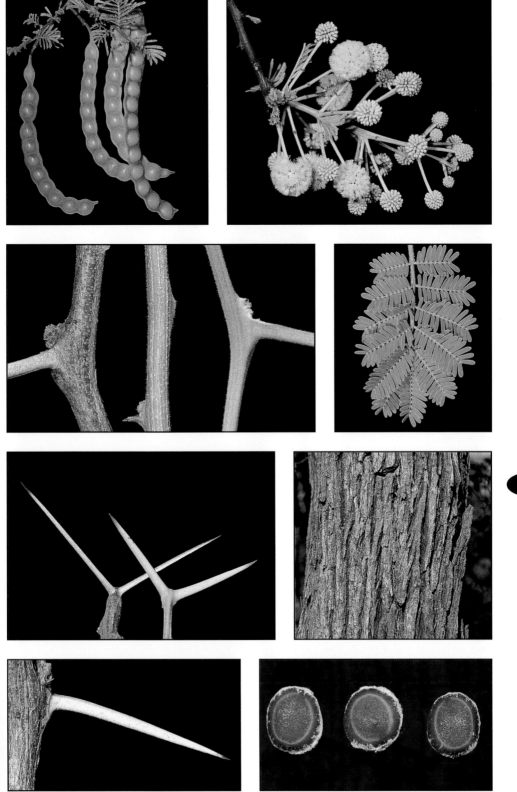

 59

Acacia grandicornuta

Horned Thorn • Horingdoring

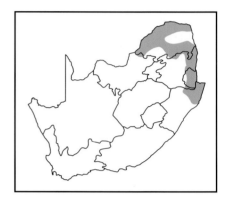

Name with authors
Acacia grandicornuta Gerstner –
Types from KwaZulu-Natal, South Africa

Synonyms
None

National Tree Number 168.1

Outstanding features

- Small to medium-sized tree, usually single-stemmed with a rounded to irregular crown,
- Bark of mature trees is coarse with deep, longitudinal fissures,
- Young shoots are smooth, hairless and grow in a marked zig-zag pattern from node to node,
- The paired spines are stout and often swollen, especially at the base,
- Leaves with 1–5 pinna pairs, petiole and rachis are hairless to slightly hairy and leaflets are comparatively large,
- Globose flowering heads are light cream to almost white with slender, hairless peduncles,
- Pods are sickle-shaped, green and hairless, dry pods with thin, brittle valves. Dangling seeds often hang from the dehiscent pods.

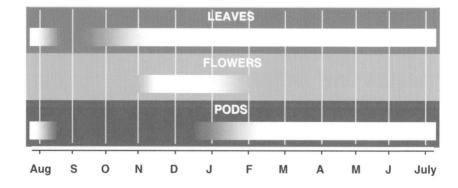

Habitat

Mostly found on deep sodic soils, as well as on heavy (clayey) soils. They are tolerant to dry conditions and under favourable conditions they can form dominant stands.

General description

A small to medium-sized tree of 5–10 m in height, occasionally up to 15 m. It is usually single-stemmed and often branches from low down with ascending branches. Its crown is rounded to irregular with a moderate horizontal spread. The foliage is dark green and fairly dense.

Main stem

The bark on the main stem of mature trees is grey to dark brown with coarse, deep, longitudinal fissures. A reddish coloration is often visible in the deep fissures. It contrasts sharply with the younger branches, which are smooth, light grey in colour with occasional darker patches that give it a striped appearance. Main stems of young trees resemble these younger branches.

Shoots

Very young new season's shoots are smooth, hairless and grow in a marked zig-zag pattern from node to node. They are dull green and are covered with small white lenticels. With maturation the colour of the shoots changes to reddish-brown. Older, previous seasons' shoots have a greyish-brown to reddish-brown colour with pronounced tufted cushions at nodes.

Thorns

The stipules are modified into hardened, spinescent spines. They are straight to slightly curved, and occur in pairs at nodes. On new season's growth the young spines are light green with reddish tips and hairless. Older spines are stout, white to greyish-white with darkened tips and often swollen, especially at the base. On older shoots and branches the spines can be very short (2–6 mm), while on other shoots they may attain a length of 100 mm. In most cases they have a mean length of between 30–60 mm with a base diameter of 3–6 mm. Spines are either oriented at right angles to the stem or raked forward or backwards up to 10° from the normal.

Leaves

The leaves are borne at the nodes, as many as 7 leaves per node. On older shoots they arise from poorly developed tufted cushions and each cluster of leaves usually consist of a pair of larger primary leaves and smaller secondary leaves. The number of pinna pairs varies from 1–5 (2–3 typical), and the number of leaflet pairs per pinna from 5–18 (8–12 typical). The petiole has a slight swelling at the base and its length may vary from 0–36 mm. Both the petiole and rachis are hairless to slightly hairy with a green colour and, combined, may attain a length of 70 mm (15–40 mm typical). The leaflets are dark green above and somewhat lighter on the underside, rounded at both sides, though narrower at the base. They are comparatively large in comparison to the size of the leaves with a mean length of 7 mm (range: 3–10 mm) and mean width of 2.4 mm (range: 1.5–4 mm). The main vein is sometimes indistinctly visible on the upper surface but is not apparent underneath. A petiolar gland is generally not visible, but there are raised, yellowish glands on the rachis at from 1 to 3 of the distal pinna junctions.

Inflorescence

Globose flowering heads are borne at the nodes, as many as 8 per node on previous seasons' shoots. The developing buds are green prior to full bloom. The open, fully developed flowering heads have a diameter that range from 8–12 mm. They are scented and have a light cream to almost white colour. Peduncles are slender and hairless with a mean length of 16 mm (range: 12–25 mm). The involucel is prominent and located at from 40 to 60 % of the length up from the base of the peduncle.

Pods and seeds

Pods are borne either single or in small bunches. They are sickle-shaped, tapered at the base and more rounded at the tip. They may attain a length that ranged from 50–170 mm and a width that ranged from 6–11 mm. Young pods are green, hairless, finely longitudinally veined and sometimes have a narrow raised edging to the valves. When dry the pods have a reddish-brown colour with thin, brittle valves. A profusion of dangling seeds can often be seen hanging from the dry dehiscent pods and the number of seeds per pod varies from 4 to 12. The seeds are reddish-brown to olive green in colour. They are flattened with an oblong shape and a mean size of 6–10 x 5–7 mm. The areole, with a mean size of 4–6 x 2.5–4.5 mm, is visible as a lighter oblong marking, either raised with a depressed central area, or occasionally recessed with a raised central area.

Similar species

A. grandicornuta is closely related to *A. robusta*, but it can be distinguished from *A. robusta* subsp. *robusta* in having more slender branches and narrower sickle-shaped pods. It differs from *A. robusta* subsp. *clavigera* in having hairless leaf rachides, fewer pinna pairs and also fewer leaflet pairs. The typically stout and slightly swollen spines further distinguish *A. grandicornuta* from *A. robusta*.

General

Name derivation: *grandicornuta* = big horns. Elsewhere in Africa, *A. grandicornuta* is found in south-eastern Botswana, Zimbabwe, Mozambique and Swaziland. The wood is relatively hard, heavy (air-dry 770 kg/m³) and light brown in colour. No heartwood is present. The wood is susceptible to damage from woodborers and is therefore seldom used.

Acacia karroo

Sweet Thorn • Soetdoring

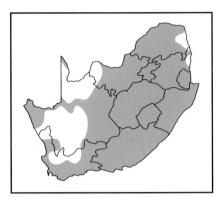

Name with authors
Acacia karroo Hayne – Type from South Africa

Synonyms
- *A capensis* (Burm. f.) Burch.
- *A. dekindtiana* A. Chev. • *A. hirtella* E. Mey.
- *A. hirtella* Willd. *var. inermis* Walp.
- *A. horrida* Willd. • *A. horrida* Willd. var. *transvaalensis* Burtt Davy • *A. inconflagrabilis* Gerstner • *A. karroo* Hayne var. *transvaalensis* (Burtt Davy) Burtt Davy
- *A. natalitia* E. Mey • *A. reticulata* (L.) Willd.
- *Mimosa capensis* Burm. f. • *M. leucacantha* Jacq. • *M. nilotica* Thunb.

National Tree Number 172

NOTE: The description below applies to the "typical" form of *A. karroo*, which occurs in the Karoo, Free State, interior regions of KwaZulu-Natal and over most of the northern parts of the country. Some of the most notable variations of *A. karroo* are discussed separately (page 68).

Outstanding features

- Small to medium-sized tree, usually single-stemmed with a rounded and somewhat spreading crown,
- Bark of mature trees is coarse, blackish-grey to black, longitudinally fissured with some horizontal cracking,
- Young shoots are smooth and mostly hairless and become progressively covered with a thin layer of bark,
- The paired spines are straight and mostly hairless,
- Leaves with 2–6 pinna pairs and 8–16 leaflet pairs per pinna, petiole and rachis are usually hairless,
- Globose flowering heads are bright yellow with hairless peduncles and a prominent involucel,
- Pods are sickle-shaped, green and mostly hairless, dry pods with thin, brittle valves, dangling seeds are often hanging from the dehiscent pods.

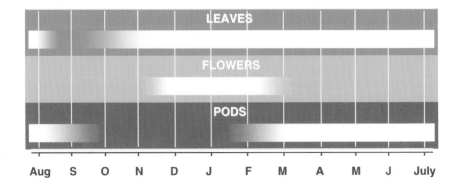

	Aug	S	O	N	D	J	F	M	A	M	J	July
LEAVES												
FLOWERS												
PODS												

Habitat

A species with a wide habitat tolerance as demonstrated by its wide distribution range. It grows on most soil types, but is often found on soils with a relatively high fertility such as clay and loam soils. It is often associated with heavy, clayey soils on the banks of rivers and streams. Of all the South African *Acacia* species it is likely the most tolerant to cold.

General description

A small to medium-sized tree of 5–12 m in height, occasionally up to 22 m. It is usually a single-stemmed tree, branching at varying heights above the ground. Multi-stemmed plants are, however, not uncommon. Its crown is rounded and somewhat spreading. The foliage is dark green and can be fairly dense.

Main stem

The bark on the main stem of mature trees is coarse, blackish-grey to black, longitudinally fissured with some horizontal cracking, forming squares that vary in size. A reddish coloration is often visible in the deep fissures. Younger branches are smoother, often red-brown in col-

our. The main stems of young trees resemble these younger branches. Copious quantities of gum are secreted at wounds.

Shoots

Young new season's shoots are smooth and usually hairless. They are green to reddish-brown and covered with small inconspicuous reddish sessile glands as well as numerous light-coloured lenticels. Older, previous seasons' shoots become progressively covered with a thin layer of light-coloured bark, which splits longitudinally to reveal a smooth green under-surface. Much older, more mature shoots are covered with thin layers of reddish-brown bark.

Thorns

The stipules are modified into hardened, spinescent spines. They are straight and occur in pairs at nodes. On new season's growth the young spines are white with yellowish or orange tips. Young spines are mostly hairless, but can sometimes be slightly hairy. Older spines are hairless, white to greyish-white, and often with some minute dark spotting. The tips are reddened or darkened. On large, mature trees the spines can be short, while on younger plants and on new growth they may attain a length of 100 mm or more. In most cases they have a mean length of 40 mm. Larger thorns usually increase slightly in diameter from base to mid-point, before tapering off to the tip. Spines are either borne at right angles to the stem or raked forward up to 20° from the normal.

Leaves

The leaves are borne at the nodes, singly or as many as 8 leaves per node. On older shoots the leaves often arise from fairly pronounced, black cushions and each cluster of leaves usually consists of larger primary leaves and smaller secondary leaves. The number of pinna pairs varies from 2–6 (3–5 typical), and the number of leaflet pairs per pinna from 8–16. The petiole has a slight swelling at the base and its length may vary from 5–18 mm. Both the petiole and rachis are mostly hairless, but can in some instances be slightly hairy when young. They are green, grooved on top and, combined, may attain a length of 100 mm (35–55 mm typical). The leaflets are the same colour above and below and with a mean length of 7.5 mm (range: 3–10 mm) and mean width of 2.1 mm (range: 1.5–5 mm). The main vein is clearly visible on the underside but indistinct above. A petiolar gland is usually present. It is green or blackish and its size and shape vary considerably. There are cupped glands on the rachis at all or most of the pinna junctions.

Inflorescence

Globose flowering heads are borne at the nodes in numbers of 2–5 per node. They are borne on new season's shoots, commencing some distance down from the tips and extending up to the tips to form a panicle, which is usually leafless. The colour of the developing buds is yellowish-green prior to full bloom. The open, fully-developed flowering heads have a diameter of 8–18 mm. They are scented and are bright yellow in colour. Peduncles are hairless with a length of 20–30 mm. The involucel is prominent and located at varying positions above or below the midpoint of the peduncle. When in full bloom the trees are very conspicuous.

Pods and seeds

Pods occur in bunches along the old panicle positions, sometimes in such profusion that they form a tangled mass. They are sickle-shaped and linear with occasional minor constrictions between seeds. They may attain a length of 150 mm and a width of 8 mm. Young pods are green and mostly hairless. The valves are thin, somewhat leathery with a narrow raised edging. They are diagonally to longitudinally venose and may also be somewhat glandular. When dry, the pods are dark brown in colour with thin, brittle valves. A profusion of dangling seeds can often be seen hanging from the dry dehiscent pods and the number of seeds per pod can be up to 12. The seeds are an olive green to light brown in colour. They are compressed with an elliptic to quadrate outline and a mean size of 4.5–7.5 x 3–5 mm. The areole, with a mean size of 3–6 x 2–3.5 mm, comprises a lighter, olive green, elliptic outline surrounding a somewhat darkened area, which in most instances is shallowly recessed, though occasionally raised.

Similar species

The glandular podded *Acacia* species (*A. tenuispina*, *A. nebrownii*, *A. permixta*, *A. swazica*, *A. exuvialis* and *A. borleae*) are all related to *A. karroo*. *A. karroo* differs from them in lacking the glandular pods. This species is highly variable and it is possible that different forms may superficially resemble various other species like *A. gerrardii*, *A. nilotica* and *A. robusta*. Hybridization with *A. tenuispina* and *A. rehmanniana* has also been reported.

General

Name derivation: *karroo* = from the Karoo. Elsewhere in Africa, *A. karroo* are widespread and occurr in every country of the Southern African Development Community (SADC) region, excluding Tanzania. The wood is hard and heavy (air-dry 800 kg/m³) and is light brown to yellowish in colour. The heartwood is reddish brown. The wood is susceptible to damage from woodborers but this may be prevented if seasoned in water for six months.

Some of the most notable variations of *Acacia karroo*

The former description of A. karroo applies to the so called "typical" form. This species is, however, extremely variable. It appears that this variation is regional with plants from different geographical areas that look distinctly different with regard to one or more features. All these variants appear to be linked to the "central A. karroo gene pool" by numerous and varied intermediate stages that become progressively less distinct until it becomes difficult to delimit each variant clearly. Apart from the "typical" form, a number of other entities are recognised within the species as described by Ross (1979) and Barnes, Filer & Milton (1996):

1. The white-barked trees or shrubs with short spines, 4–13 pinna pairs per leaf and 12–27 pairs of smaller, narrower leaflets per pinna (formerly *Acacia natalitia*) which are found chiefly in the Eastern Cape, Kwazulu-Natal, Swaziland, Mpumalanga, Zimbabwe and Mozambique. *A. hirtella*, formerly described from the Kwazulu-Natal coast, is similar but differs in having hairy young shoots, leaves, leaflets and peduncles.

2. The small slender shrubs up to 1 m high found in the Eastern Cape in the vicinity of the Kei River mouth.

3. The "fire-resistant" shrubs found in the Nongoma District of KwaZulu-Natal (formerly *Acacia inconflagrabilis*).

4. The slender, sparingly branched trees up to 6 m high found in KwaZulu-Natal, particularly in the Hluhluwe and Umfolozi Game Reserves and in the corridor linking them ("spindle" form). A "spin-

dle" growth form also occurs near the Loskop Dam. Plants typically have bright reddish-brown minutely flaking bark, blue-green foliage, large flattened petiolar glands and a large gland at the junction of each or most pinna pairs.

5. The large trees with greyish-white bark, spines up to 250 mm long and long pods found along the KwaZulu-Natal coast from the mouth of the Tugela River northwards into Mozambique. Plants are confined to a narrow belt and occur on the coastal plain, among the coastal dunes, in the mouths of river estuaries and around the shore of the fresh water Lake Sibaya. The plants, which usually form very dense pure stands and are often dominant to the exclusion of other trees, often act as pioneers in stabilising loose sand dunes, especially in disturbed areas and in patches of regenerating dune forest. Unlike in "typical" A. karroo, the paired spines often persist on the trunk.

6. On the highveld from Pretoria eastwards there is a local tendency for the production of a sparse indumentum on the young shoots, leaves, peduncles and pods (formerly *Acacia karroo* var. *transvaalensis*). However, occasionally this tendency is so extreme, for example, at Steelpoort, as to completely alter the general appearance of the plants. The latter bear a strong superficial resemblance to A. gerrardii.

7. On the Springbok flats north of Pretoria a small shrubby form of A. karroo occurs, which often can be distinguished from A. tenuispina only with difficulty (see the comments under the latter species).

68

Small multi-stemmed form of *A. karroo* on the Springbok flats near Warmbaths.

KwaZulu-Natal coastal form near Cape Vidal.

Smooth, greyish-white bark of the KwaZulu-Natal coastal form near Cape Vidal.

Flowers of the KwaZulu-Natal coastal form near Cape Vidal with a whorl of stamens at the involucel with the same colour as the florets on the head.

Shoots of the form formerly described as *A. natalitia* near Nelspruit.

Narrow leaflets of the form formerly described as *A. natalitia.*

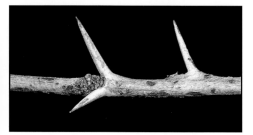

Short spines of the form formerly described as *A. natalitia* near Nelspruit.

Massive spines on specimens from Port Elizabeth.

69

Acacia gerrardii

(var. *gerrardii*)

Red Thorn • Rooidoring

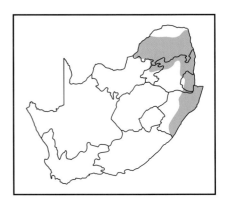

Name with authors
A. gerrardii Benth. var. *gerrardii* –
Type from KwaZulu-Natal, South Africa

Synonyms
• *A. etbaica* var. *hirta* A. Chev. • *A. hebecladoides*
Harms • *A. subtomentosa* De Wild.

National Tree Number 167

Other common names
Rooibas

Outstanding features

- A small to medium-sized tree, mostly single-stemmed with a sparse, flattish crown,
- The bark on main stem is rough and dark grey, young branches light grey, red-brown or bright orange, with traverse wrinkling,
- Young shoots are covered with short whitish hairs and have a velvety feel to the touch,
- The paired spines are straight to slightly recurved and may have thick bases,
- Leaves with 5–10 pinna pairs, petiole and rachis are hairy and leaflets are of an intermediate size,
- Globose flowering heads are cream coloured to almost white with moderately hairy peduncles,
- Pods are sickle-shaped and covered with short velvety grey hairs.

70

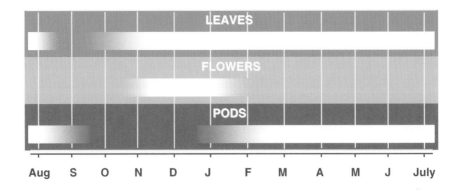

LEAVES

FLOWERS

PODS

Aug   S   O   N   D   J   F   M   A   M   J   July

Habitat

Though not uncommon within its distribution range, it seldom forms large dominant stands. Grow on a variety of soil types, including soil with a low pH. Often abundant in low lying areas on poorly drained, sodic soils.

General description

A small to medium-sized tree of 4–7 m in height, but under favourable conditions may grow to a height of 10–15 m. Undamaged plants are mostly single-stemmed, branching fairly high up. The crown is somewhat sparse, flattish with an open appearance.

Main stem

The bark on the main stem of mature trees is rough, dark grey, longitudinally fissured with some transverse cracking. A reddish coloration is often visible in the fissures. It contrasts sharply with the younger branches which are smooth, often with marked transverse wrinkling, and which vary in colour from light grey, red-brown to bright orange. The main stem of young trees resembles these younger branches. Long white persisting spines are commonly found on young stems.

Shoots

The base colour of young new season's shoots is green with some longitudinally-elongated cream-coloured lenticels. These young shoots appear whitish due to a dense cover of short whitish hairs and have a velvety feel to the touch. On older shoots the hairy layer splits longitudinally to reveal a smooth, green surface underneath. Older, previous seasons' shoots are a greyish-green in colour with orange coloured transversely-elongated lenticels. Still older shoots have grey bark, peeling to reveal a bright orange to red-brown colour.

Thorns

The stipules are modified into hardened, spinescent spines. They are straight to slightly curved, and occur in pairs at nodes. They may have thick bases and the nodes may also be swollen. On older shoots and branches the spines are usually short (about 10 mm long), while on younger shoots they may attain a length of 100 mm. They are either borne at right angles to the stem or raked backwards, occasionally forward, up to 10° from the normal. When young they are covered with whitish hairs which disappear with maturation. On new season's growth the young spines are green and their tips a light orange. Older spines are whitish with darkened tips. Long spines are sometimes present on the main trunk of younger trees.

Leaves

The leaves are borne at the nodes, usually on distinct "cushions". There can be up to 7 leaves or more per node. The number of pinna pairs varies from 5–10 and the number of leaflet pairs per pinna from 12–23. The petiole has a length of 7–25 mm, while the petiole and rachis, combined, has a mean length of 66 mm (range: 27–90 mm). Both the petiole and rachis are hairy. The leaflets are green above and somewhat lighter on the underside. Spreading hairs can be present on their margins. The leaflets have an intermediate size with a mean length of 4.5 mm (range: 3–7.5 mm) and mean width of 1.5 mm (range: 0.8–1.8 mm). A petiolar gland is usually present near the junction of the first pinna pair. There is a small raised gland at the junction of the distal 1–2 pinna pairs.

Inflorescence

Globose flowering heads are borne at the nodes in groups of up to 14 per node on both new season's and previous seasons' shoots, often in great profusion. The colour of the developing buds is green with orange tinges prior to full bloom. The open, fully developed flowering heads have a mean diameter of 16 mm (range: 10–20 mm). They are scented and are light cream to almost white in colour. Peduncles are slender, moderately hairy, with a mean length of 30 mm (range: 20–45 mm). The involucel is located from near the base to approximately one third up the peduncle.

Pods and seeds

Pods are borne either singly or in small bunches. They are sickle-shaped, tapered at both the base and the tip. They attain a mean length of 103 mm (range: 70–160 mm) and mean width of 10 mm (range: 6–12 mm). Young pods have a green base colour, but may appear greyish-green due to a covering of short velvety grey hairs. The valves are fairly thin and have a narrow raised edge. The pods dry to a colour that varies from grey to grey-brown, or occasionally reddish-brown. A profusion of dangling seeds can often be seen hanging from the dry dehiscent pods and the number of seeds per pod varies from 5 to 10. The seeds are reddish-brown to olive-grey in colour. They are flattened with a roughly rectangular shape and a mean size of 9–12 x 5–7 mm. The areole, with a mean size of 5–7.5 x 3.5–5 mm, is visible as a light coloured, U-shaped outline surrounding a slight depression with a darker colour.

Similar species

It can be distinguished from *A. robusta* by the presence of a dense cover of short whitish hairs on young shoots, as well as the velvety pods which differ from the hairless pods of *A. robusta*.

General

Name derivation: *gerrardii* = named after W. T. Gerrard who collected the type specimen from KwaZulu-Natal. There are three varieties of *A. gerrardii* of which only the type variety, var. *gerrardii,* occurs in South Africa. It is widespread in tropical Africa and occurs from Nigeria in the west to the Sudan in the north east, extending southwards to Zambia, Botswana, Zimbabwe, Mozambique, South Africa and Swaziland. The sapwood is whitish with a brown tint and the heartwood small and dark brown. The wood has a rough texture and although it is relatively hard (900 kg/m³) it is susceptible to attack by woodborers and is not used.

Mature tree

Young, immature tree

Acacia rehmanniana

Silky Thorn • Sydoring

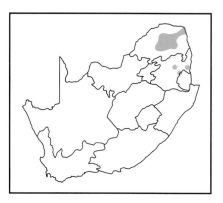

Name and authors
Acacia rehmanniana Schinz –
Type from Northern Province, South Africa

Synonyms
None

National Tree Number   182

Outstanding features

- Small to medium-sized tree, mostly single-stemmed, with a flattened, spreading crown,
- The bark on main stem is rough and dark grey, young branches are smoother with a red-brown to bright orange colour,
- Young shoots are densely covered with long hairs, golden-yellow on growing tips to whitish on slightly older parts,
- Paired spines are covered with golden-yellow to whitish hairs when young,
- The petiole and rachis are densely hairy, the leaflets are small and occur densely packed on hairy rachillae,
- Light coloured globose flowering heads with hairy peduncles are borne in panicles at terminals of new season's shoots,
- The dehiscent pods are hairless and straight without any constrictions between seeds.

74

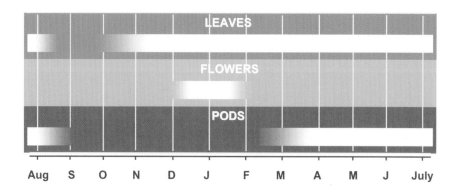

	Aug	S	O	N	D	J	F	M	A	M	J	July
LEAVES												
FLOWERS												
PODS												

Habitat

Occur in open savanna at higher altitude like the Pietersburg Plato, but also near rivers and sometimes in association with termite mounds.

General description

A small to medium-sized tree of 4–6 m in height, but under favourable conditions may grow to a height of 8–12 m. It is mostly single-stemmed, branching fairly high up. It has a somewhat flattened, spreading crown and fairly dense foliage with a velvety appearance.

Main stem

The bark on the main stem of mature trees is rough, longitudinally fissured and dark grey in colour. It contrasts sharply with the younger branches, which appear smooth, occasionally transversely wrinkled, and with a characteristic red-brown to bright orange colour. The main stem of young trees resembles these younger branches. Long white persisting spines are commonly found on young stems.

Shoots

Young new season's shoots have an unobtru-sive green ground colour and are densely covered with long hairs which vary in colour from golden-yellow on growing tips to whitish on slightly older parts. Young shoots have a velvety feel to the touch. The hairiness persists for some time but disappears gradually with maturation. Much older, previous seasons' shoots are predominantly hairless with a grey to green colour. The grey colour eventually gives way to the characteristic red-brown to bright orange colour of the main branches.

Thorns

The stipules are modified into hardened, spinescent spines. They are straight and occur in pairs at nodes. On new season's growth the young spines have a green to white colour, with reddish tips, and they are covered with golden-yellow to whitish hairs similar to those on the young shoots. The hairiness persists for some time on the base of the spines and it is only on much older shoots that the spines are hairless. The spines are borne at right angles to the stem but can be raked backwards up to 10° from the normal. They may attain a length of 55 mm, but on average are not longer than 20–30 mm.

Leaves

The leaves occur at nodes, singly or up to 3 leaves per node. New leaves unfolding at the ends of growing tips have a striking green-gold colour. The petiole and rachis are densely hairy, appear thickened and are grey-green in colour. The colour of the hairs is golden-yellow at first, turning into a greyish-white colour. The petiole is short with a mean length of 1–5 mm, while the petiole and rachis, combined, attain a mean length of 48–62 mm (range: 25–125 mm). The number of pinna pairs on primary leaves ranges from 15–44, and the number of leaflet pairs per pinna from 24–48. The leaflets are small with a mean length of 2.3 mm (range: 1–2.8 mm) and mean width of 0.8 mm (range: 0.4–0.9 mm) and occur densely packed on hairy rachillae. The undersides are a slightly lighter shade of green with hairs on the margins. Venation is not visible without magnification. The petiole base is slightly swollen and a large cupped, brown gland with a dark brown centre is present. On the rachis glands are often not visible. When present they appear small, with a pale green colour and are located at one to three of the distal pinna junctions.

Inflorescence

Globose flowering heads are borne in panicles at terminals of new season's shoots. Leaves are generally absent from the nodes at the terminals of flower-bearing shoots and these shoots are covered with dense golden-yellow hairs. Within panicles there can be as many as 7 flowering heads at the same node. The colour of the developing buds is dull green prior to full bloom. The open, fully developed flowering heads have a diameter that ranges from 10–15 mm. They are scented and are light cream to white in colour. Peduncles are light coloured (greenish-white) and hairy with a length that ranges from 5–20 mm. The involucel is inconspicuous, light coloured and located either close to the midpoint of the peduncle or lower down.

Pods and seeds

The pods are borne in bunches near terminals. The colour of the young developing pods is homogeneously green and they dry to a khaki or reddish-brown colour. The pods are straight, without any constrictions between seeds, bluntly tapered at the base and rounded at the tip. They are hairless with indistinct veins and have a distinct raised edge to the valves. They may attain a length of 70–140 mm and a width of 11–23 mm. The pods are dehiscent and the number of seeds per pod varies from 8 to 11. The seeds are olive-brown, somewhat thickened, slightly elliptic with a mean size of 4.5–9 x 4–7 mm. The areole is in the form of a raised, dark brown ring of 2.5–5 x 1.3–2.8 mm, surrounding a slightly darkened centre. When removed from the pod, the seeds may be fringed with adhering whitish pith.

Similar species

This species can be confused with *A. sieberiana*, but it can be separated by the more numerous, closely arranged pinnae, smaller and more thinly textured pods, the involucels in the lower half of the peduncle and by the way in which the flowers are clustered in panicles at the terminals of the shoots.

General

Name derivation: *rehmanniana* = named after A. Rehmann, a botanist who collected the type specimen from the Northern Province. Elsewhere in Africa, *A. rehmanniana* is found in southern Zambia, Zimbabwe and northern Botswana.

Mature tree

Young, immature tree

Acacia sieberiana

(var. *woodii*)

Paperbark Thorn • Papierbasdoring

Name with authors

Acacia sieberiana DC. var. *woodii* (Burtt Davy)
Keay & Brenan –
Type from KwaZulu-Natal, South Africa

Synonyms

• *A. amboensis* Schinz • *A. katangensis* De Wild. • *A. monga* De Wild. • *A. nefasia* (Hochst. ex A. Rich.) Schweinf. • *A. sieberiana* DC. var. *kagerensis* Troupin • *A. sieberiana* DC. var. *vermoesenii* (De Wild.) Keay & Brenan • *A sieberiana* DC. subsp. *sieberiana* var. *orientalis* Troupin • *A. sieberiana* DC. subsp. *vermoesenii (De Wild.)* Troupin var. *vermoesenii* • *A. sieberiana* DC. subsp. *vermoesenii* (De Wild.)Troupin var. *woodii* (Burtt Davy) Keay & Brenan • *A. vermoesenii* De Wild. • *A. woodii* Burtt Davy

National Tree Number 187

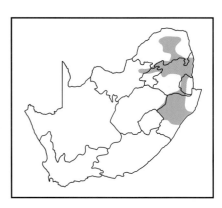

Outstanding features

- Beautiful tree, mostly single-stemmed, with a spreading, flattened crown,
- The bark on main stem is coarse, greyish to yellowish-brown and the outer layers peeling away in thin papery flakes,
- Young shoots, densely covered with long hairs, are golden-yellow on growing tips to whitish on slightly older parts,
- Paired spines are covered with whitish hairs when young,
- Leaves are fairly large, the petiole and rachis are moderately hairy and the leaflets are closely spaced,
- Globose flowering heads are cream coloured and the peduncles are hairy, involucel is located in the upper half of the peduncle,
- The indehiscent pods are large, straight to slightly curved, valves are woody, thick and hard.

78

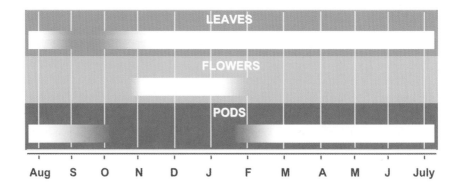

	LEAVES										
	FLOWERS										
	PODS										
Aug	S	O	N	D	J	F	M	A	M	J	July

Habitat

Habitat quite varied ranging from low altitude tropical savanna and woodland areas to high altitude grasslands. Found on alluvial soils of flood plains which are seldom under water. In general it shows a preference for well drained soils. It is fairly tolerant to cold.

General description

A beautiful tree, mostly single-stemmed, but often splitting into several stems fairly low down to form a distinctive flattened to rounded crown. It usually grows to a height of 7–9 m, but may reach a height of 12–17 m. The crown can achieve a considerable horizontal spread, often well in excess of its height.

Main stem

The colour of the bark varies from greyish to yellowish-brown, with the yellowish colour more pronounced in younger trees. The bark is coarse, especially in younger trees, with a roughly rectangular pattern and the outer layers peeling away in thin papery flakes. Below the peeling bark a yellowish inner layer is usually visible.

Shoots

Young new season's shoots have a green ground colour and are densely covered with long hairs which vary in colour from golden-yellow on growing tips to yellowish or whitish on slightly older parts. Young shoots have a velvety feel to the touch. The hairiness decreases gradually with maturation. Older, previous seasons' shoots are moderately hairy with a green or grey colour and with white to orange lenticels of varying shapes. Much older, previous seasons' shoots are predominantly hairless with a green, brown or dark grey colour and with lighter cinnamon, longitudinally elongated lenticels.

Thorns

The stipules are modified into hardened, spinescent spines. They are straight to slightly curved and occur in pairs at nodes. On new season's growth the young spines, initially, are green and covered with whitish hairs similar to that on the young shoots. The hairiness persists for some time on the spines until maturity when the spines are hairless, white with orange tips and with some dark spotting. The spines are borne at right angles to the stem but occasionally can be raked backwards or forwards up to 20° from the normal. They may attain a length of 90 mm, but on average are not longer than 20–40 mm. Some rudimentary spines may have a length of only 3 mm.

Leaves

The leaves occur at nodes, singly on new growth or up to 3 leaves per node on older shoots. New leaves unfolding at the ends of growing tips have a striking green-gold colour. The petiole and rachis are moderately hairy, with a green colour. They are grooved on top and have a thickened, robust appearance. The petiole is relatively short with a mean length of 2–10 mm, while the petiole and rachis, combined, attain a mean length of 55–70 mm (range: 25–135 mm). The number of pinna pairs on primary leaves range from 8–35 (8–20 typical), and the number of leaflet pairs per pinna from 13–45. The leaflets have a mean length of 2.8 mm (range: 1.2–6.5 mm) and mean width of 0.9 mm (range: 0.5–1.6 mm) and are closely spaced. The undersides are a slightly lighter shade of green with scattered hairs on the margins. The main vein is barely discernible. The petiole base is swollen and there is a cupped or domed petiolar gland just below the first pinna junction. On the rachis there are cupped or domed glands at from 5 to 9 of the distal pinna junctions.

80

Inflorescence

Globose flowering heads are borne at the nodes, singly or up to 5 per node, mainly on new season's shoots. The colour of the developing buds is green, turning to a yellowish colour prior to full bloom. The open, fully developed flowering heads have a mean diameter of 18 mm. They are scented and cream in colour. Peduncles are hairy, quite long with a mean length of 37 mm (range: 14–58 mm). The involucel is prominent and located in the upper half of the peduncle, often quite close to the flowering head.

Pods and seeds

Pods are borne singly or in small bunches. They are fairly large, straight to slightly curved. They are tapered at the base and rounded at the tip with no constrictions between seeds. The valves are woody, thick and hard. The young developing pods have a homogenous green colour and have a fruity smell similar to those of *A. nilotica*. Young pods can be moderately hairy. With age they become smooth and hairless and on ripening the colour change to a brown or khaki colour. They are indehiscent while still on the tree, but will open up after having lain on the ground for some time. Mature pods may attain a mean length of 150 mm (range: 50–210 mm), a mean width of 23 mm (range: 13–35 mm) and a mean thickness of 13 mm (range: 5–22 mm). The number of seeds varies from 7 to 13 and they are embedded in cream-coloured pith. The seeds are elliptic to subcircular, slightly compressed, with a size of 7–12 x 5–8 mm and 4–5 mm thick. The colour varies from brown to olive green. The central areole, 5–9.5 x 4–6 mm in diameter, is visible as an indistinct, narrow, elliptic outline that is not impressed.

Similar species

Can be confused with *A. rehmanniana* (see the comments under the latter species).

General

Name derivation: *sieberiana* = named after F.W. Sieber who collected the type specimen; *woodii* = named after the botanist J.M. Wood, former curator of the Natal Botanical Garden in Durban. There are three varieties of which only one, var. *woodii*, occurs in South Africa. It is found from the Sudan and Ethiopia southwards to Namibia, Botswana, Zimbabwe, Mozambique, South Africa and Swaziland. The wood is light (720 kg/m³), soft and of little value. Wilted leaves and green pods contain prussic acid and can thus be poisonous to stock.

Acacia haematoxylon

Grey Camel Thorn • Vaalkameeldoring

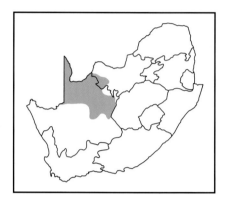

Name with authors
Acacia haematoxylon Willd. –
Type from Northern Cape, South Africa

Synonyms
A. atomiphylla Burch.

National Tree Number   169

Other common names
Vaaldoring

Outstanding features

- A shrub or medium-sized tree with distinctive sparse, grey foliage,
- The bark is light grey, coarse with deep, longitudinal fissures and has a tendency to flake,
- Young shoots have a characteristic reddish-brown colour underneath an initial thin layer of whitish hairs,
- The spines are straight, moderately hairy when young, exceptionally slender and are raked forward,
- The leaflets are very small and laterally compressed, superficially resembling a single leaflet, all parts of the leaves are densely covered with fine grey hairs,
- Globose flowering heads are golden-yellow with slender, hairy peduncles,
- Pods are sickle-shaped, circular or contorted with a dense covering of short velvety grey hairs.

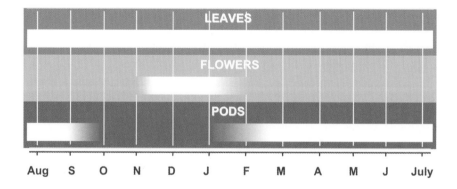

LEAVES

FLOWERS

PODS

Aug   S   O   N   D   J   F   M   A   M   J   July

Habitat

It is invariably found in arid regions on deep red Kalahari sands, either on the sandy flats between dunes or on the dune crests in association with the grass *Stipagrostis amabilis*. It is also found along dry riverbeds like the Molopo and Auob rivers.

General description

A distinctive species with sparse, grey foliage that differs from all other *Acacia* species. Two distinctive growth forms are commonly found. On the red Kalahari sands they occur as small multi-stemmed shrubs, 2–4 m high, and along dry riverbeds they occur as small to medium sized single-stemmed trees that can grow to a height of 8 m. The stems of the shrubs often emerge from the ground at an angle and then straighten up to near vertical. The crown is irregularly rounded with somewhat drooping branches. They often form dominant stands, though seldom in very dense stands.

Main stem

The bark on the main stem of mature trees is light grey to grey-brown, coarse with deep, longitudinal fissures. The bark has a tendency to flake in long strips, layer upon layer. Large branches are a medium grey, longitudinally fissured, with a darker colour in the fissures.

Shoots

Very young new season's shoots appear whitish due to a thin layer of short whitish hairs. With maturation these hairs disappear quickly to reveal a characteristic reddish-brown ground colour. Older, previous seasons' shoots have a light grey colour and the bark on these older shoots have a tendency to peel, revealing a reddish under-colour. Shoots often grow in a marked zig-zag pattern from node to node.

Thorns

The stipules are modified into hardened, spinescent spines and occur in pairs at the nodes. The spines are straight, moderately hairy when young, exceptionally slender (base diameter averaging less than 1.5 mm) and may attain a length of 55 mm. In relation to the shoots the spines are raked forward up to 10°–30° from the normal. Young spines on new season's growth are light yellow to orange in colour with the tips a darker orange colour. Older spines are yellowish-white to greyish-white with reddened tips.

Leaves

The leaves are borne at the nodes and the number of leaves per node varies from 1–2. The petiole is short (range: 1–5 mm), and the mean length of the petiole and rachis, combined, is 30–40 mm (range: 8–82 mm). The petiole and rachis are yellow-green to grey-green in colour and all parts of the leaves are densely covered with fine grey hairs. The number of pinna pairs ranges from 6–32, with an average of 15 pairs. The number of leaflet pairs per pinna ranges from 12–24, with an average of 20 pairs. The leaflets are grey-green to grey in colour and they are so small and laterally compressed that they superficially resemble a single leaflet. The leaflets have a length of 0.25–0.80 mm and a width of 0.2–0.5 mm. On the rachis there may be small raised cup-shaped glands with dark centres at 1–6 of the distal pinna junctions, as well as at the junctions of up to 3 of the basal pinna pairs.

Inflorescence

Globose flowering heads are borne at the nodes, either singly or up to four per node, mainly on new season's shoots. The colour of the developing buds is a dull grey-green. The open, fully-developed heads, with a diameter of up to 10 mm, are scented with a golden-yellow colour. The peduncles are slender and hairy with a length that varies from 10–24 mm. The involucel is located at or above the middle of the pedun-cle, or close to the apex of the peduncle and may sometimes be obscured by the head.

Pods and seeds

Pods are borne either singly or in small bunches of up to three. They are usually sickle-shaped or curled into a circle, but can also be contorted into various other shapes. Both the base and the tip are tapered. They attain a mean length of 120–140 mm (range: 80–210 mm) and mean width of 7–10 mm (range: 6–14 mm). Young pods have numerous minute dark reddish-brown glands and appear greyish-green due to a dense covering of short velvety grey hairs. They are woody, indehiscent and dry to a light grey colour. The number of seeds per pod varies from 6 to 14 and they are embedded in cream-coloured pith. The seeds are light brown to reddish-brown in colour. They are well rounded, elliptic with a mean size of 8.5–11.5 x 6–9 mm. The areole, with a mean size of 5–7 x 3.5–5 mm, is visible as a reddish-brown, elliptic outline surrounding a dark brown centre.

Similar species

As a shrub this species is so distinctive with its sparse, grey, trailing foliage that, with the exception of the *A. erioloba* x *A. haematoxylon* hybrid, it is unlikely that it will be confused with any other *Acacia* species.

General

Name derivation: *haematoxylon* = blood-coloured wood, which is a reference to the red coloured heartwood. The surrounding sapwood have a yellow colour. Elsewhere in Africa, *A. haematoxylon* is restricted to Namibia and southern parts of Botswana.

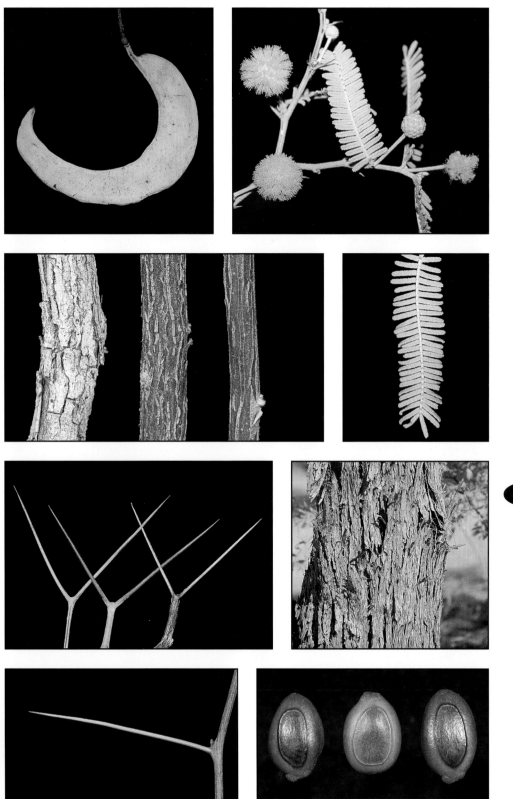

Acacia erioloba

Camel Thorn • Kameeldoring

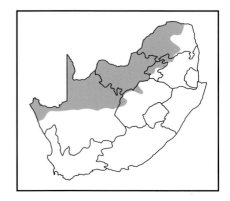

Name with authors
Acacia erioloba E. Mey. –
Type from Northwest Province, South Africa

Synonyms
• *A. giraffae* non Willd. • *A. giraffae*
var. *espinosa* Kuntze

National Tree Number 168

Outstanding features

- A single-stemmed tree up to 22 m, with main branches often considerably contorted,
- Bark of mature trees is grey, grey-brown to blackish, coarse with deep, longitudinal fissures,
- Young shoots are smooth, hairless, initially green but soon attain a dark red colour,
- Bases of paired stipular spines are often massively inflated and fused together at the base ("ant-galls"),
- Leaves with 1–5 pinna pairs, petiole and rachis are hairless and leaflets are comparatively large with prominent venation,
- Globose flowering heads are deep golden-yellow, involucel located at the apex of hairless peduncles,
- Pods are indehiscent, large and woody, sickle-shaped, greyish-green with a dense covering of velvety hairs.

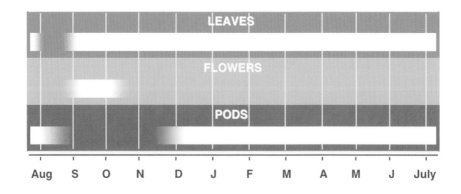

Habitat

Found mostly on deep sandy soils in arid to semi-arid areas where it occurs in open savanna or on alluvial soils along dry river beds. A typical tree species in large parts of the dry semi-desert Kalahari areas. It is adapted to dry conditions by having an extensive root system.

General description

An attractive tree, mostly single-stemmed, but often splitting into several stems fairly low down. It usually grows to a height of 6–7 m, but may reach a height of 22 m. It has a flattish, spreading crown with fairly dense foliage. The main branches are often considerably contorted, especially on trees in arid areas.

Main stem

The bark on the main stem of mature trees is grey, grey-brown to blackish, coarse with deep, longitudinal fissures. The bark has a tendency to flake in relatively thick, woody sections. In younger trees the bark may be light grey with fissuring tending to form a diamond pattern and with raised portions flaking away.

Shoots

Very young new season's shoots are smooth, hairless and grow in a marked zig-zag pattern from node to node. They are initially green but

soon attain a characteristic dark red colour. Inconspicuous orange lenticels may be present. Older, previous seasons' shoots become progressively covered with a layer of roughish grey bark. This bark displays some longitudinal and transverse cracking, giving rise to a rectangular pattern.

Thorns

The stipules are modified into hardened, spinescent spines and occur in pairs at nodes. The spines are strongly developed, almost straight and may reach a length of 60 mm. A most notable feature is the often massively inflated bases ('ant-galls'), up to 20 mm in diameter. Inflated spines of each pair are fused together at the base. In some instances the inflation can extend over the major proportion of the spine length. Smaller, almost normal spines may also be present. Spines are usually oriented at right angles to the stem, but can be raked either back or forward up to 10° from the normal. Young spines on new season's growth are red coloured, changing to white or grey-white with maturity. The bases of these older spines are of a darker grey colour. Spines are hairless.

Leaves

The leaves are borne at the nodes and the number of leaves per node vary from 1 to 7. The petiole and rachis are smooth, hairless and their colour a light green. The petiole may attain a length of 14 mm, but is usually much shorter (4 mm). The petiole and rachis, combined, may attain a length of 32 mm or more. The number of pinna pairs range from 1–5 (2–4 typical), and the number of leaflet pairs per pinna from 6–18. The rachillas are often sickle-shaped. The leaflets are hairless with prominent venation and have a characteristic bluish-green colour. Leaflets are comparatively large with a mean lenght of 9.4 mm (range: 4–13 mm) and mean width of 2.4 mm (range: 1–4 mm). A slight swelling occur at the base of the petiole. A petiolar gland is absent, but on the rachis there are small brownish-green, domed glands at each of the pinna junctions.

Inflorescence

Globose flowering heads are borne at the nodes, singly or up to 10 per node. Flowering heads at the same node are often in different stages of development. The colour of the developing buds is yellow-green prior to full bloom. The open, fully developed flowering heads are deep golden-yellow in colour with a diameter of 10–16 mm and are scented. Peduncles are green and hairless with a mean length of 35–45 mm (range: 18–55 mm). The involucel is located at the apex of the peduncle and is thus largely obscured by the flowering head.

Pods and seeds

Pods are borne singly. They are quite large and distinctive, usually sickle-shaped, tapered at the base and rounded at the tip. Mature pods can attain a length, measured on the curve, of 60–150 mm a width of 15–50 mm and a thickness of up to 15 mm. Young, developing pods often have a reddish colour. Young, fully developed pods have numerous minute dark reddish-brown to purplish glands and appear greyish-green due to a dense covering of short velvety grey hairs. They are woody, indehiscent and dry to a light grey colour. Pods can contain up to 24 seeds and they are embedded in cream-coloured pith. The seeds are dark red-brown to purplish-black in colour. They are elliptic, appreciably thickened, with a mean size of 8–14 x 7–10 mm. The areole, with a mean size of 3–9 x 2–5.5 mm, is visible as an inconspicuous, slightly indented, elliptic ring.

Similar species

With its massively inflated spines ("ant-galls") and large velvety grey pods this species is so distinctive that, with the possible exception of the *A. erioloba* x *A. haematoxylon* hybrid, it is unlikely that it will be confused with any other South African *Acacia* species.

General

Name derivation: *erioloba* = woolly lobe, referring to the woolly covering of the pods. The common name, Camel Thorn, is likely a mistranslation from the Afrikaans name "Kameeldoring", meaning "giraffe thorn", and it was this that gave the tree the previously applied specific name of *A. giraffae*. The pods are an excellent fodder for stock. The heartwood is hard and heavy with a dark reddish brown colour. It is hard, resistant to borers and termites and makes good firewood. Elsewhere in Africa, *A. erioloba* also occurs in southern Angola, Namibia, south-western Zambia, Botswana and Zimbabwe.

Acacia erioloba x Acacia haematoxylon

Bastard Camel Thorn • Basterkameeldoring

Name with authors
Acacia erioloba E. Mey. x Acacia haematoxylon Willd.

Synonyms
• A. giraffae Willd. • A. giraffae Willd. x A. haematoxylon Willd.

National Tree Number 169.1

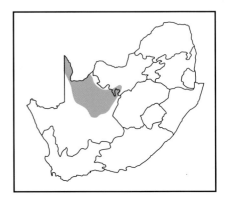

Outstanding features

• A small tree, either single- or multi-stemmed with distinctly greyish foliage,

• Bark of mature trees is light grey, grey-brown to blackish, coarse with deep, longitudinal fissures,

• Young shoots with a reddish-brown colour underneath an initial thin layer of whitish hairs,

• The spines are straight, hairless to moderately hairy when young, and are raked forward,

• The leaflets are small and all parts of the leaves are densely covered with fine grey hairs,

• Globose flowering heads are golden-yellow, involucel located at the apex of hairy peduncles,

• Pods are sickle-shaped or circular with a dense covering of short velvety grey hairs.

90

LEAVES											
FLOWERS											
PODS											
Aug	S	O	N	D	J	F	M	A	M	J	July

Habitat

Like *A. haematoxylon* it is found invariably in arid regions on deep red Kalahari sands or along dry riverbeds like the Molopo and Auob rivers.

General description

A small tree, either single- or multi-stemmed, that can grow to a height of 7 m. The crown is rounded and spreading with somewhat drooping branches. The foliage have a distinctly greyish appearance, though not as marked as that of *A. haematoxylon*.

Main stem

The bark on the main stem of mature trees is light grey, grey-brown to blackish, coarse with deep, longitudinal fissures. A reddish coloration is often visible in the fissures. The bark has a tendency to flake in long strips.

Shoots

Very young new season's shoots have a greyish-green colour and, like *A. haematoxylon*, are covered with a thin layer of short whitish hairs. With maturation these hairs disappear to reveal a characteristic reddish-brown ground colour. Older, previous seasons' shoots have a light grey

colour and the bark on these older shoots have a tendency to peel, revealing a reddish undercolour. Shoots often grow in a marked zig-zag pattern from node to node.

Thorns

The stipules are modified into hardened, spinescent spines and occur in pairs at the nodes. The spines are straight, slender and hairless to moderately hairy when young. They are never inflated and resemble those of *A. haematoxylon* more closely than those of *A. erioloba*. They may attain a length of 50 mm. In relation to the shoots the spines are raked forward up to 10° from the normal. Young spines on new season's growth are greyish-green with the tips a darker orange colour. Older spines are brownish-white to greyish-white with reddened tips.

Leaves

The leaves are borne at the nodes. The length of the petiole range from 2–9 mm, and the mean length of the petiole and rachis, combined, is 26 mm (range: 12–52 mm). The petiole and rachis are grey-green and all parts of the leaves are densely covered with fine grey hairs. The number of pinna pairs ranges from 3–12, with an average of 5–8 pairs. The number of leaflet pairs per pinna ranges from 11–22. The leaflets have a grey-green colour, which is slightly greener than those of *A. haematoxylon* and also bigger. The leaflets have a mean length of 2.7 mm (range: 1–4 mm and a mean width of 1.3 mm (range: 0.4–1.1 mm. On the rachis there are raised cup-shaped glands at the junction of each pinna pair.

Inflorescence

Globose flowering heads are borne at the nodes, either singly or 2 per node. The colour of the developing buds is a dull grey-green. The open, fully-developed heads, with a mean diameter of 8–10 mm, are scented and have a golden-yellow colour. The peduncles are hairy with a length that varies from 10–30 mm. Similar to *A. erioloba*, the involucel is located at the apex of the peduncle and is thus largely obscured by the flowering head.

Pods and seeds

Pods are usually borne singly. They are sickle-shaped or curled into a circle. Both the base and the tip are bluntly tapered. They attain a length of 70–140 mm, a width of 12–23 mm and a thickness of 8–12 mm. Young pods are glandular and appear greyish-green due to a dense covering of short velvety grey hairs. They are woody, indehiscent and dry to a light grey colour. The seeds are embedded in cream-coloured pith. The seeds are light brown to reddish-brown in colour and are almost identical in appearance to those of *A. haematoxylon*. They are well rounded, elliptic with a mean size of 9–12 x 6–8 mm. The areole, with a mean size of 6–8 x 2.5–3.5 mm, is visible as a reddish-brown, elliptic outline surrounding a dark brown centre. Despite hybridisation the seed is viable.

Similar species

Since the hybrid shares characteristics of both *A. erioloba* and *A. haematoxylon*, it is possible that the hybrid can be mistaken for either of the two pure forms. Differences and similarities are discussed above. Within its distribution range it is unlikely to be mistaken for any of the other South African *Acacia* species.

General

Elsewhere in Africa the *A. erioloba* X *A. haematoxylon* hybrid might occur wherever the distribution range of the two original species overlaps. This occurs in the south-eastern parts of Namibia as well as the southern parts of Botswana.

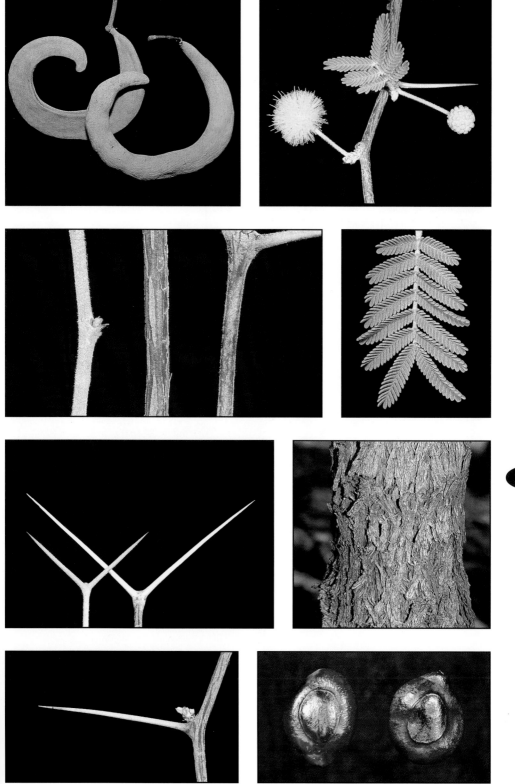

Acacia robusta

(subsp. *robusta*)

Ankle Thorn • Enkeldoring

Name with authors
Acacia robusta Burch. subsp. *robusta* – Type from Northern Cape, South Africa

Synonyms
None

National Tree Number 183

Other common names
Brosdoring

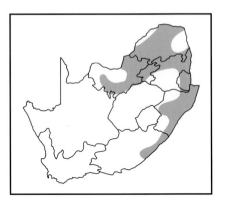

Outstanding features

- A medium to large-sized tree, single-stemmed with green foliage and thickened branches,
- Bark of mature trees is rough, dark grey with deep, longitudinal fissures,
- Shoots are smooth, hairless, appreciably thickened and the nodes pronounced,
- The paired spines on older shoots are stout and very short, on new growth they can be immense,
- Leaves with 2–7 pinna pairs, petiole and rachis are hairless and the leaflets are large and dark green,
- Globose flowering heads are light yellow to cream with mostly hairless peduncles,
- The dehiscent pods are fairly large, linear and straight to slightly curved, sub-woody, smooth and hairless.

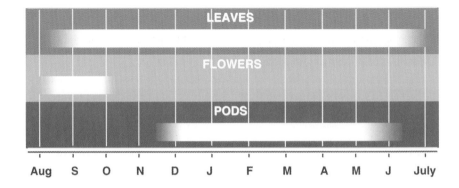

Habitat

Though not uncommon within its distribution range it never forms large dominant stands. Occurs in open savanna, grassveld and coastal areas on a variety of soil types, generally under drier conditions than subsp. *clavigera*.

General description

An attractive, medium to large-sized tree that can grow to a height of 25 m. It is mostly single-stemmed, branching fairly high up, with a dense, rounded or somewhat spreading crown. The foliage is characteristically dark green and the thickened branches and swollen nodes give the tree a rather robust appearance.

Main stem

The bark on the main stem of mature trees is rough, dark grey with deep, longitudinal fissures. A reddish coloration is often visible in the fissures. The bark higher up on the main stem becomes progressively smoother. Side branches can be almost smooth. The main stem of young trees resembles these side branches.

Shoots

Very young new season's shoots are smooth and hairless. They are initially bright green with light yellow to grey lenticels, but attain a reddish-brown colour within the same season. Light-coloured, almost orange, lenticels are distinctly visible on these shoots. Older, previous seasons' shoots remain smooth and vary in colour from slightly reddish-brown to grey with light-coloured lenticels still visible. The shoots are often appreciably thickened and the nodes pronounced.

Thorns

The stipules are modified into hardened, spinescent spines. They are straight to substantially curved, and occur in pairs at nodes. On new season's growth the young spines are bright green with yellowish or orange tips and they are hairless. Older spines are white to greyish-white with darkened tips. On older shoots and branches the spines can be stout and very short (2–6 mm), while on new growth they can be immense with a length of 125 mm and base diameter of 4.5 mm. The short spines are oriented at right angles to the stem or raked forward to an angle of 20° from the normal, but where long and recurved, they are usually raked backwards up to 10° from the normal.

Leaves

The leaves are borne at the nodes, usually on distinct "cushions". There can be up to 6 leaves per node, though more commonly only one or two. The average number of pinna pairs is 3 (range: 2–7 pairs), and the number of leaflet pairs per pinna varies from 10–27 pairs. There is a slight swelling at the base of the petiole. The petiole has a length of 7–20 mm, while the petiole and rachis, combined, have a mean length of 45–65 mm (range: 26–102 mm). Both the petiole and rachis are hairless and grooved on top. The leaflets are dark green and the main veins are readily visible, particularly on the undersides. The leaflets are fairly large with a length of up to 12.5 mm and a width of up to 5 mm. A petiolar gland, when present, is massive and located near the junction of the first pinna pair. There is a prominent domed or cup-shaped gland at the junction of the distal 1–2 pinna pairs.

Inflorescence

Globose flowering heads are borne at the nodes in groups of up to 12 per node on previous seasons' shoots only, often in great profusion. The colour of the developing buds is predominantly green prior to full bloom. The open, fully-developed flowering heads have a mean diameter of 12–18 mm. They are scented and light yellow to cream in colour. Peduncles are green, mostly hairless, with a mean length of 20–35 mm (range: 12–54 mm). The involucel is located at varying positions below the middle of the peduncle.

Pods and seeds

Pods are borne singly or in pairs at the nodes. They are fairly large, linear and straight to slightly curved. They may be somewhat thickened, ta-

pered at the base and rounded at the tip. The valves are sub-woody, smooth and hairless with distinct venation in the shape of a chevron. There may often be a considerable number of raised glands. The young developing pods have a homogenous green colour and on ripening the colour changes to a medium to dark brown colour. They are dehiscent and mature pods may attain a length of 60–130 mm and a width of 16–30 mm. Mature pods contain up to 12 seeds. They are circular or elliptic, thickened, with a size of 7.5–15 x 5–9 mm. The colour is a dark chocolate brown. The areole with a mean size of 5.5–9 x 3.5–6.5 mm is visible in the form of a lighter brown, raised ring surrounding a well defined depression.

Similar species

The distinction between subsp. *robusta* and subsp. *clavigera* is sometimes not very clear due to the occurrence of intermediates which show various combinations of characters. Some of the most notable differences between the two subspecies are the young shoots and leaf-rachides of subsp. *clavigera* which are sparsely to densely covered with whitish hairs (smooth and hairless in subsp. *robusta*), the difference in shape of the pods and the habitat preference of subsp. *clavigera*, which are mostly found near water. *Acacia robusta* can also be confused with *A. grandicornuta* and *A. gerrardii* (see the comments under the latter species).

General

Name derivation: *robusta* = well built, referring to the robust, thick young shoots. There are three subspecies of *A. robusta* of which only two occur in South Africa. Elsewhere in Africa, *A. robusta* subsp. *robusta* also occurs in western Zimbabwe and Botswana. The wood is relatively heavy, but is of little use. The sapwood is yellowish with the heartwood dark brown.

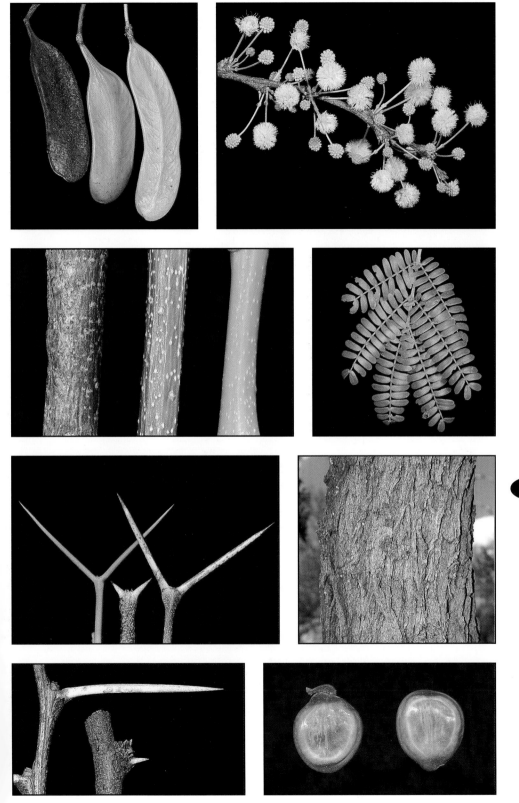

Acacia robusta

(subsp. *clavigera*)

Brack Thorn • Brakdoring

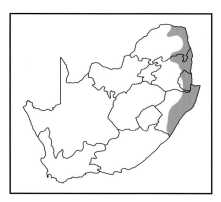

Name with authors

Acacia robusta Burch. subsp. *clavigera* (E. Mey.) Brenan – Type from KwaZulu-Natal, South Africa

Synonyms

• *A. clavigera* E. Mey. • *A. clavigera* E. Mey. subsp. *clavigera*
• *A. sambesiaca* Schinz

National Tree Number 183.1

Outstanding features

- A medium to large-sized tree, upright, single-stemmed with dark green foliage and thickened branches,
- Bark of mature trees is rough, dark grey with longitudinal fissures,
- Young shoots are sparsely covered with whitish hairs, appreciably thickened and the nodes pronounced,
- The paired spines on older shoots are stout and very short, on new growth they can be immense,
- Leaves with 2–7 pinna pairs, petiole and rachis are covered with hairs and the leaflets are large and dark green,
- Globose flowering heads are light yellow to cream with mostly hairless peduncles,
- The dehiscent pods are narrow, linear and straight to slightly curved, sub-woody, smooth and hairless.

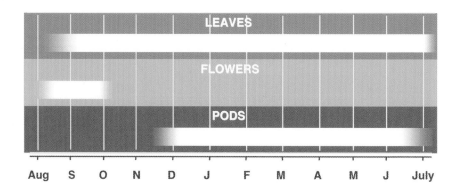

Habitat

Mostly found near water along river banks and in coastal areas. With its predominantly tropical distribution in the east of the country it is possibly less tolerant to cold and drought than subsp. *robusta*.

General description

In general appearance it resembles subsp. *robusta*, though it tends, in some instances, to be more upright. It is an attractive, medium to large-sized tree that can grow to a height of 25 m. It is mostly single-stemmed, branching at varying heights. It has a dense, rounded or somewhat spreading crown with branches that are occasionally trailing. The foliage is characteristically dark green and the thickened branches and swollen nodes, give the tree a rather robust appearance.

Main stem

The bark on the main stem of mature trees is rough, dark grey with longitudinal fissures, which are generally not as deep as those of subsp. *robusta*. A reddish coloration is often visible in the fissures. The bark higher up on the main stem becomes progressively smoother. Side branches can be almost smooth. The main stem of young trees resembles these side branches.

Shoots

Very young new season's shoots are sparsely covered with whitish hairs. They are initially green with light yellow to grey lenticels, but attain a reddish-brown to light brown colour within the same season. Light-coloured, almost orange, lenticels are distinctly visible on these shoots. Older, previous seasons' shoots remain smooth and vary in colour from slightly reddish-brown to light grey with light-coloured lenticels still visible. The shoots are often appreciably thickened and the nodes pronounced.

Thorns

The stipules are modified into hardened, spinescent spines. They are straight to slightly curved, and occur in pairs at nodes. On new season's growth the young spines are bright green with yellowish or orange tips and they can be sparsely covered by hairs. Older spines are white to greyish-white with darkened tips and hairless. On older shoots and branches the spines can be stout and very short (2–6mm), while on new growth they can be long with a length of 100 mm or more. The spines are oriented at right angles to the stem or raked forward to an angle of 10°–30° from the normal.

Leaves

The leaves are borne at the nodes, usually on distinct "cushions". There can be up to 5 leaves per node, though more commonly only one or two. The average number of pinna pairs is 3 (range: 2–7 pairs), and the number of leaflet pairs per pinna varies from 8–25 pairs. There is a slight swelling at the base of the petiole. The petiole has a length of 7–20 mm, while the petiole and rachis, combined, have a mean length of 45–65 mm (range: 26–90 mm). Both the petiole and rachis are sparingly to densely covered with hairs and grooved on top. The leaflets are dark green and may have a few marginal cilia. The leaflets are fairly large with a length of up to 12 mm and a width of up to 4 mm. A petiolar gland, when present, is prominent and located near the junction of the first pinna pair. There is a domed or cup-shaped gland at the junction of the distal 1–2 pinna pairs.

Inflorescence

Flowers are indistinguishable from those of subsp. *robusta*. Globose flowering heads are borne at the nodes in groups of up to 12 per node on previous seasons' shoots only, often in great profusion. The colour of the developing buds is predominantly green prior to full bloom. The open, fully developed flowering heads have a mean diameter of 12–18 mm. They are scented and light yellow to cream in colour. Peduncles are green, mostly hairless, with a mean length of 20–35 mm (range: 12–54 mm). The involucel is located at varying positions below the middle of the peduncle.

Pods and seeds

The pods are linear and straight to slightly curved. They may be somewhat thickened, tapered at the base and rounded at the tip. The valves are sub-woody, smooth and hairless with longitudinal venation. There may be a number of raised glands. The young developing pods are homogenously green and on ripening the colour change to a brown or reddish-brown colour. They are dehiscent and mature pods may attain a length of 100–180 mm and a width of 12–18 mm, which is appreciably narrower than those of subsp. *robusta*. Mature pods contain up to 13 seeds. They are circular or elliptic, thickened, with a maximum size of approximately 12 x 10 mm. The colour is a dark brown. The areole with a mean size of 9 x 7 mm is visible in the form of a darker raised ring surrounding a slight depression.

Similar species

The distinction between subsp. *robusta* and subsp. *clavigera* is sometimes not very clear due to the occurrence of intermediates which show various combinations of characters. Some of the most notable differences between the two subspecies are the young shoots and leaf-rachides of subsp. *clavigera* which are sparsely to densely covered with whitish hairs (smooth and hairless in subsp. *robusta*), the difference in shape of the pods and the habitat preference of subsp. *clavigera*, which are mostly found near water. *Acacia robusta* can also be confused with *A. grandicornuta* and *A. gerrardii* (see the comments under the latter species).

General

Name derivation: *robusta* = well built, referring to the robust, thick young shoots. There are three subspecies of *A. robusta* of which only two occur in South Africa. Elsewhere in Africa, *A. robusta* subsp. *clavigera* also occurs in northern Namibia, Zambia, Malawi, Zimbabwe Mozambique and Swaziland. The wood is relatively heavy (air-dry 880 kg/m^3), but is of little use. The sapwood is yellowish with the heartwood dark brown.

100

Acacia xanthophloea

Fever Tree • Koorsboom

Name and authors
Acacia xanthophloea Benth. –
Types from Malawi and Mozambique

Synonyms
A. songwensis Harms

National Tree Number 189

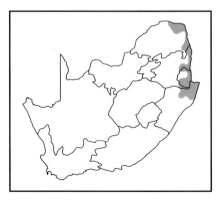

Outstanding features

- A tall, single-stemmed, upright tree with a sparse rounded or flattened crown,
- The bark is smooth, powdery with a characteristically lime-green to greenish-yellow colour,
- Young shoots are smooth, hairless with a homogeneous bright green colour,
- The paired spines are hairless, white with darkened tips and raked forward,
- Leaves with 2–9 pinna pairs, petiole and rachis are largely hairless and grooved on top,
- Globose flowering heads are bright yellow with slender, hairy peduncles and prominent involucels,
- The indehiscent pods are straight, hairless with constrictions between seeds and slight swellings that mark the positions of the seeds.

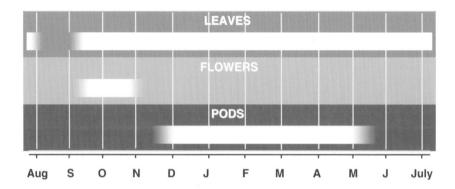

	Aug	S	O	N	D	J	F	M	A	M	J	July
LEAVES												
FLOWERS												
PODS												

Habitat

Found in low lying areas in association with water. Grows in swampy areas, margins of lakes and pans and along river banks. Often forms dominant stands in seasonally flooded areas on alluvial soils.

General description

A tall striking tree, mostly with a single upright stem and with branching commencing fairly high up. It grows to an average height of 10–15 m, but may reach a height of 25 m. The crown is somewhat sparse, rounded or flattened and in the absence of competition from neighbouring trees the canopy can achieve a spread in excess of the height of the tree. The greenish-yellow bark makes the trees very distinctive. Dead branches are almost black.

Main stem

The bark on the main stem of mature trees is smooth, with occasional irregular depressions and flaking, and has a characteristically lime-green to greenish-yellow colour. The yellowish colour is due to a fine sulphorous, powdery covering which can be rubbed off to reveal the smooth,

green bark. Scars due to broken branches or other injury are dark brown to black.

Shoots

Young new season's shoots are smooth and hairless with a homogeneously bright green colour. Older, previous seasons' shoots are light green. Yellow, transversely elongated lenticels may be present, as well as occasional dark brown flaking patches. On much older shoots a yellow powdery covering that can be rubbed off with the finger tips, is present.

Thorns

The stipules are modified into hardened, spinescent spines. They are straight and occur in pairs at nodes. On new season's growth the young spines are hairless, greenish-white to pink, with reddish-brown tips. Older spines are white with darkened tips. On some older shoots and branches, especially those of large mature trees, the spines can be short and rudimentary, while on younger trees they are well-developed and robust. In most cases they have a mean length of about 40 mm, but can attain a length of 85 mm or more with a base diameter in excess of 3.6 mm.

On older wood there is often a distinct, dark brown, tufted cushion at the node on which the spines are borne. Spines are raked forward at an angle that range from 10°–20° from the normal.

Leaves

The leaves are borne at the nodes, as many as 8 leaves per node. Each cluster of leaves usually consists of one or two larger primary leaves and smaller secondary leaves. The number of pinna pairs ranges from 2–9 (4–6 typical), and the number of leaflet pairs per pinna varies from 7–17 (10–12 typical). The petiole has a slight swelling at the base and its length may vary from 1–15 mm. Both the petiole and rachis are pale green, grooved on top and largely hairless. Combined they may attain a mean length of 50 mm (range: 20–95 mm). The leaflets are green above and slightly lighter on the underside. The main vein is indistinctly visible on the underside. The leaflets have a mean length of 5 mm (range: 2.5–6.5 mm) and mean width of 1.4 mm (range: 0.7–1.8 mm). A petiolar gland is generally not visible, but there is usually an inconspicuous, raised, cupped gland at the junction of the distal 1–2 pinna pairs.

Inflorescence

Globose flowering heads are borne at the nodes in groups of up to 10 per node, mainly on previous seasons' shoots. The colour of the developing buds is initially green, turning to a yellowish or orange colour prior to full bloom. The open, fully developed heads, with a mean diameter of 10–14 mm, are scented and bright yellow in colour. The peduncles are green, slender and hairy with a mean length of 18 mm (range: 8–30 mm). The involucel is fairly prominent and located at or just below the middle of the peduncle.

Pods and seeds

The pods are borne in bunches. They are straight, often with marked constrictions between seeds and slight swellings that mark the positions of the seeds. They are hairless, transversely venose and there is a narrow raised edging to the valves. The colour of the young developing pods is homogeneously green and they dry to a dark brown colour. They may attain a mean length of 60 mm (range: 30–75 mm) and a mean width of 11 mm (range: 7–14 mm). The pods are indehiscent, breaking up transversely into segments after being shed. The number of seeds per pod varies from 2 to 9. The seeds are olive green to brown, elliptic with a size of 4.5–6.5 x 3.5–5 mm. The areole is in the form of an indistinct lighter-coloured, narrow, horseshoe-shaped marking of 3–4.5 x 2–3 mm, surrounding a slightly darkened centre.

Similar species

With its characteristic smooth greenish-yellow bark it is unlikely to be confused with any other South African *Acacia* species.

General

Name derivation: *xanthophloea* = yellow bark. These trees were associated with malaria by early travellers before the cause of malaria was understood, hence the name "fever tree". The association arises from the fact that the tree grows in wet habitats, which are also the breeding grounds of the malaria mosquito. The wood is relatively hard, heavy (air-dry 910 kg/m^3) and is occasionally used as a general purpose timber. Elsewhere in Africa, *A. xanthophloea* is found from Kenya southwards to Botswana, Zimbabwe, Mozambique and Swaziland.

Group Two

Straight and recurved thorns, paired, located at the nodes

Additional characteristics and variations

- stipules that are modified into hardened, spinescent spines
- recurved and straight spines usually occur separately in pairs at the nodes, but mixed pairs do also occur
- bases of straight spines may be inflated or not
- tips of straight spines may be recurved

Acacia hebeclada subsp. *hebeclada*
Acacia luederitzii var. *luederitzii*
Acacia luederitzii var. *retinens*
Acacia tortilis subsp. *heteracantha*

Acacia hebeclada

(subsp. *hebeclada*)

Candle Thorn • Trassiedoring

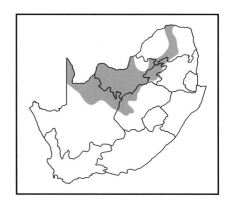

Name with authors
Acacia hebeclada DC. subsp. *hebeclada* –
Type from Northern Cape, South Africa

Synonyms
• *A. hebeclada* DC. • *A. hebeclada* DC. var.
stolonifera (Burch.) Dinter • *A. stolonifera* Burch.

National Tree Number 170

Other common names
Trassiebos

Outstanding features

- Growth form varies from a prostrate multi-stemmed shrub to a more upright shrub or small tree,
- The bark of the tree form is thickened, dark coloured and longitudinally fissured, in the prostrate form it is fairly smooth,
- Young shoots are covered with short whitish hairs and have a velvety feel to the touch,
- The paired spines are straight with only the tips slightly recurved, some shorter spines are strongly recurved,
- Leaves with 2–12 pinna pairs, petiole and rachis and to some extent the leaflets are hairy,
- Globose flowering heads are pale yellow to cream coloured with hairy peduncles,
- Pods are straight and stand erect, the valves are thick, woody and densely hairy with a felt-like appearance.

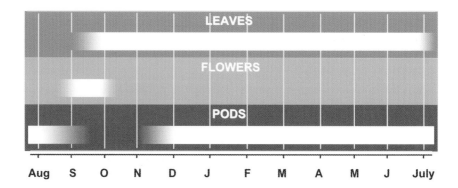

	Aug	S	O	N	D	J	F	M	A	M	J	July
LEAVES												
FLOWERS												
PODS												

Habitat

As a low growing shrub it is found in dry savanna and grassland areas and on soils ranging from Kalahari sands to sandy alluvium soils, often associated with calcrete. As a more upright shrub or tree it is usually found on more moist soils with a higher clay content. It is considered to be a good indicator of calcium-rich soils. It is fairly tolerant to cold.

General description

Growth form can vary considerably. Over large parts of its distribution range it occurs as a prostrate, spreading, multi-stemmed shrub with dense branches near ground level or with stems rising from branching underground stems. It this form it may be no more than 1 or 2 m high, but can achieve a diameter several times its height. In appearance it is thus often reminiscent of a large, flattened cushion. In some areas it occurs as a more upright shrub or small tree of 3–8 m high with a rounded, spreading crown and drooping branches, also with a considerable horizontal spread.

Main stem

The bark on the main stem of the tree form is thickened, dark brown to dark grey and longitudinally fissured, giving the stem a striped appearance. In the prostrate form the bark on the numerous main stems is dark-coloured and fairly smooth.

Shoots

Young, new season's shoots appear light grey due to a dense cover of short whitish hairs and have a velvety feel to the touch. Older, previous seasons' shoots are smooth, hairless, olive green to reddish-brown in colour with light-coloured transversely-elongated lenticels. Still older shoots have grey bark, peeling to reveal an orange to reddish-brown colour.

Thorns

The stipules are modified into hardened, spinescent spines and occur in pairs at nodes. The size and shape vary considerably. Larger spines are mostly straight with only the tips slightly recurved, while shorter spines may be strongly recurved. These recurved spines have a length of 5–15 mm, while the larger, predominantly straight spines can reach a length of 60 mm, with a mean of 20–25 mm. They are usually borne at right angles to the stem, but can be raked backwards or forward up to 10° from the normal. On new season's growth the young spines are grey-green with orange tips and are densely covered with whitish hairs. Old spines are hairless and white with reddish tips.

Leaves

The leaves are borne at the nodes, singly or up to 4 leaves per node. The number of pinna pairs varies from 2–12 (5–9 typical) and the number of leaflet pairs per pinna varies from 6–18 pairs. The petiole has a length of 3–9 mm, while the petiole and rachis, combined, have a length of 10–66 mm. The petiole and rachis are light green, grooved on top and hairy. The leaflets are bluish-green with spreading hairs on their margins. The leaflets have an intermediate size with a mean length of 4.9 mm (range: 2.5–7 mm) and mean width of 1.2 mm (range: 1.0–1.5 mm). A petiolar gland, if present, is fairly large and located near the junction of the first pinna pair. There is a small raised gland at the junction of the distal 1–3 pinna pairs.

Inflorescence

Globose flowering heads are borne at the nodes, either singly or in groups of up to 8 per node on both new season's and previous seasons' shoots. The colour of the developing buds is green prior to full bloom. The open, fully developed flowering heads have a diameter of 13–17 mm. They are scented and are pale yellow to cream in colour. Peduncles are hairy with a length of up to 20 mm. The involucel is small and located just above the base of the peduncle.

Pods and seeds

The pods are quite large and very distinctive. They are borne at the nodes on stout stems and stand erect. They are straight or nearly so, tapered at the base and rounded at the tip. The valves are thick, woody and densely hairy with a felt-like appearance. Mature pods have a mean length of 125 mm (range: 40–210 mm), a mean width of 20 mm (range: 10–45 mm) and a mean thickness of 7 mm (range: 6–15 mm). Young pods are green to greyish-green in colour and they dry to a light grey colour. The pods are tardily dehiscent, only splitting partially. They can contain up to 10 seeds. The seeds are reddish-brown, roughly elliptic and thickened, with a size of 6–15 x 4–11 mm. The areole, with a size of 5–12 x 2–7 mm, is visible as a yellowish, open-ended, elliptic line surrounding a dark reddish-brown centre and is not impressed.

Similar species

With its characteristic prostrate growth form and distinctive straight spines with recurved tips it is unlikely to be confused with any other South African *Acacia* species, especially when the large upright pods are present.

General

Name derivation: *hebeclada* = having shoots covered in soft hairs. There are three subspecies of *A. hebeclada* of which only the type subspecies, subsp. *hebeclada,* occurs in South Africa. This subspecies is also found in Namibia and Botswana. The wood is dark brown and very hard.

Acacia luederitzii

(var. *luederitzii*)

False Umbrella Thorn • Baster Haak-en-steek

Name with authors
Acacia luederitzii Engl. var. *luederitzii* –
Type from Namibia

Synonyms
• *A. goeringii* Schinz • *A. luederitzii* Engl.

National Tree Number 174

Other common names
Bastard Umbrella Thorn, Rooidoring

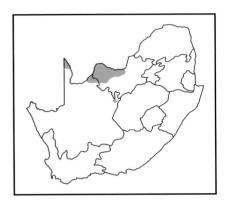

Outstanding features

- A small to medium-sized tree, mostly single-stemmed with a rather open appearance,
- The bark on main stem is rough, dark coloured and longitudinally fissured, stems of young trees are fairly smooth with a red-brown colour,
- Young shoots are covered with short whitish hairs and have a velvety feel to the touch,
- Both long straight spines and smaller strongly recurved spines are present and occur in pairs,
- Leaves typically with 5–8 pinna pairs, petiole and rachis are hairy and leaflets are small,
- Globose flowering heads are cream-coloured to almost white with light-green, hairy peduncles,
- Pods are flat and straight, dehiscent and the valves are thin and brittle.

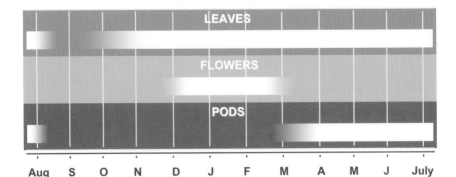

LEAVES

FLOWERS

PODS

Aug S O N D J F M A M J July

Habitat

Found in low rainfall savanna areas in the west of the country, typically on Kalahari sands where it often occurs in co-dominance with *A. erioloba.*

General description

A small to medium-sized tree of 5–7 m in height, but under favourable conditions may grow to a height of 12–15 m. Undamaged plants are mostly single-stemmed, branching from about 2 m above ground. The crown is flattened and spreading or somewhat rounded, often with a rather open appearance. The canopy spread may exceed the tree height. When leafless, the trees have a distinct reddish appearance, especially in the case of young plants.

Main stem

The bark on the main stem of mature trees is moderately rough, longitudinally fissured, often with closely-spaced transverse cracks. The colour of the bark varies from dark grey to almost black. A distinct reddish coloration is often visible in the fissures. The main stem of young trees is fairly smooth with a characteristic red-brown colour. Long white persisting spines are commonly found on young stems.

Shoots

The colour of young new season's shoots is whitish due to a dense cover of short whitish hairs and they have a velvety feel to the touch. On older shoots the hairy layer splits longitudinally to reveal a smooth surface underneath with a characteristic reddish-brown colour. Older, previous seasons' shoots are grey to reddish-brown in colour and are sparsely dotted with inconspicuous grey or brown longitudinally-elongated or circular lenticels.

Thorns

The stipules are modified into hardened, spinescent spines and occur in pairs at nodes. The size and shape vary considerably, with both long straight or slightly curved spines and smaller strongly recurved spines present. The small recurved spines have a length of 3–10 mm, while the larger, predominantly straight spines can reach a length of 70 mm, with a mean of 30–50 mm. The recurved spines of each pair are orientated at an angle that ranges from 70° to 90°. The straight spines are usually borne at right angles to the stem, but can be raked backwards or forward up to 10° from the normal. On new season's growth the young spines are whitish and are covered with whitish hairs. Old spines are hairless and greyish-white with darkened tips.

Leaves

The leaves are borne at the nodes and the number of leaves per node varies from 2–6. The number of pinna pairs varies from 3–10 (5–8 typical) and the number of leaflet pairs per pinna from 10–26. The petiole has a length of 3–14 mm, while the petiole and rachis, combined, may attain a length of 60 mm (35–50 mm typical). Both the petiole and rachis are distinctly hairy. The leaflets are green and spreading hairs are present on their margins. The leaflets are small with a mean length of 3 mm (range: 2–5 mm) and a mean width of 0.9 mm (range: 0.5–1.5 mm). A raised, dark brown, petiolar gland may be present fairly close to the first pinna junction, but is often absent. There is a small raised gland at the junction of the distal 2–3 pinna pairs.

Inflorescence

Globose flowering heads are borne at the nodes, singly or as many as 5 per node. The colour of the developing buds is initially green, turning to orange-red prior to full bloom. The open, fully developed flowering heads have a diameter that ranges from 10–22 mm with a rather sparse appearance. They are light cream to almost white in colour. Peduncles are light green, slender and hairy with a mean length of 26 mm (range: 12–42 mm). The involucel may have a reddish colour and is located on the lower half of the peduncle.

Pods and seeds

The pods are borne at the nodes, singly or in bunches of up to 4. The colour of the young developing pods is green and they dry to a conspicuous reddish-brown colour. When not ripe they can be finely hairy, especially on margins and near the base, but are hairless when mature. The pods are flat and straight, without significant constrictions between seeds, tapering at the base and rounded at the tip. They are dehiscent and the valves are rather thin and brittle, longitudinally to diagonally venose with a narrow, inconspicuous raised edging which may be darkened. They attain a length of up to 130 mm and a width of 10–19 mm. The number of seeds per pod varies from 6–10. The seeds are flattened, subcircular or elliptic in shape with a size of 5.5–11.5 x 5–8 mm and vary in colour from brown to olive green. The areole is horseshoe-shaped with a size of 3–7 x 2.8–5 mm and is not indented.

Similar species

The most distinctive difference between the two varieties of *A. luederitzii* is the inflated spines of var. *retinens*. These may not always be present. Other, inconsistent, differences include differences in growth form and habitat, fewer pinna pairs of var. *retinens* (at least in the western part of its distribution range), and the pods of var. *retinens* which are often narrower than those of var. *luederitzii*. An other South African *Acacia* species with a similar combination of short recurved and long non-inflated straight spines is *A. tortilis* subsp. *heteracantha*. The differences between the two are discussed under the latter species.

General

Name derivation: *luederitzii* = named after the German explorer A. Luederitz who spent considerable time in Namibia. There are two varieties, both of which occur in South Africa. Elsewhere in Africa, *A. luederitzii* var. *luederitzii* also occurs in Namibia, western Zambia, western Zimbabwe and Botswana. The wood is hard and heavy with a light brown colour.

Mature tree   Young, immature trees

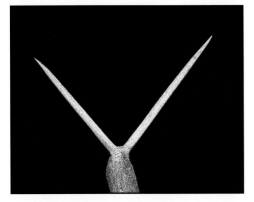

Acacia luederitzii

(var. *retinens*)

Belly Thorn • Buikdoring

Name with authors
Acacia luederitzii Engl. var. *retinens* (Sim) J.H. Ross & Brenan – Type from Mozambique

Synonyms
• *A. gillettiae* Burtt Davy • *A. retinens* Sim

National Tree Number 174.1

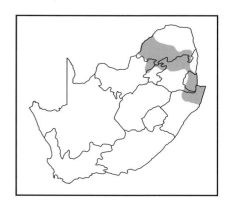

Outstanding features

- A small, multi-stemmed shrub or a small to medium-sized, single-stemmed tree,
- The bark on main stem is rough, dark-coloured and longitudinally fissured, stems of young trees are fairly smooth with a grey colour,
- Young shoots are covered with short whitish hairs and have a velvety feel to the touch,
- Both long straight spines and smaller strongly recurved spines are present and occur in pairs, the straight spines are often massively inflated ('ant-galls'),
- Leaves typically with 4–6 pinna pairs, petiole and rachis are hairy and leaflets are small to intermediate in size,
- Globose flowering heads are cream-coloured to almost white with hairy peduncles,
- Pods are flat and straight to slightly curved, dehiscent and the valves are thin and brittle.

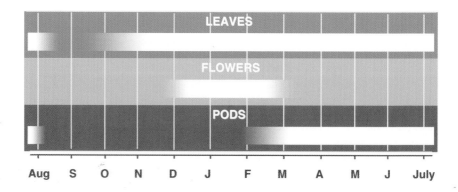

LEAVES											
FLOWERS											
PODS											
Aug	S	O	N	D	J	F	M	A	M	J	July

Habitat

It is commonly found on heavy, clayey soils, unlike var. *luederitzii* which shows a preference for sandy soils.

General description

It is usually a multi-stemmed shrub, which grows to a height of 2–5 m. It has a dense, rounded crown, often trailing down to ground level and with a substantial horizontal spread that can well exceed its height. It may form localised dominant stands, which can become fairly dense. It also occurs as a single-stemmed tree which can grow to a height of 10 m.

Main stem

The bark on the main stem of mature trees is rough, longitudinally fissured, occasionally with a tendency to peel in strips. The colour of the bark varies from dark grey to almost black. The main branches higher up are fairly smooth and grey in colour. The main stem of young trees resembles these younger branches.

Shoots

The colour of young new season's shoots is whit-

ish due to a dense cover of short whitish hairs and they have a velvety feel to the touch. On older shoots the hairy layer split longitudinally, giving the shoots a striped appearance. Underneath the hairy layer the shoots are smooth, green and covered with orange to yellowish transversely-elongated lenticels. Older, previous seasons' shoots have a dark grey to orange colour, sparsely dotted with greyish lenticels.

Thorns

The stipules are modified into hardened, spinescent spines and occur in pairs at nodes. The size and shape vary considerably, with both long straight or slightly curved spines and smaller recurved spines present. A most notable feature is the longer straight spines that are often massively inflated ('ant-galls'), up to 18 mm in diameter. The smaller recurved spines have a length of 4–10 mm, while the larger, predominantly straight spines can reach a length of 70 mm. The recurved spines of each pair are orientated at an angle of approximately 70°. The straight spines are usually borne at right angles to the stem, but can be raked backwards or forward up to 10° from the normal. On new season's growth the young spines are green with reddened tips and are covered with whitish hairs. With maturation the spines can take on a reddish colour, while much older spines are light grey, usually with some dark spotting, and with darkened tips.

Leaves

The leaves are borne at the nodes and the number of leaves per node varies from 2–6. The number of pinna pairs varies from 2–13 (4–6 typical) and the number of leaflet pairs per pinna from 7–24. The petiole has a length of 3–14 mm, while the petiole and rachis, combined, may attain a length of 60 mm (35–50 mm typical). Both the petiole and rachis are distinctly hairy. The leaflets are green and spreading hairs are present on their margins. The leaflets are small to intermediate in size with a length of 3–6 mm and a width of 0.5–1.6 mm. A raised, dark brown, petiolar gland may be present fairly close to the first pinna junction, but is often absent. There is a small raised gland at the junction of the distal 1–2 pinna pairs.

Inflorescence

Globose flowering heads are borne at the nodes, singly or as many as 5 per node, mainly on previous seasons' shoots. The colour of the developing buds is initially green, turning to orange-red prior to full bloom. The open, fully developed flowering heads have a diameter that range from 8–18 mm with a rather sparse appearance. The flowering heads appear to be smaller in diameter in the east of its distribution range (KwaZulu-Natal). They are light cream to almost white in colour. Peduncles are light-green, slender and hairy with a mean length of 18–24 mm (range: 12–42 mm). The involucel may be reddish and is located on the lower half of the peduncle.

Pods and seeds

The pods are borne at the nodes, singly or in bunches of up to 4. The colour of the young developing pods is green and they dry to a khaki or dark brown colour. When not ripe they can be finely hairy, especially on margins and near the base, but hairless when mature. The pods are flat and straight to slightly curved, without significant constrictions between seeds, tapering at the base and more rounded at the tip. They are dehiscent and the valves are rather thin and brittle, longitudinally to diagonally venose with a narrow, inconspicuous raised edging which may be darkened. They attain a length of up to 80 mm and a width of up to 15 mm. The number of seeds per pod varies from 6–10. The seeds are flattened, subcircular or elliptic in shape with a size of 5.5–11.5 x 5–8 mm and vary in colour from brown to olive green. The areole is horseshoe-shaped with a size of 3–7 x 2.8–5 mm and is not indented.

Similar species

The most distinctive difference between the two varieties of *A. luederitzii* is the inflated spines of var. *retinens*. These may not always be present. Other inconsistent differences between the two varieties are discussed under var. *luederitzii*.

General

Name derivation: *luederitzii* = named after the German explorer A. Luederitz who spent a lot of time in Namibia, and *retinens* = hooked or retaining. There are two varieties, both of which occur in South Africa. Elsewhere in Africa, *A. luederitzii* var. *retinens* also occurs in southern Mozambique and Swaziland. The wood is hard and heavy (1 000 kg/m^3) with a light brown colour.

Acacia tortilis

(subsp. *heteracantha*)

Umbrella Thorn • Haak-en-Steek

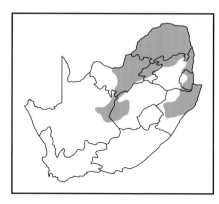

Name with authors
Acacia tortilis (Forssk.) Hayne subsp.
heteracantha (Burch.) Brenan –
Type from Northern Cape, South Africa

Synonyms
• *A. heteracantha* Burch. • *A. litakunensis* Burch.
• *A. maras* Engl. • *A. spirocarpoides* Engl.

National Tree Number 188

Outstanding features

- A small to medium-sized tree, mostly single-stemmed with a conspicuously flattened crown,
- The bark on main stem is rough, dark grey and longitudinally fissured, stems of young trees are fairly smooth with marked transverse wrinkling,
- Young shoots are reddish-green to reddish-brown and sparingly covered with whitish hairs,
- Both long straight spines and smaller strongly recurved spines are present and occur in pairs,
- Leaves typically with 4–8 pinna pairs, petiole and rachis are hairy and leaflets are small,
- Globose flowering heads are small, light yellow to cream coloured with slender, hairy peduncles,
- Pods are twisted into a tight circle or into a helix of three to four turns, indehiscent and hairless.

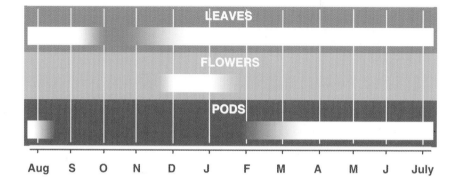

| | LEAVES | | | | | | | | | | |
| Aug | S | O | N | D | J | F | M | A | M | J | July |

Habitat

May grow on a variety of soil types, but show some preference to heavy, clayey soils. Adapted to dry conditions and is often one of the first woody plants to establish on disturbed areas like old lands. Also occurs along dry river beds and it is tolerant to cold.

General description

A distinctive tree, mostly single-stemmed but branching fairly low down. In arid areas it grows to a height of 3–6 m, but under favourable conditions it may reach a height of 15 m. Smaller trees often have a rounded crown, while larger trees have a conspicuously flattened crown. The crown can achieve a considerable horizontal spread, often in excess of its height. In large trees the lower branches are often leafless with the leaves concentrated on the upper perimeter of the canopy.

Main stem

The bark on the main stem of mature trees is rough, dark grey, longitudinally fissured with some transverse cracking. The bark higher up on the main stem becomes progressively smoother. Side branches can be almost smooth, often with marked transverse wrinkling. The main stem of young trees resembles these younger branches. The main stem of young trees may have a yellowish-red sheen. Long white persisting spines are commonly found on young stems.

Shoots

Very young new season's shoots are initially green with light yellow to grey lenticels, but attain a reddish-green to reddish-brown colour within the same season. These young shoots are sparingly covered with whitish hairs. Older, previous seasons' shoots are hairless and vary in colour from light brown to olive green with light coloured lenticels.

Thorns

The stipules are modified into hardened, spinescent spines and occur in pairs at nodes. Both long, straight spines and smaller, strongly recurved spines are present. The spines of each pair are usually similar, but some pairs may have a combination of one straight spine and one recurved spine. The small recurved spines have a length of 3–5 mm, while the larger, straight spines can reach a length of 100 mm with a base diameter in excess of 3 mm. The average length of the straight spines is, however, not more than 30–60 mm. The spines of each pair are orientated at an angle of approximately 110°. The straight spines are borne at right angles to the stem, or raked forward up to 20° from the normal. On new season's growth the young spines are green to greenish-white with orange tips and they are hairless. Old spines are white to greyish-white with darkened tips.

Leaves

The leaves are borne at the nodes, as many as 8 leaves per node. The number of pinna pairs ranges from 2–10 (4–8 typical) and the number of leaflet pairs per pinna from 5–22 (10–16 typical). The petiole has a length of 2–14 mm, while the length of the petiole and rachis, combined, ranges from 6–46 mm (12–35 mm typical). The petiole and rachis are green and hairy. The leaflets are green and of the same shade above and below. Their margins are fringed with sparse hairs and the main vein is visible on the underside, but only barely visible on the upper surface. Leaflets are small with a mean length of 2.7 mm (range: 0.5–4 mm) and mean width of 0.8 mm (range: 0.3–1.0 mm). A green or brown, domed or cupped petiolar gland is usually present immediately below the first pinna pair. Small, inconspicuous raised dark glands may be present on the rachis at 1–3 of the distal pinna junctions.

Inflorescence

Globose flowering heads are borne at the nodes in groups of up to 10 per node on previous seasons' shoots. The colour of the developing buds is predominantly green prior to full bloom. The open, fully developed flowering heads are relatively small with a mean diameter of 7 mm. They are scented and are light yellow to cream in colour. Peduncles are slender and hairy with a mean

length of 12 mm (range: 4–24 mm). The involucel is located in the lower third of the peduncle.

Pods and seeds

The pods, which are borne at the nodes in bunches, are very distinctive. They are twisted into a tight circle or into a helix of three to four turns, like a coil spring. The mean width is 8 mm (range: 5–13 mm) and the length up to 125 mm. Young pods are homogenously green and they dry to a light yellowish-brown colour. They are longitudinally venose, somewhat woody and hairless. The number of seeds per pod varies from 8–14. They have an elliptic shape with a mean size of 4–7 x 3–6 mm and are brown to greenish-brown. The areole, with a mean size of 3–6 x 2–4 mm, is dark brown and horseshoe-shaped.

Similar species

An other South African *Acacia* species with a similar combination of short recurved and long non-inflated straight spines is *A. luederitzii* var. *luederitzii*. The twisted pods, characteristic flat spreading crown and the less hairy young shoots and spines of *A. tortilis* should make it easy to separate the two species.

General

Name derivation: *tortilis* = twisted, referring to the shape of the pods, and *heteracantha* = different thorns. The species has been divided into several subspecies, two of which occur south of the Zambezi River. Only subsp. *heteracantha* is represented in South Africa. Elsewhere in Africa, subsp. *heteracantha* also occurs in southern Angola, Namibia, Botswana, Zimbabwe, Mozambique and Swaziland. The sapwood is light brown and the heartwood reddish-brown. The wood is relatively heavy (990 kg/m³) and tough, but unless water seasoned, not durable.

Mature tree

Young, immature tree

Group Three

Recurved thorns, paired, located at the nodes

Additional characteristics and variations
- prickles
- stipules not spinescent and they do not persist

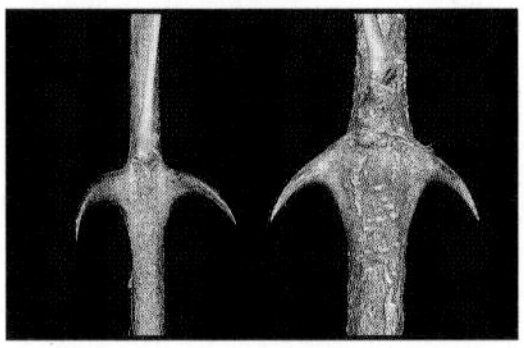

Acacia mellifera subsp. *detinens*

Acacia fleckii

Acacia erubescens

Acacia caffra

Acacia hereroensis

Acacia goetzei subsp. *microphylla*

Acacia welwitschii subsp. *delagoensis*

Acacia burkei

Acacia nigrescens

Acacia polyacantha subsp. *campylacantha*

Acacia galpinii

Acacia mellifera

(subsp. *detinens*)

Black Thorn • Swarthaak

Name with authors
Acacia mellifera (Vahl) Benth. subsp.
detinens (Burch.) Brenan –
Type from Northern Cape,
South Africa

Synonyms
• *A. detinens* Burch. • *A. ferox* Benth.
• *A. tenax* Marloth

National Tree Number 176

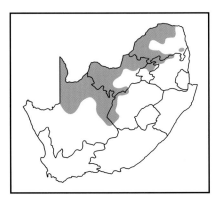

Outstanding features

- A multi-stemmed shrub or small tree of which the crown may reach down to ground level,
- The bark is roughish with longitudinal fissures or fairly smooth,
- Young shoots are green and hairless, older shoots are reddish-brown, greyish-green or light grey,
- The paired prickles are well developed, strongly recurved, sharp-pointed and hairless,
- Leaves with 2–3 pinna pairs and 1–4 leaflet pairs per pinna, leaflets are large, petiole and rachis are sparsely hairy,
- Flowering spikes are short with a light cream to white colour, buds are green to reddish-purple prior to full bloom,
- Pods are straight with minor constrictions between seeds, dehiscent and papery.

126

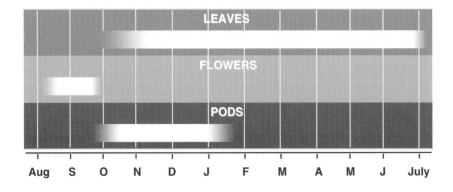

LEAVES

FLOWERS

PODS

Aug S O N D J F M A M J July

Habitat

May grow on a variety of soil types, ranging from Kalahari sands to heavy, clayey soils. In sandveld it often tends to be associated with more calcium-rich soils on drainage lines. It is usually found in arid areas where it is well adapted to dry conditions with its shallow, wide spreading root system.

General description

This is usually a multi-stemmed shrub up to 3 m high, or occasionally a tree that can grow to a height of 7 m. It has a spreading, rounded to flattened crown which may reach down to ground level. As a tree it usually branches low down with a substantial horizontal spread that can well exceed its height. Its bluish-green foliage, when seen from a distance, is also distinctive. As a shrub it may form large dominant stands which can become so dense (mostly as a result of some disturbance) as to be almost impenetrable.

Main stem

The bark on large mature trees is light to dark grey, roughish with longitudinal fissures that are generally darker. More often, however, the main stems are fairly smooth with a light grey or grey-

brown colour, covered with numerous pale grey, raised, transversely-elongated lenticels.

Shoots

Very young new season's shoots have a light green colour. They are smooth and largely hairless. With maturation the colour of the shoots change to a reddish-brown, greyish-green or light grey colour. On older shoots this light coloured layer splits longitudinally to reveal a smooth, green surface underneath. Older, previous seasons' shoots are grey, grey-brown to dark olive green with numerous pale grey, raised, transversely-elongated lenticels.

Thorns

The stipules are unmodified and not spinescent. They do not persist and senesce early. Prickles are well developed, strongly recurved, sharp-pointed, paired and located at the nodes. They often occur closely spaced and there are thus more prickles per unit shoot length than with other species. They may attain a length that ranges from 2.5–6 mm. The prickles of each pair are orientated at an angle that ranges from 10° to 80°, occasionally as much as 180° on older shoots. Their colour on young, new season's shoots varies from green to yellowish with reddened tips and with a grey base. They are hairless. On older shoots and stems the prickles vary in colour from dark red to grey-black and in all cases the prickle base is lighter in shade than the prickle itself.

Leaves

The leaves are borne at the nodes, singly or up to 4 leaves per node (1–2 typical). The number of pinna pairs ranges from 2–3 (rarely 4). The petiole has a length of 2–12 mm, while the mean length of the petiole and rachis, combined, is 14–18 mm (range: 6–40 mm). This petiole and rachis are slender, light green and sparsely hairy. The number of leaflet pairs per pinna varies from 1–4. Though the overall size of individual leaves is small, the leaflets are quite large. They are green when young, becoming bluish-green when older. The margins of the leaflets are sparsely fringed with white hairs and the main and lateral veins are visible on both surfaces. The size of the leaflets tends to vary, depending on the number of pinna pairs, as well as the number of leaflets per pinna. The leaflets from leaves with only a single leaflet pair per pinna are larger than when there is more than one pair. In the latter case they also tend to decrease in size towards the tips of the pinnae. The length of the leaflets can be up to 12 mm (7–10 mm typical), and their width up to 6 mm (3–4.8 mm typical). There is usually a small, raised, darker green or brown gland on the petiole. Glands on the rachis can be absent, or when present, visible between the two distal pinna pairs.

Inflorescence

Flowering spikes are borne at the nodes, singly or up to 5 per node on previous seasons' shoots, often in great profusion before the appearance of the new foliage. The colour of the developing buds varies from green to a characteristic reddish-purple prior to full bloom. The open, fully developed flowering spikes are very short with their length almost equal to their diameter, thus resembling globose flowering heads. They are scented and have a light cream to white colour with a mean length (or diameter) of 18 mm (range: 15–35 mm). Peduncles are very short with a length of 3–11 mm.

Pods and seeds

The pods are borne at the nodes. They are straight, sometimes with some minor constrictions between seeds, sharply tapered at the base and bluntly pointed to rounded at the tip. They are dehiscent, papery when dry and may attain a length of 70 mm and a width of 20 mm. They are flat, indistinctly venose, with a thin raised edging to the valves. The colour of the young pods is green, sometimes with a reddish tinge, and they dry to a light brown or khaki colour. The pods develop and ripen rapidly and the seeds are dispersed early in the season. The number of seeds per pod varies from 1 to 5 and they have an olive green to khaki colour. They are flattened, circular to elliptic in shape with a size of 7–10 x 6–8 mm. The areole is horseshoe-shaped with a diameter of 2–3 mm and it is indented.

Similar species

With the combination of low branching, well developed, strongly recurved paired prickles and bluish-green foliage, it is unlikely, within its distribution range, to be confused with any other South African *Acacia* species.

General

Name derivation: *mellifera* = honey bearing, referring to the fact that this tree is a good source of nectar to honeybees, and *detinens* = to hold, referring to the ability of the sharp, hooked prickles to hold on to the unwary. There are two subspecies of *A. mellifera* of which only subsp. *detinens* occurs in South Africa. It also occurs in Tanzania, extending southwards to Angola, Namibia and Botswana. The wood is widely used as fuel and for making charcoal. The dark heartwood becomes almost black when oiled and polished.

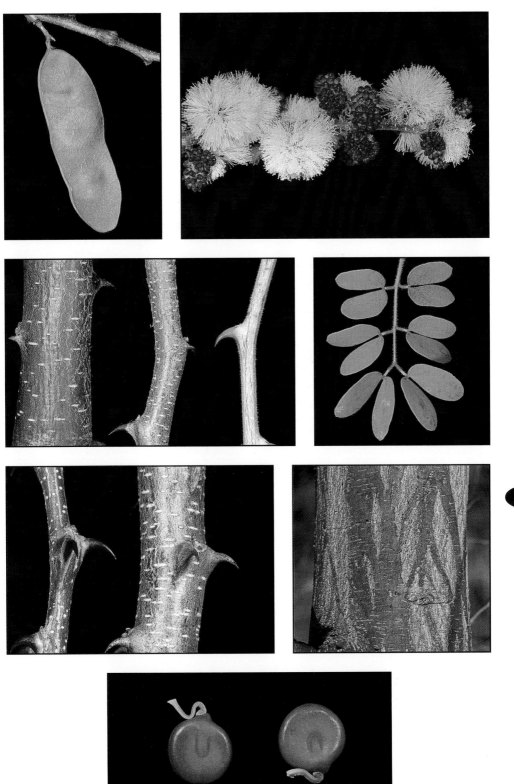

Acacia fleckii

Blade Thorn • Bladdoring

Name with authors
Acacia fleckii Schinz – Type from Botswana

Synonyms
• *A. catechu* (L.f.) Willd. subsp. *suma* (Roxb.)
Roberty var. *baumii* Roberty • *A. cinerea* Schinz

National Tree Number 165

Common Names
Plate Thorn, Plaatdoring

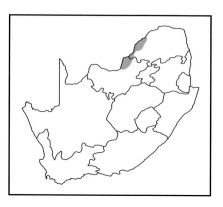

Outstanding features

- A multi-stemmed shrub or small, single-stemmed tree with a rounded to flattened crown,
- The bark on the main stem is light grey, peeling longitudinally to reveal a yellowish ground colour,
- Young shoots are homogeneously green and sparsely covered with whitish hairs, older shoots have a whitish or greyish covering with a green under-colour,
- Prickles are strongly recurved, sharp-pointed, paired and located at the nodes,
- Leaves with 8–16 pinna pairs, petiole and rachis are hairy, leaflets are small and the petiolar gland is conspicuous,
- Flowering spikes have a yellow-white to cream colour, peduncles are green and moderately hairy,
- Pods are flat, hairless, predominantly straight with occasional constrictions between seeds and are dehiscent.

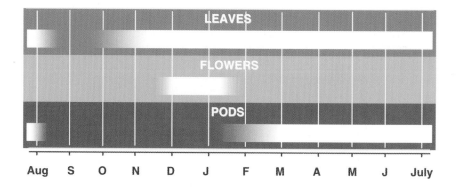

LEAVES

FLOWERS

PODS

Aug   S   O   N   D   J   F   M   A   M   J   July

Habitat

This species is confined to dry savanna areas where it is usually found growing on sandy soils. They may form localized dominant stands.

General description

This is usually a multi-stemmed shrub up to 3 m high, or occasionally a small single-stemmed tree that can grow to a height of 6 m. As a shrub it may form impenetrable thickets. It has a crown that varies in shape from rounded to flattened and which can equal or exceed its height in diameter.

Main stem

The bark on the main stem of large, mature trees is light grey and tends to strip off longitudinally, revealing a yellowish ground colour. Viewed from a distance the bark appears striped. The main stems of shrubs have a grey to yellowish-grey covering that tends to flake off. Main branches are predominantly smooth with a colour that varies from yellowish to green or grey with small yellow patches.

Shoots

Young new season's shoots are homogeneously green and sparsely covered with whitish hairs.

Slightly older, previous seasons' shoots are predominantly hairless with a whitish or greyish covering which tends to split, revealing a green under-colour. Much older, previous seasons' shoots have a green colour with numerous small, light coloured transversely-elongated lenticels.

Thorns

The stipules are unmodified, not spinescent and do not persist. Prickles are strongly recurved, sharp-pointed, paired and located at the nodes. They vary in length from 5–8 mm. The prickles of each pair are orientated at an angle of 120° to 160°. Young prickles on new season's shoots are green, sometimes partially reddish, and their tips are a dark red. The colour of older prickles are reddish-brown. The bases of these prickles are characteristically elongated and of the same reddish-brown colour which contrasts sharply with the light-coloured shoots on which they are borne.

Leaves

The leaves are borne at the nodes, usually singly, but sometimes up to 3 leaves per node. The number of pinna pairs varies from 8–16 and the number of leaflets pairs per pinna from 12–28. The petiole has a length of 3–10 mm, while the length of the petiole and rachis, combined, varies from 18–75 mm (30–50 mm typical). Both the petiole and rachis are green and hairy when young. The ventral side of the rachis is commonly armed with a number of small recurved prickles. The leaflets are green with spreading hairs on their margins. The main vein is visible on both sides. Leaflets are small with a mean length of 4.6 mm (range: 2–6.5 mm) and a mean width of 1.4 mm (range: 0.5–1.6 mm). A large petiolar gland, 0.8–2.2 mm long, is usually present close to the first pinna junction. No glands are present on the rachis.

Inflorescence

Flowering spikes are borne at the nodes, singly or 2 per node on new season's shoots. The colour of the developing buds is green prior to full bloom. The open, fully developed flowering spikes are yellow-white to cream in colour and are scented. The spikes have a length of 35–100 mm and a diameter of 18–22 mm. The peduncles are green, moderately hairy, with a length of 10–18 mm.

Pods and seeds

The pods are borne at the nodes, singly or in bunches of up to 4. The colour of the young developing pods is dark green and they dry to a light brown colour. The pods are flat, predominantly straight with only occasional constrictions between seeds and tapered at both ends. They are dehiscent and hairless with a narrow, but distinct raised edging to the valves with transverse venation radiating inwards. They have a mean length of 80–100 mm (range: 40–135 mm) and a mean width of 18 mm (range: 11–22 mm. The number of seeds per pod varies from 1–4. The seeds are flattened, circular and quite large with a diameter of 8–12 mm. Their colour varies from light brown to green. The areole is visible as a small, light coloured marking, 2–4 mm in diameter and is slightly indented.

Similar species

This species closely resembles *A. erubescens*. In *A. fleckii* the petiole is shorter, being not more than 10 mm long, while the petiole in *A. erubescens* is over 10 mm long. The leaf petiole of *A. fleckii* bears a fairly conspicuous gland up to 2.2 mm long, while the leaf rachis bears no glands at all. The number of pinna pairs usually exceeds those of *A. erubescens* and the leaflets of *A. fleckii* are also smaller.

General

Name derivation: *fleckii* = named after Fleck, a German collector who collected the type specimen from the Ghanzi district in Botswana. Elsewhere in Africa, *A. fleckii* is also found in Angola, northern Namibia, Zambia, western and southern Zimbabwe and Botswana.

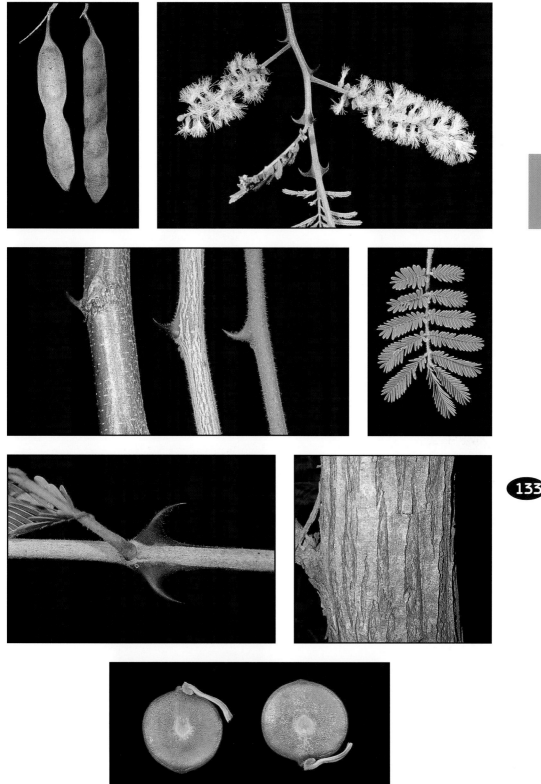

Acacia erubescens

Blue Thorn • Blouhaak

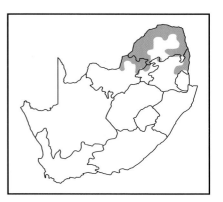

Name with authors
Acacia erubescens Welw. ex Oliv. –
Type from Angola

Synonyms
• *A. caffra* Willd. var. *pechuelii* Kuntze • *A. dulcis*
Marloth & Engl. • *A. kwebensis* N.E. Br.
• *A. longipetiolata* Schinz

National Tree Number   164

Other common names
Geelhaak

Outstanding features

- A small to medium-sized, low branching, multi-stemmed shrub or single-stemmed tree,
- The bark on the main stem is yellowish and covered with thickened or papery, peeling bark,
- Young shoots are smooth and hairless with a dark reddish-purple colour that changes to light brown or greyish-white,
- Prickles are strongly recurved, sharp-pointed, paired and located at the nodes,
- Leaves with 3–7 pinna pairs, petiole and rachis are moderately hairy and edges of leaflets reddish when young,
- Flowering spikes have a light yellow to cream colour, sometimes with a pink tinge, peduncles are densely hairy,
- Pods are flat, hairless, predominantly straight with occasional constrictions between seeds and are dehiscent.

134

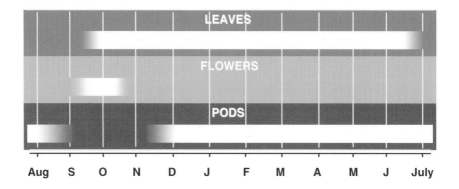

	Aug	S	O	N	D	J	F	M	A	M	J	July
LEAVES												
FLOWERS												
PODS												

Habitat

May grow on a variety of soil types ranging from sandy soils to fine textured, poorly drained soils. Occur in dry savanna areas where they often form dominant stands, or along dry river banks on poorly drained soils. Well adapted to dry conditions.

General description

A small to medium-sized, multi-stemmed shrub or single-stemmed tree that can grow to a height of 8 m. It has a rounded crown, which can attain a spread in excess of its height. As a single-stemmed tree it branches fairly low down and in large individuals the branches can droop down to ground level at the periphery. When leafless the yellowish fluted trunk and branches are conspicuous.

Main stem

The main stem is yellowish and covered with thickened or papery, peeling bark that varies in colour from grey, greyish-yellow to yellow. Underneath the peeling bark the stem is fairly smooth. The main stems of young trees are predominantly smooth with the peeling bark largely absent, except for some very thin papery layers. The stems of these young trees are characteristically yellowish.

Shoots

Very young new season's shoots initially are a dark reddish-purple, which changes to light brown or greyish-white within the same season. These young shoots are smooth and hairless. Previous seasons' shoots are brown or grey with some small transversely-elongated lenticels. Older shoots become progressively covered with thin layers of grey or yellowish papery bark. Underneath the papery bark the shoots usually have a pale yellowish colour.

Thorns

The stipules are unmodified, not spinescent and do not persist. Prickles are paired and located at the nodes. They are strongly recurved and sharp-pointed, often with pronounced basal buttresses. They vary in length from 5–7 mm. On older shoots they are often much smaller than on new growth. The prickles of each pair are orientated at an angle of 120° to 180°. Young prickles on new season's shoots are sparingly hairy with a reddish colour, becoming darker towards the tips. Older prickles are hairless and vary in colour from grey-black to grey. The prickle bases are usually of the same colour as the shoots on which they are borne.

Leaves

The leaves are borne at the nodes, usually singly, but occasionally in pairs. The number of pinna pairs varies from 3–7 and the number of leaflet pairs per pinna from 6–27 (8–14 pairs typical). The petiole has a length of 13–25 mm, while the petiole and rachis, combined, have a mean length of 38 mm (range: 28–52 mm). The petiole and rachis are yellow-green or reddish and moderately hairy when young. The rachis is glandular and its ventral side is commonly armed with a number of small recurved prickles. The leaflets are green with spreading hairs on their margins. In young plants the edges of the leaflets are often reddish. Leaflets have a mean length of 6.4 mm (range: 3–7.5 mm) and a mean width of 1.6 mm (range: 1–2 mm). A small petiolar gland, 0.3–1 mm long, is commonly present, usually in the middle of the petiole. There can be a small raised gland at the junction of the distal 1–2 pinna pairs.

Inflorescence

Flowering spikes are borne at the nodes, singly or up to 5 per node, sometimes in the form of a rachis splitting into 2 or more pedicels each with a spike. Flowers are borne on previous seasons' shoots before the appearance of the new foliage. The colour of the developing buds is yellowish-green prior to full bloom. The open, fully developed flowering spikes are short with a mean length of 28 mm and a mean diameter of 12 mm. They are scented and have a light yellow to cream colour, sometimes with a pink tinge. Peduncles are densely hairy with a mean length of 8 mm.

Pods and seeds

The pods are borne in bunches near terminals, often in abundance. The colour of the young developing pods is initially green, changing to a characteristic dark reddish colour. This reddish colour is often confined to one side of the pod only. With ripening the colour changes to a light brown or khaki. The pods are flat and straight, occasionally with minor constrictions between seeds. They are venose with numerous small reddish glands. Both ends are sharply tapered and they are dehiscent and hairless, except for some hairiness at the base. They attain a mean length of 80–90 mm (range: 40–135 mm) and a mean width of 14–18 mm (range: 11–23 mm). The number of seeds varies from 2 to 3, occasionally up to 5. The seeds are flattened, roughly circular, 8–12 mm in diameter and have a brown colour with a slightly darker edging. The central areole is small, 1–4 mm in diameter and is visible as a lighter brown marking which is not impressed.

Similar species

Can be confused with *A. fleckii* (see the comments under the latter species).

General

Name derivation: *erubescens* = turning red or blushing, probably referring to the pinkish colour of the young flowers or to the edges of the leaflets, particularly on young plants, that are often reddish. Elsewhere in Africa, *A. erubescens* also occurs in northern Botswana, southern Mozambique, northern Namibia, Zimbabwe and extends further north to Zaire and Tanzania. The wood is heavy (1 070 kg/m^3) and fairly long-grained, but is susceptible to attack by woodborers. The sapwood is yellowish and the heartwood dark brown.

Acacia caffra

Common Hook-thorn • Gewone Haakdoring

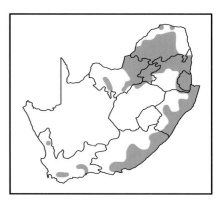

Name with authors
Acacia caffra (Thunb.) Willd. –
Type from Western Cape, South Africa

Synonyms
• *A. caffra* Willd. var. *longa* Glover • *A. caffra*
Willd var. *namaquensis* Eckl. & Zeyh. • *A. caffra*
Willd. var. *tomentosa* Glover • *A. caffra*
Willd. var. *transvaalensis* Glover • *A. fallax*
E. Mey • *A. multijuga* Meisn.

National Tree Number 162

Other common names
Cat Thorn, Katdoring

Outstanding features

- Small to medium-sized, single-stemmed tree with a rounded or irregular shaped crown or a small multi-stemmed shrub,
- The bark on the main stem is light grey to dark grey-brown, rough, longitudinally fissured with some horizontal cracking,
- New season's shoots are mostly hairless and green to reddish-brown,
- The paired prickles are recurved, hairless and often small and poorly developed on older shoots,
- The leaves are highly variable, but typically with 10–18 pinna pairs and are fairly large,
- Light yellow to cream coloured flowering spikes are grouped in clusters towards the tips of predominantly previous seasons' shoots,
- The dehiscent pods are flat and straight with occasional constrictions between seeds.

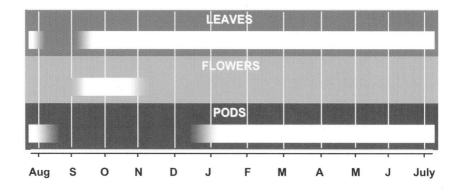

	Aug	S	O	N	D	J	F	M	A	M	J	July
LEAVES												
FLOWERS												
PODS												

Habitat

A species with a wide habitat tolerance and can be found from the coast to highveld areas. At high altitude they occur widely spaced in tall grassveld, while in coastal areas they occur among coastal scrub. This species is tolerant to a low soil pH and is often found on leached acidic sandy soils in high rainfall areas. Also favours rocky slopes. It is fire tolerant.

General description

A small to medium-sized, single-stemmed tree or a small multi-stemmed shrub. Single-stemmed plants often split into a number of stems fairly low down and the stems are often contorted. The crown is rounded, spreading or irregularly shaped and the branches ascending. It usually grows to a height of 5–7 m, but may reach a height of 14 m.

Main stem

The bark on the main stem is light grey to dark grey-brown in colour. It is rough, longitudinally fissured with some horizontal cracking, forming small squares. The bark often flakes in places. The main stem of young trees is smoother with a light grey colour.

Shoots

The colour of very young new season's shoots are homogenously green with raised striations of the same colour. With maturation the colour of the shoots changes to greenish-brown or reddish-brown with numerous slightly raised, light-brown to orange transversely-elongated lenticels. The shoots are mostly hairless, but depending on the location, new growth can be moderately hairy. Older, previous seasons' shoots are grey with dark grey, olive green or dark brown striations.

Thorns

The stipules are unmodified and not spinescent. They do not persist and senesce early. Prickles are recurved, paired and located at the nodes. They vary in length from 2–9 mm. The prickles of each pair are orientated at an angle of almost 180°. Young prickles on new season's shoots are hairless, green and their tips orange. The colour of older prickles ranges from reddish-brown to grey with darkened tips. Scattered prickles are sometimes present on the main stem. On much older shoots and branches the prickles can be very small and poorly developed or absent.

Leaves

The leaves are fairly large and occur singly at the nodes. The petiole and rachis vary from hairless to moderately hairy, depending on the location. The petiole and rachis are light green and grooved on top. The petiole has a length of 5–30 mm, and the combined length of the petiole and rachis varies from 60–230 mm. The number of pinna pairs varies from 8–38 (10–18 pairs typical), and the number of leaflet pairs per pinna from 13–64. The leaflets have a length of 2–8 mm and width of 0.7–1.8 mm. Venation is visible on the undersides of the leaflets. A slight swelling occurs at the base of the petiole. A raised petiolar gland is commonly present, usually in the middle of the petiole. There is a raised gland at the junction of the distal pinna pairs, occasionally at the junction of all pinna pairs.

Inflorescence

Flowering spikes are grouped in clusters of 1 to 5 at the nodes towards the tips of predominantly previous seasons' shoots, often in profusion. The colour of the developing buds is green or yellow-green, occasionally with reddish tinges. The open, fully developed flowering spikes have a mean length of 78 mm (range: 60–140 mm) and a mean diameter of 17 mm. They are scented and have a light yellow to cream colour. The spike rachides often have a reddish colour. Peduncles are sparsely hairy with a length that ranges from 2–41 mm.

Pods and seeds

The pods are borne in bunches near terminals, often in abundance. The young developing pods are green and sparsely to densely covered with dark reddish glands. With ripening they change to a dark brown colour. The pods are flat and straight, with occasional constrictions between seeds and tapering sharply at both ends. The valves are indistinctly venose, but with a distinct raised edge. The pods are early dehiscent and, depending on the location, are hairless or moderately hairy when young. They attain a mean length of 100–140 mm (range: 45–198 mm) and a mean width of 10–14 mm (range: 7–27 mm). The pods can contain up to 10 seeds. The seeds are flattened, roughly circular or elliptic with a size of 6–12 x 4–8 mm. They vary in colour from light brown to greenish-yellow. The central areole, 2–5 x 2–4 mm in size, is visible as a horseshoe-shaped depression.

Similar species

A. caffra is a very variable species and the extremes of the species may differ appreciably. Its superficial resemblance with other species will thus differ accordingly. *A. caffra* is closely related to *A. hereroensis* and the differences between the two species are discussed under the latter species. It may also resemble *A. ataxacantha*, *A. goetzei* subsp. *microphylla* and *A. polyacantha* subsp. *campylacantha* (see the comments under the latter species).

General

Name derivation: *caffra* = native of the land. Elsewhere in Africa, *A. caffra* is found in south-eastern Botswana, southern Mozambique and Swaziland. The wood is heavy (air-dry 980 kg/m^3), close-grained, with a light coloured sapwood and nearly black heartwood. It is not used commercially, but makes good fencing poles and firewood.

140

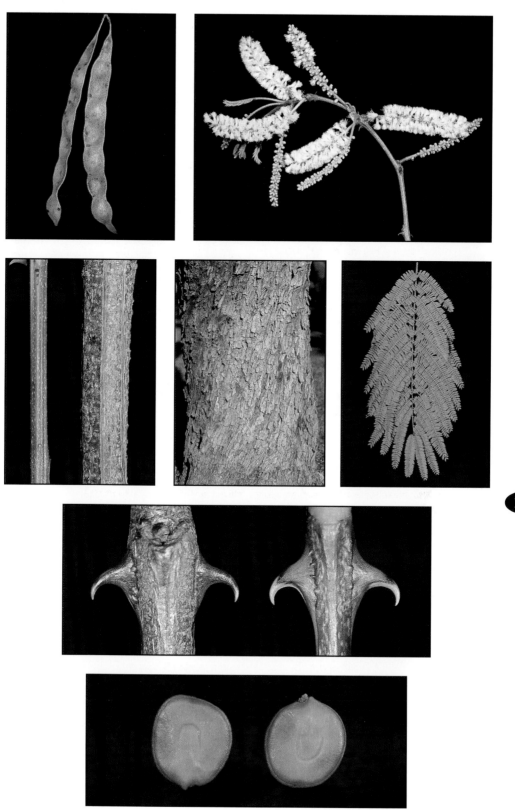

Acacia hereroensis

Mountain Thorn • Bergdoring

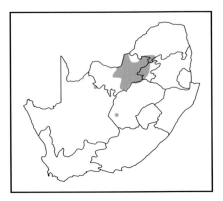

Name with authors
Acacia hereroensis Engl. – Type from Namibia

Synonyms
• *A. gansbergensis* Schinz
• *A. mellei* Verdoorn

National Tree Number 171

Outstanding features

- Small to medium-sized, single-stemmed tree with an irregular rounded crown or a small multi-stemmed shrub,
- The bark on the main stem is dark grey to greyish-brown and longitudinally fissured,
- New season's shoots are sparsely hairy and green to reddish-brown,
- The paired prickles are slightly recurved and sparsely covered with hairs when young,
- The leaves typically with 10–18 pinna pairs, the petiole and rachis are sparsely hairy and the leaflets are small and compact,
- Light yellow to cream coloured flowering spikes are borne singly or in pairs at the nodes on hairy peduncles,
- The dehiscent pods are flat and straight with occasional constrictions between seeds.

142

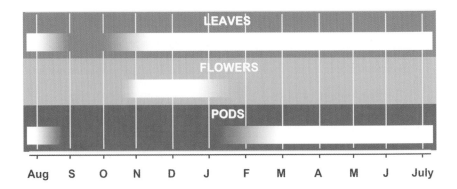

Habitat

Found in open savanna and dry grassland, notably on rocky hillsides and along shallow watercourses. May grow on a variety of soil types, but often associated with dolomite formations. It is fairly tolerant to cold.

General description

A small to medium-sized, single-stemmed tree that can grow to a height of 11 m, or a small multi-stemmed shrub. It has trailing branches and an irregular rounded crown that can attain a horizontal spread equal to its height.

Main stem

The bark on the main stem of mature trees is rough, dark grey to greyish-brown and longitudinally fissured. A reddish coloration is often visible in the fissures. The main stem of young trees is fairly smooth with a light grey colour.

Shoots

Very young new season's shoots are green to reddish-brown and are sparsely hairy. Older, previous seasons' shoots are smooth and hairless with a predominantly light grey colour. Shoots are finely striated and minute, indistinct light coloured lenticels are visible on the older shoots.

Thorns

The stipules are unmodified and not spinescent. They do not persist and senesce early. Prickles are slightly recurved. They are located at the nodes in pairs but may occasionally occur singly. Lengths vary from 5 to 10 mm. The prickles of each pair are orientated at an angle that ranges from 80° to almost 180°. On young, new season's shoots they are reddish with green tips, changing to purple with maturation. The very young prickles are sparsely covered with whitish hairs. On older shoots and stems the prickles are grey, similar to the colour of the shoots on which they are borne.

Leaves

The leaves are borne at the nodes, singly or up to 3 leaves per node. The petiole and rachis are green, sparsely hairy and are dotted with minute dark glands. The ventral side of the rachis may be armed with a number of small recurved prickles. The petiole has a length of 3–22 mm, and the combined length of the petiole and rachis

143

varies from 20–100 mm (40–70 mm typical). The number of pinna pairs varies from 8–26 (10–18) pairs typical), and the number of leaflet pairs per pinna from 14–48. Rachillas are hairy and usually sickle-shaped and particularly in the case of young plants, may be armed underneath with a series of minute prickles. The leaflets are small with a mean length of 2.9 mm (range: 1–4 mm) and a mean width of 0.9 mm (range: 0.25–1.1 mm). The leaflets are green and spreading hairs are sometimes present on their margins. The main vein can be distinguished on both the upper and lower surface, while some lateral venation can also be seen underneath. A slight swelling occurs at the base of the petiole. The stalked petiolar gland can be large and often projects at an angle towards the rachis. There are cupped, green or light-coloured glands on the rachis at the junction of 1–3 of the distal pinna pairs and occasionally at the lowest 1–3 pairs.

Inflorescence

Flowering spikes are borne at the nodes, usually singly, but occasionally two per node. The colour of the developing buds is light green prior to full bloom. The open, fully developed flowering spikes have a mean length of 40–56 mm (range: 22–86 mm) and a mean diameter of 16–18 mm. They are scented and light yellow to cream in colour. The spike rachides are hairy and may have a reddish colour. Peduncles are hairy with a mean length of 12–16 mm (range: 3–28 mm).

Pods and seeds

The pods are borne in bunches of up to 5. The colour of the young developing pods varies from green to partially reddish. The reddish colour is often confined to one side of the pod only. With ripening the colour changes to brown. The pods are flat and straight, occasionally with constrictions between seeds. They are indistinctly venose with numerous small reddish-brown glands. Both ends are sharply tapered. They are dehiscent and can either be hairless or hairy to varying degrees. They attain a length of 50–140 mm and a width of 12–23 mm. The number of seeds varies from 3 to 6, occasionally up to 8. The seeds are flattened, circular to elliptic with a size of 7–10 x 5–10 mm and have a brown to olive-green colour. The central areole appears as a dark brown, recessed marking of 4–2 x 3–2 mm.

Similar species

A. hereroensis is closely related to *A. caffra*. It differs from *A. caffra* in having a shorter leaf petiole, as well as shorter and smaller leaves with more compact leaflets. The lateral veins are not visible on the under surface of the leaflets while they are fairly prominent in *A. caffra*. In *A. hereroensis* the leaves tend to be held erect, while in *A. caffra*, being longer, they tend to droop. The spines are better developed than they are in *A. caffra,* the young shoots are hairy and the flower spikes are mostly produced singly and not in clusters. *A. caffra* flowers in early spring and *A. hereroensis* later in midsummer.

General

Name derivation: *hereroensis* = refer to Hereroland in Namibia from where the species was first described. Elsewhere in Africa, *A. hereroensis* also occurs in Namibia, Zimbabwe and south-eastern Botswana.

Acacia goetzei

(subsp. *microphylla*)

Purple-pod Thorn • Perspeuldoring

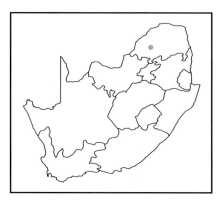

Name with authors
Acacia goetzei Harms subsp. *microphylla*
Brenan – Type from Malawi

Synonyms
• *A. gossweileri* Bak. f. • *A. joachimii* Harms
• *A. kinionge* De Wild. • *A. ulugurensis* Taub.
ex Harms • *A. van-meelii* Gilbert & Boutique

National Tree Number 167.1

Outstanding features

- A medium-sized, single-stemmed tree with a rounded or somewhat spreading crown,
- The bark on the main stem is light grey to dark grey, moderately rough with irregular longitudinal fissures and some horizontal cracking,
- Young shoots are mostly hairless and green to reddish-brown while older shoots are grey with reddish-brown striations,
- The paired prickles are recurved, hairless and often small and poorly developed on older shoots,
- Leaves with 3–10 pinna pairs, the petiole and rachis are mostly hairless and the leaflet size variable,
- Light yellow to cream coloured flowering spikes are borne at the nodes, singly or grouped in clusters,
- The dehiscent pods are flat and straight with occasional constrictions between seeds, prominently veined and hairless.

146

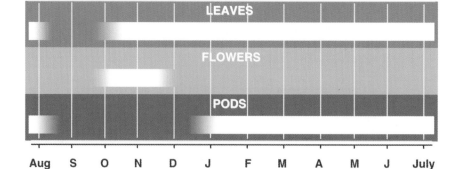

	LEAVES										
FLOWERS											
PODS											
Aug	S	O	N	D	J	F	M	A	M	J	July

Habitat

Habitat quite variable. May grow on a variety of soil types in open savanna and woodland with an occasional preference for riverine habitats.

General description

A medium-sized tree, mostly single-stemmed and branching at varying heights above ground level. The crown is rounded or somewhat spreading. It usually grows to a height of 6–10 m, but may reach a height of 15–20 m.

Main stem

The bark on the main stem is light grey to dark grey. It is moderately rough with irregular longitudinal fissures and some horizontal cracking. A reddish coloration is often visible in the fissures. The main stem of young trees is fairly smooth with a light grey colour and often has persisting prickles.

Shoots

The colour of young new season's shoots is green to reddish-brown with raised striations of the same colour. Indistinct, light coloured lenticels are visible on these young shoots. They are usually hairless, but may occasionally be sparsely hairy.

Older, previous seasons' shoots are grey and hairless with reddish-brown striations and are covered with numerous light coloured lenticels.

Thorns

The stipules are unmodified and not spinescent. They do not persist and senesce early. Prickles are strongly recurved, paired and located at the nodes. They can be up to 7 mm long and the prickles of each pair are orientated at an angle of up to 180°. Young prickles on new season's shoots are mostly hairless, green to dark reddish-brown and their tips orange. The colour of older prickles is mostly grey with darkened tips. On much older shoots and branches the prickles can be very small and poorly developed or absent.

Leaves

The leaves are borne at the nodes, singly or up to 3 per node. The petiole and rachis are light green and mostly hairless. The petiole has a length of 13–50 mm, and the combined length of the petiole and rachis varies from 35–140 mm. The number of pinna pairs varies from 3–10 and the number of leaflet pairs per pinna from 5–23. The leaflet size is highly variable with a length of 3–10.5 mm and width of 1–3.5 mm. A raised petiolar gland is usually present at the top of the petiole, close to the junction of the basal pinna pair. There is a small gland at the junction of the distal 1–3 pinna pairs.

Inflorescence

Flowering spikes are borne at the nodes, singly or grouped in clusters. The colour of the developing buds is green or yellow-green prior to full bloom. The open, fully developed flowering spikes have a length of 30–120 mm. They are scented and light yellow to cream in colour. Peduncles are sparsely hairy with a length of 4–45 mm.

Pods and seeds

The pods are borne singly or in bunches. The young developing pods vary in colour from green to a deep reddish or purplish-brown colour and they dry to a brown colour. The pods are flat and straight, occasionally with minor constrictions between seeds. They are prominently veined, dehiscent, hairless and tapered at both ends. They attain a length of 80–180 mm and a width of 20–35 mm. The pods contain 3–5 seeds. The seeds are flattened, circular to elliptic in outline with a brown to greenish-brown colour. They have a size of 8–11 x 8–10 mm. The areole, visible as a horseshoe-shaped outline, is recessed with a size of 4.5–6 x 2.5–4 mm.

Similar species

This species can resemble *A. caffra* but differs in having shorter and smaller leaves, but with leaflets that are generally larger than those of *A. caffra*. In *A. goetzei* subsp. *microphylla* the leaves tend to be held erect, while in *A. caffra*, being longer, they tend to droop. On average the pods of *A. goetzei* subsp. *microphylla* are shorter and broader than those of *A. caffra*.

General

Name derivation: *goetzei* = named after Goetze, a plant collector, and *microphylla* = small leaflets. There are two varieties of *A. goetzei* of which only var. *microphylla* is represented in South Africa. With a predominantly northernly distribution range, which includes southern Ethiopia, Kenya, Tanzania, Zaire, Malawi, Angola, Zambia, Zimbabwe and Mozambique, it was likely introduced into South Africa.

Mature tree

Young, immature tree

149

Acacia welwitschii

(subsp. *delagoensis*)

Delagoa Thorn • Delagoadoring

Name with authors
Acacia welwitschii Oliv. subsp. *delagoensis*
(Harms) J.H. Ross & Brenan –
Type from Mozambique

Synonyms
A. delagoensis Harms

National Tree Number 163

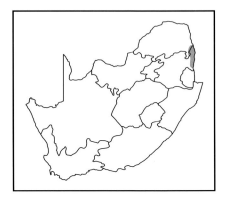

Outstanding features

- A medium-sized, single-stemmed tree with lateral branches often down to ground level,
- The bark on the main stem is fairly smooth, longitudinally fissured with a light grey to dark grey colour,
- New season's shoots are smooth, predominantly hairless and green with occasional reddish tinges,
- The paired prickles are strongly recurved, sharp-pointed and hairless,
- Leaves with 2–5 pinna pairs, the petiole and rachis are usually hairless and the leaflets are fairly large,
- Light yellow to cream-coloured flowering spikes are borne singly or in pairs at or between nodes of new season's shoots,
- The dehiscent pods have a reddish colour and are hairless, flat and straight with occasional constrictions between seeds.

150

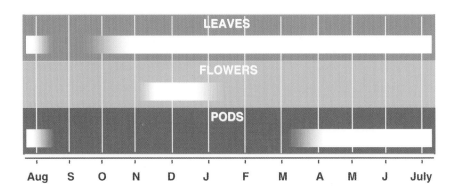

	LEAVES										
FLOWERS											
PODS											
Aug	S	O	N	D	J	F	M	A	M	J	July

Habitat

In South Africa they are mainly found on heavy soils and brackish flats on the transition between granite and basalt in the Kruger National Park.

General description

A medium-sized, usually single-stemmed tree that can grow to a height of 15 m. It usually branches low down with lateral branches down to ground level, which gives the tree a bushy appearance at the base. The crown is rounded, somewhat uneven in outline and there is a tendency for the foliage to be stratified into roughly horizontal layers.

Main stem

The bark on the main stem of large, mature trees is fairly smooth with longitudinal fissures. The colour of the bark varies from light grey to dark grey with some biscuit to light brown patches. A yellow coloration is often visible in the fissures. Persisting prickles on the apices of knobs may be present on the main stems of young plants.

Shoots

Very young new season's shoots are green, occasionally with reddish tinges and they are smooth and predominantly hairless. Older, previous sea-sons' shoots are greyish-green to grey with numerous light coloured, transversely-elongated lenticels.

Thorns

The stipules are unmodified and not spinescent. They do not persist and senesce early. Prickles are well-developed, strongly recurved, sharp-pointed, paired and located at the nodes. They may attain a length of 9 mm. The prickles of each pair are orientated at an angle that ranges from 90° (mainly young prickles) to 180° (mainly older prickles). On young, new season's shoots they are predominantly yellowish-green with a red-dened tip. With maturity they change to a deep red colour with a reddish-grey base and a pur-plish-black tip. On older, previous seasons' shoots the prickles are grey with a dark grey to black tip. The prickles are hairless.

Leaves

The leaves are borne at the nodes, singly or as many as 3 leaves per node. The number of pinna pairs vary from 2–5 (3 pairs typical) and the number of leaflet pairs per pinna from 2–9 (3–5 pairs typical). The petiole and rachis are usually hairless, except, occasionally, for a few scattered hairs when young. Small recurved prickles can be present on the underside of the rachis, but are often absent. The petiole length varies from 6–28 mm, while the petiole and rachis, combined, have a mean length of 25–35 mm (range: 16–46 mm). The leaflet size is extremely variable, but they are usually fairly large with a mean length of 5.5–9.5 mm (range: 4–20 mm) and a mean width of 2.6–5.5 mm (range: 2.2–13 mm). The upper surface is dark green and the underside is a paler green. Both surfaces are hairless with visible venation. There is usually a dark, raised gland close to the basal pinna junction, but its position can vary appreciably. Glands are usually absent from the rachis, or when present they are small, inconspicuous and located at 1–3 of the top pinna junctions.

Inflorescence

Flowering spikes are borne singly or in pairs at or between nodes towards the tips of predominantly new season's shoots, often in great profusion. The colour of the developing buds are initially green, changing to a slight yellowish colour prior to full bloom. The open, fully developed flowering spikes have a mean length of 60 mm and a mean diameter of 14 mm. They are scented and light yellow to cream in colour. Peduncles are hairless with a mean length of 10 mm.

Pods and seeds

The pods are borne singly or in bunches. The young developing pods have a characteristic deep reddish or purplish-brown colour. The reddish colour is often confined to one side of the pod only. With maturation the colour changes to dark green and later, when dry, to dark brown or purplish black. The pods are flat and straight, occasionally with minor constrictions between seeds. They are prominently veined, dehiscent, hairless, tapering at the base and rounded at the tip. The valves have a narrow raised edge. They attain a length of 52–122 mm and a width of 13–20 mm. The pods can contain up to 6 seeds. The seeds are flattened, elliptic to quadrate in outline with a small projection at the hilum. They are fairly large with a size of 7–13 x 7–13.5 mm and have an olive green colour. The areole, visible as a horseshoe-shaped outline, is appreciably recessed with a size of 4–8 x 4–9 mm.

Similar species

This species can be confused with *A. burkei*, but it differs by having hairless leaves and hairless shoots (growing tips).

General

Name derivation: *welwitschii* = named after F.M.J. Welwitsch, a German botanist who collected the type specimen, and *delagoensis* = refers to Delagoa bay (Maputo) in Mozambique. All the material from South Africa is assigned to subsp. *delagoensis*; the typical subsp. *welwitschii* occurs only in Angola. Elsewhere in Africa, *A. welwitschii* subsp. *delagoensis* is found in Malawi, eastern Zimbabwe and Mozambique. The wood is hard and heavy (air-dry 960 kg/m^3) with yellow-brown sapwood and black heartwood. The wood is, however, susceptible to damage from woodborers.

Acacia burkei

Black Monkey Thorn • Swartapiesdoring

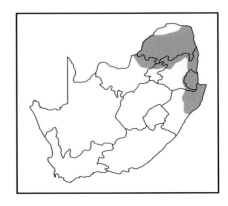

Name with authors
Acacia burkei Benth. –
Type from Gauteng, South Africa

Synonyms
A. *ferox* Benth.

National Tree Number 161

Other common names
Basterknoppiesdoring

Outstanding features

- A medium-sized, upright, single-stemmed tree with branching fairly high above the ground, a "small-leaflet" and a "large leaflet" form has been described,
- The bark on the main stem of young trees is yellowish and papery, on older trees it is grey and fairly smooth to coarse,
- New season's shoots are sparsely hairy and green with reddish tinges,
- The paired prickles are strongly recurved, sparsely hairy when young and often occur on knobs on old stems,
- Leaves with 3–14 pinna pairs, the petiole and rachis are moderately hairy and the leaflet size extremely variable,
- Yellowish-white flowering spikes are borne at the nodes on both new season's and previous seasons' shoots,
- The dehiscent pods are hairless, prominently venose, flat and straight with occasional constrictions between seeds.

154

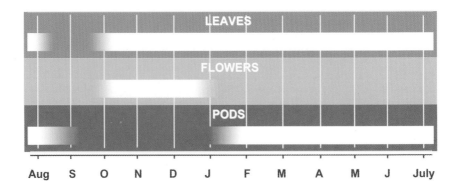

| | Aug | S | O | N | D | J | F | M | A | M | J | July |

LEAVES

FLOWERS

PODS

Habitat

Habitat quite variable. May grow on a variety of soil types, but shows some preference to sandy soils (not leached) – mainly on granite in the Kruger National Park. Commonly found in mixed savanna, often widely spaced. Also occurs on rocky slopes, in low lying areas or along dry river beds.

General description

Usually a medium sized tree which grows to a height of 6–12 m. Under optimal conditions it can grow to a height of 25–30 m with a crown diameter approximately two thirds of its height. Trees are mostly single-stemmed, upright and branching fairly high above the ground. It is an attractive tree and the shape of the spreading crown varies from open, rounded to flat-topped. There appear to be two forms of this species, notably in Kwazulu-Natal: a "small-leaflet" form which is characteristically flat-topped, and a "large-leaflet" form which more frequently has a rounded crown.

Main stem

Very variable. In young trees the main stem is distinctly yellowish in colour with papery flakes, while that of mature trees is predominantly grey.

The bark on the main stem varies from fairly smooth and scaly to coarse with longitudinal fissures. In the latter case some transverse cracking occur, as well as a tendency to flake. A yellow colour is often discernible in deep fissures.

Shoots

Very young new season's shoots have a green colour, often with a reddish tinge, and are sparsely covered with fine white hairs. Previous seasons' shoots are greyish with light coloured, transversely-elongated lenticels. Older, thickened shoots are smooth, dark green to grey with light-coloured transversely elongated lenticels. These older shoots are partially covered with thin layers of yellow, papery bark.

Thorns

The stipules are unmodified and not spinescent. They do not persist and senesce early. Prickles are paired and located at the nodes. They are well-developed, strongly recurved, sharp-pointed and may attain a length of 9 mm. The prickles of each pair are orientated at an angle that ranges from 110° to almost 180°. On much older stems they often occur on knobs, almost like those of *A. nigrescens*. The colour on young, new season's shoots ranges from green to reddish brown.

The very young prickles are covered with sparse, minute hairs which disappear with maturity. On older shoots and stems the prickles are dark-grey, often with an elevated base which has a grey colour, lighter in shade than the prickle itself.

Leaves

The leaves are borne at the nodes, singly or up to 4 per node. The number of pinna pairs varies from 3–14 and the number of leaflet pairs per pinna from 4–19. The petiole and rachis are light green, slender and mostly moderately hairy. Small recurved prickles can be present on the underside of the rachis. The base of the petiole is swollen and its length varies from 10–35 mm. The petiole and rachis, combined, have a length of 25–120 mm. The leaflet size is extremely variable and reference is made in literature of a "small-leaflet" form and a "large-leaflet" form. There appears to be no clear-cut distinction between the two forms, as many intermediates do occur. The length of leaflets varies from 4.5–20.5 mm and the width from 1.6–13 mm. The colour is slightly paler underneath. Main and lateral venation is visible, particularly on the underside and their margins are usually sparsely fringed with hairs. There is a small, brown, raised gland located on the lower half of the petiole and there may be a small gland on the rachis at 1–3 of the distal pinna junctions.

Inflorescence

Flowering spikes are borne at the nodes, singly or up to 6 per node towards the tips on both new season's and previous seasons' shoots. The colour of the developing buds are initially green, changing to a slight yellowish colour prior to full bloom. The open, fully developed flowering spikes have a mean length of 70 mm (range: 14–146 mm) and a mean diameter of 16 mm. They are scented and light yellow to yellowish-white in colour. Peduncles are moderately hairy with a mean length of 15 mm (range: 4–30 mm).

Pods and seeds

The pods are borne in bunches of up to 20 near terminals, often in abundance. The colour of the young developing pods is initially green, changing to a characteristic dark reddish or purplish-brown colour. This reddish colour is often confined to one side of the pod only. The pods dry to a dark brown colour. The pods are flat and straight, occasionally with minor constrictions between seeds. They are prominently venose, dehiscent, hairless and sharply tapered at both ends. They attain a length of 40–170 mm and a width of 9–25 mm. The pods contain 5 or more seeds. The seeds are flattened, elliptic with a small projection at the hilum. They are fairly large with a size of 6–13 x 6–11 mm and have a dark brown colour. The areole, visible as a slightly darker horseshoe-shaped outline, is recessed with a size of 4–8 x 3–8 mm.

Similar species

This species can, in its larger leafed form, resemble *A. nigrescens* but the leaves of the former are generally narrower and, even in their largest form, are still smaller than those of *A. nigrescens*. It may also develop knobs on which prickles are borne, but these are neither as large, nor as conspicuous, as those of *A. nigrescens*. In *A. burkei* a yellow colour is visible in deep fissures in the bark, but not in *A. nigrescens*. *A. burkei* also resembles *A. welwitschii* subsp. *delagoensis* (see comments under the latter species).

General

Name derivation: *burkei* = named after the English botanist Joseph Burke who collected this species in 1840 near the Magaliesberg. Elsewhere in Africa, *A. burkei* is also found in south-eastern Botswana, south-eastern Zimbabwe, Mozambique and Swaziland. The wood is hard and heavy (air-dry 900 kg/m^3) with a yellow-brown to dark brown colour. It is used for furniture but is difficult to work.

Mature tree

Young, immature tree

"Small-leaflet" form

"Large-leaflet" form

157

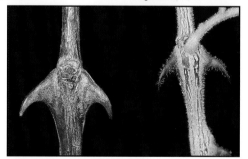

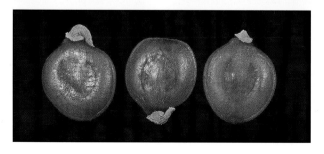

Acacia nigrescens
Knob Thorn • Knoppiesdoring

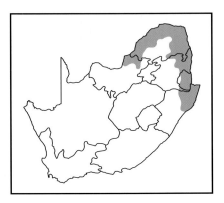

Outstanding features

- A tall, upright, single-stemmed tree with an irregular, rounded crown,
- The bark on the main stem of young trees is yellowish and papery, on older trees it is dark grey, coarse and longitudinally fissured,
- New season's shoots are smooth, hairless and green or reddish-brown, older shoots are partially covered with papery bark,
- The paired prickles are recurved, hairless and on older stems occur on conical knobs,
- Leaves with 1–4 pinna pairs and usually only 1–2 pairs of large leaflets per pinna, the petiole and rachis are hairless,
- Light yellow to cream coloured flowering spikes are borne in clusters towards the tips of previous seasons' shoots,
- The dehiscent pods are flat and straight, hairless, prominently venose, leathery with a green to reddish colour.

158

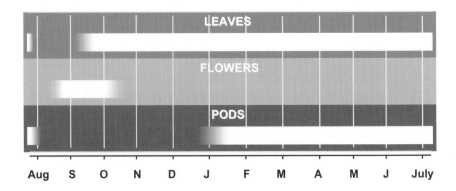

Habitat

Habitat quite variable. May grow on a variety of soil types, except sandy soils. In the Kruger National Park it is commonly found on basalt, granite and dolomite soils. Also occurs on shallow rocky soils, alluvial soils and hillsides. It is fire and drought resistant, but is sensitive to cold.

General description

A tall tree, mostly with a single upright stem and with branching commencing fairly high up. It grows to an average height of 10–15 m, but may reach a height of 30 m. The crown is somewhat irregular and rounded with ascending branches.

Large individuals tend to grow much taller than the surrounding vegetation, and are thus very conspicuous. May also form localize dominant stands.

Main stem

Very variable. In young trees the main stem is distinctly yellowish in colour with papery flakes, while that of mature trees is dark grey, coarse and longitudinally fissured. The occurrence of persisting prickles on the apices of large dark brown knobs is a characteristic feature of the main stems of small to intermediate sized trees. These knobs are often absent from the main stems of very large trees, but may still be visible on some of the side branches.

Shoots

Young new season's shoots have a homogeneous green or reddish-brown colour and are smooth and hairless. Older, previous seasons' shoots are partially covered with a thin layer of greyish-white to brown papery bark. Underneath the papery bark the shoots are smooth and green with numerous light-coloured transversely-elongated lenticels. The papery bark, even on older shoots, is dark grey to yellow.

Thorns

The stipules are unmodified and not spinescent. They do not persist and senesce early. Prickles are paired, well-developed, strongly recurved, sharp-pointed and located at the nodes. They may attain a length of 7 mm. The prickles of each pair are orientated at an angle of up to 180°. Their colour on young, new season's shoots ranges from green to reddish brown and they are hairless. On older shoots and stems the prickles retain the reddish brown colour for some time, but age to a grey colour with dark, almost black points. On much older stems they occur on prominent conical knobs, hence the name "Knob Thorn".

Leaves

The leaves are borne at the nodes, singly or in pairs. The number of pinna pairs varies from 1–4 (2–3 typical). The petiole length is highly variable from 5–55 mm, while the mean length of the petiole and rachis, combined, is 65 mm (range: 15–120 mm). The petiole and rachis are slender, light green and hairless. There are usually only one or two pairs of large leaflets per pinna. The ventral side of the rachillas is occasionally armed with a number of small recurved prickles. The undersides of the leaflets are markedly paler in colour than the upper surfaces. Venation, both main and lateral, is clearly visible above but less so underneath and the leaflets are mostly hairless. The leaflet size is highly variable. Their length varies from 6.5–50 mm (16–25 mm typical), and their width from 5.3–50 mm (8–12 mm typical). There can be a small raised gland on the petiole, located in the middle or on the lower half of the petiole. Glands on the rachis are often absent, or when present, located at the junctions of the pinna pairs.

Inflorescence

Flowering spikes are grouped at the nodes in clusters of up to 5 towards the tips of previous seasons' shoots, often in great profusion before the appearance of the new foliage. The colour of the developing buds prior to full bloom varies from green to yellow or purplish-red. The open, fully developed flowering spikes have a mean length of 50–60 mm (range: 10–100 mm) and a mean diameter of 10–13 mm. They are scented and light yellow to cream in colour. The peduncles and spike rachides have a characteristic reddish colour. Peduncles are hairless with a mean length of 8–10 mm (range: 3–24 mm). When in full bloom the trees are very conspicuous.

Pods and seeds

The pods are borne in bunches. The colour of the young developing pods is initially green, changing to a dark reddish or purplish-brown colour. This reddish colour is often confined to one side of the pod only. The pods dry to a dark brown, almost black colour, but if they persist on the tree they weather to a light grey colour. The pods are flat and straight, prominently venose, leathery, hairless and tapered at both ends. They attain a length of 60–178 mm and a width of 14–24 mm. The pods are dehiscent and contain 3–6 seeds. The seeds are flattened, circular, fairly large with a diameter of 10–13 mm and have a dark brown colour. The areole is visible as a distinct dark brown horseshoe-shaped outline, appreciably recessed with a diameter of 5–8 mm.

Similar species

A. nigrescens could be confused with *A. galpinii* if flowering when leafless. It also resembles *A. burkei* (see comments under the latter species).

General

Name derivation: *nigrescens* = blackish or becoming black, and refers to the dark colour of the dry pods. Elsewhere in Africa, *A. nigrescens* is found from Tanzania southwards to Namibia, Botswana and Swaziland. The heartwood is hard and heavy (air-dry 1 100 kg/m^3) with a dark brown colour, surrounded by yellowish-white sapwood.

Acacia polyacantha

(subsp. campylacantha)

White Thorn • Witdoring

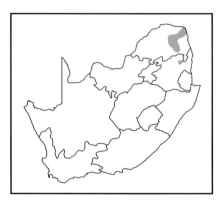

Name and authors
Acacia polyacantha Willd. subsp.
campylacantha (Hochst. ex A. Rich.) Brenan –
Types from Ethiopia

Synonyms
• *A. caffra* (Thunb.) Willd. var. *campylacantha*
(Hochst. ex A. Rich.) Roberty
• *A. campylacantha* Hochst. ex A. Rich.
• *A. catechu* (L. f.) Willd. subsp. *suma* (Roxb.)
Roberty • *A. erythrantha* Steud. ex A. Rich.

National Tree Number 180

Outstanding features

• A tall, upright, single-stemmed tree with a sparse, flattish crown which often exhibits stratification,

• The bark on the main stem is smooth and greyish-white or rough and peeling, on young trees it is yellowish and papery,

• New season's shoots are smooth, moderately hairy and green,

• The paired prickles are recurved, well-developed on new growth, mature trees are almost without prickles, on older stems and main stems of young plants they often occur on knobs,

• The leaves are large with 14–60 pinna pairs, the petiole and rachis are moderately hairy,

• Light yellow to cream coloured flowering spikes are borne at the nodes towards the tips of new season's shoots,

• The dehiscent pods are hairless, flat and straight with prominent venation.

162

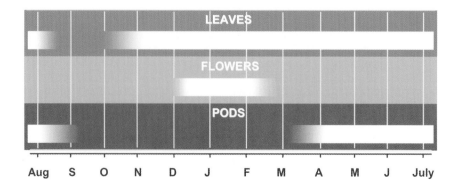

	Aug	S	O	N	D	J	F	M	A	M	J	July
LEAVES												
FLOWERS												
PODS												

Habitat

Shows a preference for moist conditions. Found on alluvial, loam or clay soils along rivers and streams in riverine woodland and seasonally flooded areas. Often grows grouped together.

General description

Large trees are striking. They are tall and erect, mostly with a single stem and with branching commencing fairly high up. Upper branches are erect, those further down more arcuate and the lowest branches almost horizontal. They grow to an average height of 10–15 m, but may reach a height of 25 m. In large trees the crown is rather sparse, flattish, spreading and it often exhibits stratification.

Main stem

In young trees the bark is papery with a distinct yellowish colour. Persisting, dark coloured prick-les on light coloured conical bases are often present on these young stems. The bark of mature trees can be quite smooth with a whitish-grey colour. Some rough bark may be present, which peels in papery flakes to reveal the smooth under surface.

Shoots

Young, new season's shoots are smooth, homogeneously green, covered with light coloured lenticels and are moderately hairy. Older, previous seasons' shoots are grey-green to brown, also covered with light-coloured lenticels and there may be some dark-coloured striations. Much older shoots can become covered with thin layers of light brown, papery bark.

Thorns

The stipules are unmodified and not spinescent. They do not persist and senesce early. Paired prickles are located at the nodes. They are slightly to strongly recurved and the prickles of each pair are orientated at an angle that ranges from 110° to 180°. Mature trees may be almost without prickles, while the prickles on new growth can be well-developed, sharp-pointed and up to 15 mm long. On much older stems as well as the main stems of young plants they often occur on knobs, almost like those of *A. nigrescens*. Their colour on young, current season's shoots are initially green, which may change to dark red brown with maturity. On older shoots and stems the prickles have a grey coloured base, similar to the colour of the shoots, and the apex has a dark gunmetal blue or dark reddish colour.

Leaves

The leaves are fairly large and arranged singly along the shoots. The petiole and rachis are green and moderately hairy, particularly in newly-emerged leaves. The petiole has a length of 5–40 mm and the combined length of the petiole and rachis varies from 60–200 mm (100–130 mm typical). The number of pinna pairs varies 14–60 (14–20 pairs typical), and the number of leaflet pairs per pinna from 15–68 (25–30 pairs typical). The leaflets have a length of 2–6 mm and width of 0.4–1.4 mm. The upper surface is darker than the underside and hairs are limited to the margins only. A slight swelling occurs at the base of the petiole. A large, elongated petiolar gland with a size of 1.5–4 x 1.5–3 mm is commonly present, usually close to the base of the petiole. There is a cupped gland at the junction of the distal 2–16 pinna pairs.

Inflorescence

Flowering spikes are borne at the nodes, singly or in clusters of up to 4 towards the tips of new season's shoots. The colour of the developing buds prior to full bloom varies from green to yellowish-green. The open, fully-developed flowering spikes have a mean length of 90–105 mm (range: 30–120 mm) and a mean diameter of 10–12 mm. They are scented and are light yellow to cream in colour. Peduncles have a mean length of 15–19 mm (range: 5–30 mm). The peduncles and spike rachides are covered with orange hairs.

Pods and seeds

The pods are borne at the nodes, singly or in bunches of up to 5 per node. The colour of the young developing pods is a dark green and they have a shiny appearance. The pods dry to a light brown colour. The pods are flat and straight with only occasional constrictions between seeds and are tapered at both ends. The valves are hairless with a narrow, but distinct raised edging. Venation is quite distinct with the veins commencing at the margins and spreading inwards diagonally. The pods have a mean length of 100 mm (range: 65–180 mm) and a mean width of 15 mm (range: 9–21 mm). They are dehiscent with horizontal cracks forming between individual seeds as the pods dry. The number of seeds per pod varies from 3–10. The seeds are flattened, elliptic to quadrate with a size of 7–9 x 6–8 mm. Their colour varies from dark olive green to brown. The areole is visible as a lighter green outline surrounding a slightly paler area and is not impressed. The size of the areole is 3–4 x 2.5–3.5 mm.

Similar species

This species can be confused with *A. caffra*, but it differs by having a relatively straight trunk and yellowish-brown flaking bark, large petiolar glands and a crown which often exhibits stratification.

General

Name derivation: *polyacantha* = many thorns, and *campylacantha* = curved thorns. All African material of this tree is placed in subsp. *campylacantha*; the typical subspecies is known only from India and possibly Sri Lanka. Elsewhere in Africa, *A. polyacantha* subsp. *campylacantha* occurs widespread from Gambia in the west to Ethiopia in the north-east, southwards to South Africa. The wood is light coloured without any heartwood and is fairly light (air-dry 640 kg/m³).

164

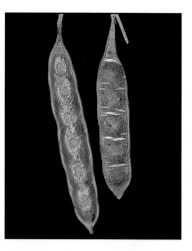

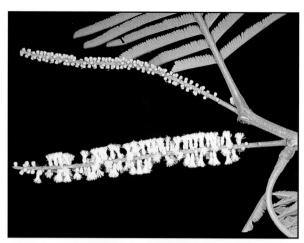

Mature tree

Young, immature tree

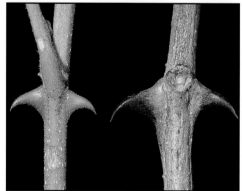

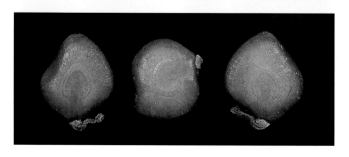

Acacia galpinii

Monkey Thorn • Apiesdoring

Name with authors
Acacia galpinii Burtt Davy –
Type from the Northern Province, South Africa

Synonyms
None

National Tree Number 166

Other common names
Geelapiesdoring

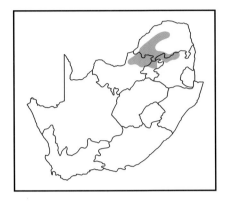

Outstanding features

- A large and distinctive tree, usually single-stemmed with a rounded crown,
- The bark on the main stem is grey to yellowish, coarse, corky, longitudinally fissured with the outer layers peeling away,
- Young shoots are green, smooth and hairless, while older shoots become covered with a thin layer of light brown bark,
- The paired prickles are hairless and recurved to almost straight,
- Leaves with 5–14 pinna pairs, petiole and rachis are hairless and the petiole is slender,
- Light yellow to cream coloured flowering spikes are grouped in clusters towards the tips of previous seasons' shoots, developing buds are purplish-red,
- The large dehiscent pods are flat, straight and hairless with distinct venation.

166

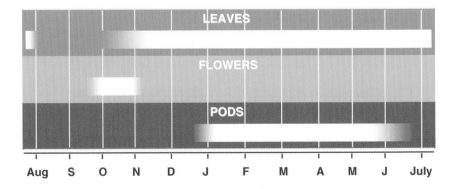

LEAVES

FLOWERS

PODS

Aug S O N D J F M A M J July

Habitat

In its natural habitat it is mostly found along river banks or near water. Also occurs in open savanna. Prefers deep, well drained soils. It is moderately tolerant to cold.

General description

A large and distinctive tree, which can grow to a height of 30 m or more. It is usually single-stemmed, branching at varying heights above the ground. It has a rounded crown, which can attain a considerable spread. When leafless the yellowish fluted trunk and branches are conspicuous.

Main stem

The colour of the bark varies from grey to yellowish. The bark is coarse, corky, longitudinally fissured and the outer layers peel away in more or less rectangular flakes. The colour of the bark on the main branches varies from brown to yellowish-brown. It is rough and corky with papery flakes and often has persisting prickles on swollen bases.

Shoots

Very young new season's shoots are green, smooth and hairless. With maturation they attain a brownish-green colour with numerous transversely-elongated grey to orange lenticels. Older, previous seasons' shoots become progressively covered with a thin layer of light brown bark. This bark displays some longitudinal cracking, giving rise to a striped pattern.

Thorns

The stipules are unmodified and not spinescent. They do not persist and senesce early. Prickles are recurved to almost straight, paired and located at the nodes. They are hairless and vary in length from 8–12 mm. The prickles of each pair are orientated at an angle of almost 180°. Young prickles on new season's shoots are green and their tips a light orange. The colour of older prickles ranges from gun-metal blue, purplish-red to dark brown. Scattered prickles are sometimes present on the main stem.

Leaves

The leaves occur at the nodes, usually singly or in pairs, but occasionally up to 4 leaves per node. The petiole and rachis are hairless and green, but may be reddish in the case of new growth. The petiole is slender with a length of 14–36 mm, while the petiole and rachis, combined, have a mean length of 85 mm (range: 50–145 mm). The number of pinna pairs ranges from 5–14, and the number of leaflet pairs per pinna from 12–35. Leaflets have a mean length of 7 mm (range: 4–10 mm) and mean width of 2.2 mm (range: 0.8–3 mm). They are a somewhat lighter shade underneath and are mostly hairless, though sometimes with minute short hairs on the margins. Only the main vein can be discerned on the upper surface. The petiole base is slightly swollen and a small, green to dark coloured petiolar gland is usually present in the middle of the petiole. On the rachis there are small, green glands at some of the distal pinna junctions and sometimes at some of the basal pinna junctions as well.

Inflorescence

Flowering spikes are grouped in clusters of 2 to 12 towards the tips of previous seasons' shoots, often in great profusion before the appearance of the new foliage. The colour of the developing buds is strikingly purplish-red prior to full bloom. The open, fully developed flowering spikes have a mean length of 78 mm (range: 50–110 mm) and a mean diameter of 14 mm. They are scented and light yellow to cream in colour and the spike rachides a reddish colour. Peduncles are normally hairless with a mean length of 8 mm (range: 3–15 mm). When in full bloom, the trees are very conspicuous.

Pods and seeds

The pods are borne in bunches near terminals. The colour of the young developing pods is homogeneously green and they dry to a brown colour. The pods are flat, straight and tapered at both ends, though less sharply at the tip. They are hairless with distinct venation. The valves are somewhat woody with slightly raised edges. The pods are large with a mean length of 160–200 mm (range: 110–280 mm) and a mean width of 26 mm (range: 22–35 mm). They are dehiscent and can contain up to 10 seeds per pod. The seeds are brown to reddish-brown, subcircular with a size of 8–15 x 8–12.5 mm. The areole is recessed, dark brown and horseshoe-shaped with a size of 5–8 x 3.5–7 mm.

Similar species

If leafless but in flower, *A. galpinii* can be confused with *A. nigrescens*.

General

Name derivation: *galpinii* = named after E. E. Galpin, a plant collector. Elsewhere in Africa, *A. galpinii* is also found in central Tanzania, Zambia, Malawi, Mozambique, Botswana and Zimbabwe. The wood is hard, heavy (air-dry 980 kg/m^3) and coarsely grained. It is light brown in colour and the heartwood is smallish with a dark brown colour. It is said to make good furniture, but is difficult to work. The trees adapt well to cultivation.

Group Four

Recurved thorns, scattered irregularly along the internodes

Additional characteristics and variations
- prickles
- stipules not spinescent and they do not persist

Acacia ataxacantha
Acacia kraussiana
Acacia brevispica subsp. *dregeana*
Acacia schweinfurthii var. *schweinfurthii*

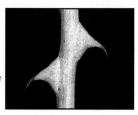

Acacia ataxacantha

Flame Thorn • Vlamdoring

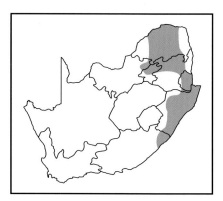

Name with authors
Acacia ataxacantha DC. – Type from Senegal

Synonyms
• *A. ataxacantha* DC. var. *australis* Burtt Davy
• *A. eriadenia* Benth. • *A. lugardiae* N.E. Br.

National Tree Number 160

Other common names
Rank wag-'n-bietjie

Outstanding features

• Often grows densely entangled with other vegetation, forming thick impenetrable thickets,

• Bark on the main stem of young trees is fairly smooth with longitudinal striations on which prickles are born,

• Very young new season's shoots are covered with short, densely packed orange hairs,

• Unpaired recurved prickles are scattered along dark-grey or brown striations on shoots and stems,

• Leaves are large, the petiole and rachis are hairy and the stalked petiolar gland is distinctive,

• Creamy-yellow flowering spikes are grouped in clusters towards the tips of new season's shoots,

• Ripe pods have a striking deep red to purple-red colour.

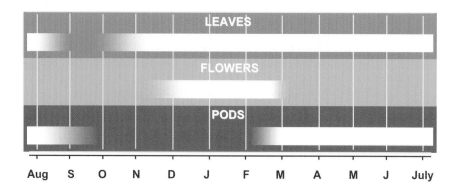

Habitat

Generally not a species of the open savannas. It is mostly confined to riverine habitats, rocky hillsides, mountainous areas and forest margins.

General description

Growth form variable from a multi-stemmed semi-scandent untidy shrub to a free-standing small tree (5–10 m). It often grows densely entangled with other vegetation, forming thick impenetrable thickets almost down to ground level. When growing in such dense entanglements it is unobtrusive until in flower or covered with their conspicuous translucent red pods (late summer). As a free-standing tree it has a rounded crown of which the spread may equal or exceed its height.

Main stem

The bark on the main stem of young trees is fairly smooth with a light grey to buff colour, often with dark, longitudinal striations on which prickles are born. In older trees the bark is dark-grey, coarsely flaking with some transverse splitting. Longitudinal fissures may reveal an orange ground colour.

Shoots

The base colour of very young new season's shoots are green, or purplish above and green underneath, but may appear orange due to short, densely packed orange hairs. These hairs disappear with maturation. Older, previous seasons' shoots vary in colour from green to greyish with minute, buff coloured, transversely-elongated lenticels. They also have longitudinal dark-grey or brown striations.

Thorns

The stipules are unmodified and not spinescent. They are large, rather shield-like with an ovate or triangular shape, up to 12 x 7 mm, and located on either side of the leaf petioles. They are sometimes absent, but when present may persist up to the end of the growing season. Unpaired recurved prickles are scattered along dark-grey or brown striations on shoots and stems. They are short, sharp-pointed and have thick bases. On very young, new season's shoots they may appear orange due to densely packed orange hairs. These hairs quickly disappear and the prickles then have a dark or dark-green colour with a brown apex. Much older prickles have a light to dark-grey colour, the same as that of the older shoots and stems, while their apex have a faint orange colour.

Leaves

The leaves are fairly large and arranged singly along stems. The leaflets may vary in colour from bright green when young, to a darker blue-green. The petiole and rachis are hairy, particularly in newly-emerged leaves, and their ventral sides are commonly armed with a number of recurved prickles. The colour of the petiole and rachis may vary from green, occasionally purplish on the upper side, to orange (due to the orange colour of the covering hairs). The petiole have a length of 7–18 mm, and the combined length of the petiole and rachis range from 65 mm (older leaves) to 160 mm (young leaves). The number of pinna pairs range from 6–28 (9–16 typical), and the number of leaflet pairs per pinna from 10–62. Individual pinnae may attain a maximum length of 66 mm or more. Leaflet size is highly variable in length (2–7 mm) and width (0.5–2.5 mm). A slight to appreciable swelling occur at the base of the petiole. The petiolar gland (occasionally more than one), if present, is distinctive, stalked and can project as much as 2 mm at an angle towards the rachis. On the rachis there are small green to dark domed glands at one to three of the distal pinna junctions.

174

Inflorescence

Flowering spikes are grouped in clusters towards the tips of new season's shoots, often in great profusion. They are scented and creamy-yellow in colour. The colour of the developing buds are initially green, turning to yellow and orange prior to full bloom. Peduncles are hairy with a length of 4–25 mm. The flowering spikes have a mean length of 60 mm (range: 22–115 mm) and a mean diameter of 14.5 mm. The involucel is distinct and located at the base of the peduncle. When in full bloom the trees are very conspicuous.

Pods and seeds

The pods are borne in bunches near terminals, often in abundance. The colour of the young developing pods is green. With ripening they change to a deep red to purple-red colour which is very striking, hence the common name "Flamethorn". With age the colour changes to brown or a light khaki. The pods are flat and straight, without significant constrictions between seeds, tapering sharply at both ends. They are dehiscent, leathery with some transverse venation and may attain a length of 70–100 mm and a width of 14–19 mm. The number of seeds vary from 3 to 8 and the cords which attach the seeds to the pod give rise to raised ridges which reveal the positions of the seeds in the unopened pod. The seeds are flattened, roughly circular, 6–9 mm in diameter and vary in colour from olive green to brown. The central areole, 2.5–3 mm in diameter, is visible as a depression.

Similar species

Without flowers or pods, this species can be confused with *A. brevispica*. With the latter, however, the foliage is yellowish-green in colour and the petiole and rachis are hairless. In addition the inflorescences of *A. brevispica* are globose and the pods lack the striking red colour. As a small tree it may be confused with *A. caffra* but the stalked gland on the petiole of *A. ataxacantha,* as well as the large and triangular stipules, is usually diagnostic. The unpaired, scattered prickles differ from the paired prickles of *A. caffra*.

General

Name derivation: *ataxacantha* = scattered thorns. Elsewhere in Africa, *A. ataxacantha* is widely distributed occurring from Senegal in the west to the Sudan in the north-east, extending down to Zimbabwe, Mozambique, Botswana, Namibia and Swaziland in the south.

Acacia kraussiana

Coast Climbing Thorn • Kusrankdoring

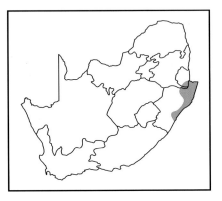

Name with authors
Acacia kraussiana Meisn. ex Benth. –
Type from KwaZulu-Natal, South Africa

Synonyms
None

National Tree Number 173.1

Outstanding features

- A scandent shrub with long trailing branches, often only visible on the crowns of surrounding vegetation,
- Main stems are characteristically angular (5-sided), fairly smooth with occasional minor longitudinal fissures,
- Shoots are angular and slightly hairy and dark-green when young, some shoots are modified into tendrils,
- Small, unpaired recurved prickles arise from striations at the angular edges of shoots and stems,
- Leaves with 3–6 pinna pairs, the leaflets are large and the petiole and rachis are slightly hairy with a large petiolar gland near the petiole base,
- Yellowish-white globose flowering heads are borne in panicles at terminals of new season's shoots,
- The pods are hairless, flat and straight, tardily dehiscent to indehiscent with swellings over the seeds.

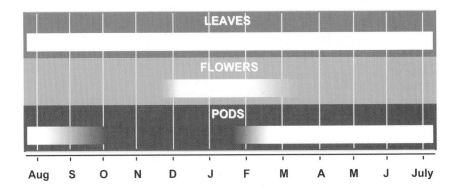

Habitat

It occurs mostly in coastal dune forest, thickets, dry riverine habitats and forest margins. Most commonly found along the coast, but may also be found inland.

General description

Occurs as a multi-stemmed scandent shrub with long trailing branches. It can be unobtrusive and is often only visible on the crowns of surrounding trees and shrubs. It depends on surrounding vegetation for support and its height is largely determined by the surrounding vegetation. It has tendrils, which are coiled around the branches of supporting vegetation. The tendrils are leafless and are armed with prickles.

Main stem

The main stems do not attain a large diameter. They are characteristically angular (5-sided), fairly smooth, though sometimes with minor longitudinal fissures. They are brown with a green cast in places. The bark may peel in places in thin, papery strips.

Shoots

Young new season's shoots are slightly hairy with a homogeneous dark green colour. They are inconspicuously glandular with numerous, minute, light-coloured lenticels. These shoots are angular (5-sided), which become more pronounced as they mature. Older, previous seasons' shoots have a light-brown to grey-brown colour with a green cast in places. Light coloured striations, which are armed with minute prickles, occur at the angular edges of the shoots. Some shoots are modified into tendrils. They have the same colour as the shoots, depending on their age, and are also armed with minute prickles.

Thorns

The stipules, which can be up to 4.5 x 1.1 mm in size, are not spinescent and are deciduous. Small, unpaired recurved prickles are scattered along the internodes of shoots and stems and are placed along the striations. They are short, often a mere 1 mm long, but may attain a length of 2 mm. They are sharp-pointed. On very young, new season's shoots they are green to dark-reddish with yellowish tips. Older prickles are brown to light grey.

Leaves

The leaves are large and arranged singly along stems. The petiole and rachis are slightly hairy, reddish when young and their ventral sides are commonly armed with a number of recurved prickles. The petiole has a length of 8–35 mm, and the petiole and rachis, combined, may attain a length of 130 mm (65–75 mm typical). The number of pinna pairs varies from 3–6 and the number of leaflet pairs per pinna from 6–17 (9–14 pairs typical). Leaflets are large and their size tends to increase along individual pinnae. They have a mean length of 12 mm (range: 5–23 mm) and a mean width of 4.6 mm (range: 2–8 mm). Leaflets are dark-green above and slightly lighter below. Main and transverse venation is visible on both surfaces and the upper and lower surfaces are slightly hairy. The petiole base is appreciably swollen and immediately above the swelling is a large, cupped or domed petiolar gland, up to 4 mm long. On the rachis are small glands at 1–2 of the distal pinna junctions.

Inflorescence

Globose flowering heads are borne in panicles at terminals of new season's shoots. Leaves are initially absent from the nodes at the terminals of flower-bearing shoots. The colour of the developing buds is homogeneously green. The open, fully-developed flowering heads have a mean diameter of 14–20 mm. They are yellowish-white in colour, and turn to a deeper yellow as they fade. They are borne on light-green, moderately hairy peduncles with a mean length of 10–15 mm. The stipules at the base of the peduncles are small and inconspicuous and they senesce early. The flowering heads at each panicle are often in various stages of development.

Pods and seeds

The pods are borne in bunches near terminals. The pods are flat and straight, mostly linear with occasional slight constrictions between seeds. They are tapered at the base and more rounded at the tip. The valves are hairless with a coarse papery texture and have a narrow raised edging. Transverse venation is visible and swellings over the seeds give a clear indication of their position. The colour of the developing pods is green and they dry to a dark brown colour. The pods attain a mean length of 100 mm (range: 60–160 mm) and a mean width of 17 mm (range: 14–25 mm). They are tardily dehiscent to indehiscent and contain up to 14 seeds. The seeds are somewhat compressed, elliptic with a size of 5.5–9 x 4–6 mm and have an olive-brown to dark brown colour. The areole takes the form of an indistinct, darker brown elliptic or horseshoe-shaped outline, 4–7 mm x 2.5–4 mm, which may or may not be slightly impressed.

Similar species

The large leaves, including large leaflets, and the presence of tendrils, separate this species from other South African *Acacia* species. It has a superficial resemblance to *Entada spicata* (E. Meyer) Dtuce, but the pods of the latter are so distinctive, splitting transversely into one-seeded segments, that confusion is not likely to arise.

General

Name derivation: *kraussiana* = named after the German botanist F.F von Krauss. Elsewhere in Africa, *A. kraussiana* is restricted to Mozambique and Swaziland.

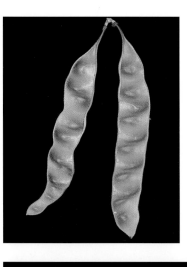

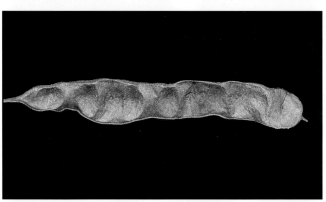

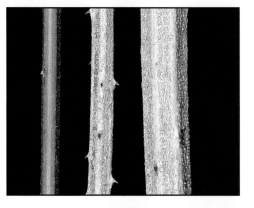
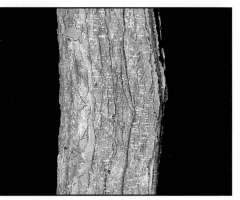

Acacia brevispica

(subsp. *dregeana*)

Prickly Thorn • Dorinkiedoring

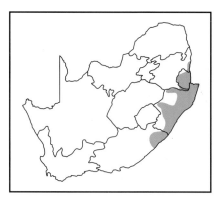

Name with authors
Acacia brevispica Harms subsp. *dregeana*
(Benth.) Brenan –
Type from Eastern Cape, South Africa

Synonyms
• *A. brevispica* Harms var. *dregeana*
(Benth.) J.H. Ross & Gordon-Gray • *A. pennata*
var. *dregeana* Benth.

National Tree Number 160.2

Outstanding features

- A scandent shrub, often growing densely entangled with other vegetation, forming thick impenetrable thickets,
- Bark on the main stems is fairly smooth, light-grey with light-coloured, longitudinal striations on which prickles are borne,
- Young shoots are sparsely hairy, homogeneously green, while older shoots are light-grey with darker, slightly raised, striations,
- Unpaired recurved prickles arise from raised striations on shoots and stems,
- Leaves are large with 6–20 pinna pairs, the petiole and rachis are hairless and the undersides of the leaflets are often densely hairy,
- Yellowish-white globose flowering heads are borne in panicles at terminals of new season's shoots,
- The dehiscent pods are leathery, flat and straight with distinct transverse venation.

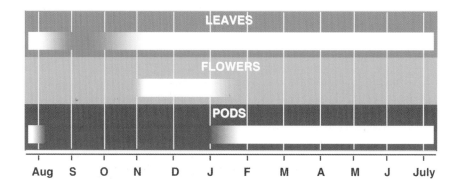

Habitat

Generally not a species of the open savannas. It is mostly found in thickets, dry riverine habitats and forest margins, from sea-level to an altitude of approximately 2 000 m. Plants from higher altitudes are moderately tolerant to cold.

General description

Growth form variable from a multi-stemmed scandent shrub (up to 12 m) to a single-stemmed free-standing small tree (2.5–7 m). It grows profusely, often densely entangled with other vegetation, forming thick impenetrable thickets almost down to ground level.

Main stem

The bark on the main stems is fairly smooth with a light grey colour, often with light-coloured, longitudinal striations on which prickles are borne. In older trees there may occasionally be some minor longitudinal fissuring.

Shoots

Young new season's shoots are green, longitudinally grooved, sparsely hairy and dotted with small dark glands. Growing tips can be reddish. Older, previous seasons' shoots are smooth and hairless with a light grey colour and with grey, brown to reddish-brown, slightly raised, longitudinal striations. They are also covered with inconspicuous, light-coloured lenticels.

Thorns

The stipules, which can be up to 4.5 x 1.2 mm in size, are not spinescent and are deciduous. Unpaired recurved prickles are scattered along the internodes. They arise from raised striations on shoots and stems. They are short, often a mere 1 mm long, but may attain a length of 7 mm. They are sharp-pointed. On very young, new season's shoots they are distinctly green to yellow-green, without hairs and are marked with small, dark, raised glands. Prickles on older shoots and stems have thickened bases and are of the same colour as the striations from which they arise. The apex of these older prickles is almost black.

Leaves

The leaves are large and arranged singly along stems, not confined to the nodes. The leaflets are initially dark-green, becoming yellowish-green as they age. The petiole and rachis are slightly grooved, largely hairless and their ventral sides are commonly armed with a number of recurved prickles. The petiole has a length of 5–35 mm, and the petiole and rachis, combined, may attain a length of 125 mm or more. The number of pinna pairs ranges from 6–20, and the number of leaflet pairs per pinna from 18–62. Leaflets vary from 2.5–6.0 mm in length and 0.5–1.0 mm in width. The undersides of the leaflets may be hairless, but are often densely hairy, the hairs being flattened against the surface. A slight to appreciable swelling occurs at the base of the petiole. The petiolar gland, if present, varies in position, shape and size. They are usually green, elongated (occasionally round) with a depression on top. On the rachis there are small green, cupped glands at one or two of the distal pinna junctions.

Inflorescence

Globose flowering heads are borne in panicles at terminals of new season's shoots. Leaves are initially absent from the nodes at the terminals of flower-bearing shoots. Some flower heads may also be found among leaves at axils some way down from the tip of the shoots. The colour of the developing buds is green prior to full bloom. The open, fully-developed flowering heads have a mean diameter of 10–12 mm. They are yellowish-white in colour, and turn to a deeper yellow as they fade. They are borne on light-green, hairy peduncles with a mean length of 20–25 mm. The stipules at the base of the peduncles are small and inconspicuous and they senesce early. The flowers at each panicle are often in various stages of development.

Pods and seeds

The pods are borne in bunches near terminals. The colour of the developing pods is homogeneously green and they dry to a dark-brown to almost black colour. The pods are flat and straight, without significant constrictions between seeds, tapered at the base and more rounded at the tip. They are dehiscent, leathery with distinct transverse venation and with numerous minute reddish glands. The valves have a distinct raised edge and sometimes there are swellings at the seed positions. They can be hairy or hairless and attain a length of 60–150 mm and a width of 18–28 mm. The pods can contain up to 12 seeds. They are flattened, elliptic with a size of 8–12 x 6–10 mm and are dark-brown, olive-brown or reddish-brown in colour. The areole is in the form of an elliptic outline, slightly to appreciably indented and with a size of 6–8 x 3–5 mm.

Similar species

This species can be confused with *A. schweinfurthii* var. *schweinfurthii*. It can be distinguished from the latter species by its shorter leaf petioles, smaller leaflets, often densely hairy undersides of the leaflets and the yellowish-green colour of the mature leaves, as compared to the dark green of *A. schweinfurthii*. In *A. schweinfurthii* a large, elongated yellow or dark-coloured petiolar gland occurs immediately above the swelling at the base of the petiole, while in *A. brevispica*, if present, it varies in position, shape and size. Another distinguishing character is the dehiscent pods of *A. brevispica* that split readily opposed to the pods of *A. schweinfurthii* that are tardily dehiscent to indehiscent.

General

Name derivation: *brevispica* = short prickles, and *dregeana* = named after the collector J.F. Drège. There are two subspecies of *A. brevipica* of which only subsp. *dregeana* is represented in South Africa. Subspecies *dregeana* is also found in Swaziland and southern Mozambique.

Acacia schweinfurthii

(var. schweinfurthii)

River Climbing Thorn • Rivierrankdoring

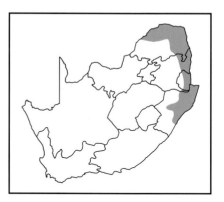

Name with authors

Acacia schweinfurthii Brenan & Excell var.
schweinfurthii – Type from Sudan

Synonyms

A. brevispica Harms var. *schweinfurthii*
(Brenan & Exell) Ross & Gordon-Gray

National Tree Number 184.1

Outstanding features

- A scandent shrub with long trailing branches, often growing densely entangled with other vegetation, forming thick impenetrable thickets,
- Bark on the main stems is fairly smooth, light brown with dark coloured, longitudinal striations on which prickles are borne,
- Young shoots are hairless and green, while older shoots are light yellowish-grey with light grey striations,
- Unpaired recurved prickles arise from raised striations on shoots and stems,
- Leaves are large with 6–17 pinna pairs, the petiole and rachis are hairless with a large petiolar gland near the petiole base,
- Yellowish-white globose flowering heads are borne in panicles at terminals of new season's shoots,
- The pods are leathery, hairless, flat and straight, tardily dehiscent to indehiscent.

184

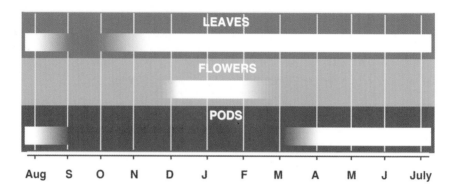

	LEAVES										
		FLOWERS									
		PODS									
Aug	S	O	N	D	J	F	M	A	M	J	July

Habitat

Mostly confined to wet, riverine habitats where there is the likelihood of seasonal flooding. Also occurs in coastal areas, woodland and forest margins away from water.

General description

Occurs as a multi-stemmed scandent shrub with long trailing branches, forming thick impenetrable thickets down to ground level. Its height is largely determined by the surrounding vegetation, which it uses as support, and branches can grow to the top of tall trees. Isolated plants occur as low growing, spreading shrubs.

Main stem

The bark on the main stems is fairly smooth with a light brown colour, often with dark coloured, longitudinal striations on which prickles are borne. In older trees there may occasionally be some irregular longitudinal fissuring.

Shoots

Young new season's shoots are longitudinally grooved and hairless with a homogeneous dark green colour and with numerous, minute, light coloured lenticels. Older, previous seasons' shoots

are smooth and are light yellowish-grey in colour with a green ground colour that becomes more visible as the shoots mature. Light-grey longitudinal striations and numerous, closely spaced, transversely-elongated lenticels are visible on these older shoots.

Thorns

The stipules, which can be up to 5 x 1.2 mm in size, are not spinescent and are deciduous. Unpaired recurved prickles are scattered along the internodes. They arise from raised striations on shoots and stems. They are well developed, strongly recurved and sharp-pointed with thickened bases that spread both laterally and longitudinally. They can attain a length of 9.5 mm or more, but shorter prickles of a mere 1 mm long may also be present. On very young, new season's shoots they are dark green and hairless. Prickles on older shoots have light-grey bases and their apex is almost black.

Leaves

The leaves are large and arranged singly along stems, not confined to the nodes. The petiole and rachis are slightly grooved, largely hairless and their ventral sides are commonly armed with a number of recurved prickles. The petiole has a length of 15–55 mm, and the petiole and rachis, combined, may attain a length of 190 mm (130–160 mm typical). The number of pinna pairs ranges from 6–17 (12–13 typical), and the number of leaflet pairs per pinna from 17–60 (30–40 typical). Leaflets have a mean length of 6.8 mm (range: 2.5–8.5 mm) and a mean width of 1.5 mm (range: 0.8–2.5 mm). Leaflets are slightly darker above than below and the main vein and some lateral veins can be seen on the underside. Except for some hairs on the margins the leaflets are predominantly hairless. A distinct elongated swelling occurs at the base of the petiole and immediately above the swelling is a large, elongated yellow or dark-coloured petiolar gland. There is occasionally a further domed, yellowish gland on the petiole, about two thirds of the distance from the end of the swelling to the first pinna pair. On the rachis are small green, domed glands at 1–3 of the distal pinna junctions.

Inflorescence

Globose flowering heads are borne in panicles at terminals of new season's shoots. Leaves are initially absent from the nodes at the terminals of flower-bearing shoots. Some flowering heads may also be found among leaves at axils some way down from the tip of the shoots. The colour of the developing buds is initially green, but changes to a yellowish colour prior to full bloom. The open, fully-developed flowering heads have a mean diameter of 8–12 mm. They are yellowish-white in colour, and turn to a deeper yellow as they fade. They are borne on light-green, hairy peduncles with a mean length of 10–15 mm. The stipules at the base of the peduncles are small and inconspicuous and they senesce early. The flowering

heads at each panicle are often in various stages of development.

Pods and seeds

The pods are borne near terminals, singly or in bunches. The colour of the developing pods is green and they dry to a dark or medium brown colour. The pods are flat and straight, without significant constrictions between seeds, tapered at the base and more rounded at the tip. The valves are leathery, venose, glandular and have a distinct, narrow, raised edging. Swellings over the seeds give a clear indication of their position. The pods are hairless and attain a length of 80–190 mm and a width of 14–29 mm. The pods are tardily dehiscent to indehiscent and contain 8–16 seeds. They are thickened to 3.5 mm, elliptic with a size of 8–12 x 6–8 mm and have a dark-brown or blackish colour. The areole takes the form of an open-ended elliptic, lighter brown, impressed outline with a size of 6–8 x 3–5 mm.

Similar species

This species can be confused with *A. brevispica* subsp. *dregeana* (see the comments under the latter species).

General

Name derivation: *schweinfurthii* = named after the German explorer G. Schweinfurth who collected the type specimen from the Sudan. There are two varieties of *A. schweinfurthii* of which only the type variety, var. *schweinfurthii*, occurs in South Africa. Elsewhere in Africa, *A. schweinfurthii* var. *schweinfurthii* is also found in the Sudan, Tanzania, Malawi, Zambia, Botswana, Zimbabwe and Mozambique.

186

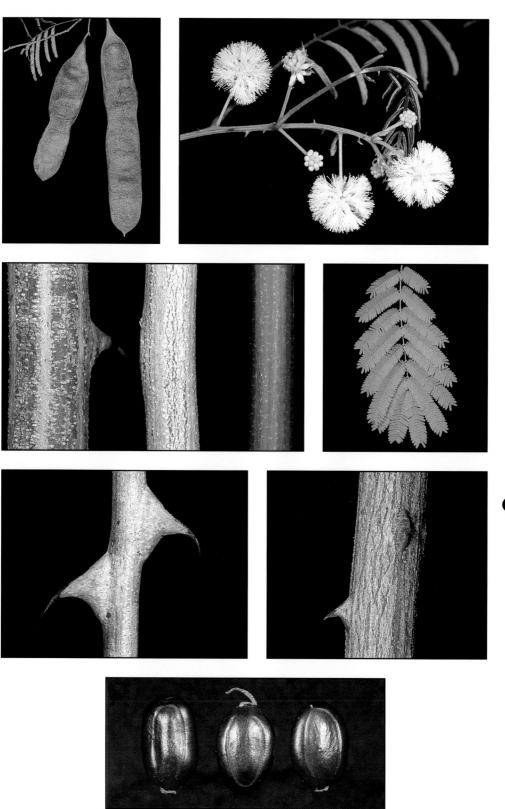

Group Five

Recurved thorns, in threes at the nodes

Additional characteristics and variations
- prickles
- stipules not spinescent and they do not persist

Acacia senegal var. *rostrata*
Acacia senegal var. *leiorhachis*

Acacia senegal

(var. *rostrata*)

Three-hook Thorn • Driehaakdoring

Name with authors
Acacia senegal (L.) Willd. var. *rostrata* Brenan –
Type from Northern Province

Synonyms
• *A. oxyosprion* Chiov. var. *oxyosprion*
• *A. rostrata* Sim • *A. senegal* (L.) Willd. subsp.
trispinosa (Stokes) Roberty • *A. spinosa* Marloth &
Engl. • *A. trispinosa* Marloth & Engl.
• *A. volkii* Süsseng.

National Tree Number 185.1

Other common names
Three-thorn Acacia, Geelhaak

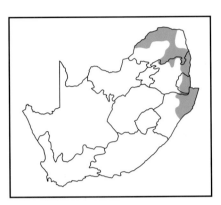

Outstanding features

- Usually a low-growing, multi-stemmed shrub with a compact, flattened crown,
- The bark on the main stem is dark-grey and fairly smooth or light-grey and corky,
- Young shoots are greenish-white and covered with whitish hairs, older shoots are light-grey, smooth and hairless,
- Prickles are located at the nodes in threes, the central prickle is hooked downwards, the lateral prickles are curved upwards,
- Leaves with 3–8 pinna pairs, 10–22 leaflet pairs per pinna and the petiole and rachis are hairy,
- Flowering spikes are yellowish-white and the peduncles are short and hairy,
- The dehiscent pods are slightly hairy when young, flat and straight, tapered at both ends and their apices strongly beaked.

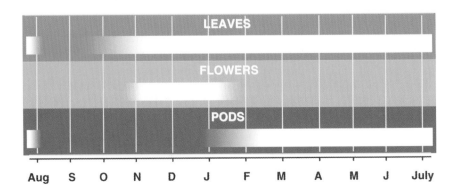

	Aug	S	O	N	D	J	F	M	A	M	J	July
LEAVES												
FLOWERS												
PODS												

Habitat

Found in low rainfall, arid areas, often on slightly alluvial or calcium-rich soils in low lying areas and higher up along dry river beds on poorly drained soils. It also occurs in sandveld areas and in association with calcrete outcrops.

General description

In growth form it differs markedly from var. *leiorhachis*. It is usually a multi-stemmed shrub, which grows to a height of 2–4 m. It can also be single-stemmed, but branching low down. It has a compact, flattened crown with a substantial horizontal spread that can well exceed its height. It may form localised dominant stands, which can become fairly dense.

Main stem

The bark on large mature trees is dark-grey and fairly smooth or light-grey and corky, splitting longitudinally to reveal a biscuit colour. Persisting prickles are often present on the main stem.

Shoots

Young growing tips may initially be reddish, but soon changes to a greenish-white colour. Young

shoots are covered with whitish hairs and light-coloured lenticels are also visible. The greenish-white layer that covers the young shoots tends to split, revealing a green under-colour. Older, previous seasons' shoots are smooth and hairless and have a light-grey colour with some inconspicuous, transversely-elongated lenticels of the same colour. Much older shoots take on a yellowish colour with some flaking of the bark.

Thorns

The stipules are unmodified, not spinescent and do not persist. Prickles are located at the nodes in threes. The central prickle is hooked downwards and the two lateral prickles curved upwards and arranged relative to each other at an angle of about 180°. The central prickle is usually better developed with a pronounced basal buttress. It is also more strongly recurved than the lateral prickles. The lateral prickles are also recurved, more so than in the case of var. *leiorhachis* where they can be almost straight. They vary in length from 4–7 mm. Young prickles on new season's shoots are sparingly hairy with a deep reddish-brown colour, becoming darker towards the tips. Older prickles are hairless and vary in colour from dark-reddish to grey-black. The prickle-bases of these older prickles are usually of the same colour than the shoots on which they are borne.

Leaves

The leaves are borne at the nodes, singly or up to 4 per node. The petiole and rachis are green and hairy. The petiole has a length of 2–20 mm, and the combined length of the petiole and rachis varies from 10–50 mm (25–35 mm typical). The ventral side of the rachis is occasionally armed with a number of small recurved prickles. The number of pinna pairs varies from 3–8, occasionally up to 14, and the number of leaflet pairs per pinna from 10–22. The leaflets have a mean length of 4–5 mm and a mean width of 1.0–1.6 mm. The leaflets are fringed with hairs. The petiole has a basal swelling and immediately above it a small, inconspicuous green or dark-coloured petiolar gland. The petiolar gland may, however, be absent. A small, inconspicuous raised gland may occur on the rachis at some or all of the pinna junctions.

Inflorescence

Flowering spikes are borne at the nodes, singly or 2 per node on previous seasons' shoots. The colour of the developing buds is green to slightly yellowish prior to full bloom. The open, fully-developed flowering spikes are yellowish-white and scented. The spike rachides are densely hairy. The spikes have a length of 35–80 mm and a diameter of 13–20 mm. The peduncles are hairy with a length of 2–8 mm.

Pods and seeds

The pods are flat, straight and more or less parallel-sided. The pods are tapered at both ends and their apices are usually strongly beaked. They are quite broad in relation to their length, giving them a broad leaf-like appearance. The valves are thin and parchment-like with narrow but distinctly raised edging and with marked venation, the veins extending inwards from the edges. They are dehiscent and slightly hairy when young. The young pods are green and they dry to a light-brown or khaki colour. They attain a length of 45–70 mm and a width of 20–32 mm. The pods contain up to 4 olive-brown to light-brown seeds. The seeds are flattened and circular with a diameter of 9–10 mm, or elliptic with a mean size of 8 x 10 mm. The areole with a size of 2.5–6 x 2.5–5 mm is visible as a central U - or horseshoe-shaped marking that is appreciably recessed.

Similar species

With the combination of a compact, flattened crown and hooked prickles that are located in threes at the nodes, it is unlikely to be confused with any other South African *Acacia* species. Specific differences between the two varieties of *A. senegal* are discussed in the text.

General

Name derivation: *senegal* = from Senegal in West Africa, and *rostrata* = beaked, which is a reference to the pods with their beaked apices. There are four varieties of this species of which two are found in South Africa. Elsewhere in Africa, *A. senegal* var. *rostrata* also occurs in Somalia, Kenya, Uganda, Angola, Namibia, Botswana, Zimbabwe, Mozambique and Swaziland. The wood is hard and heavy (air-dry 990 kg/m^3) with a light colour. No heartwood is present. The wood is susceptible to damage from woodborers and is not used.

Acacia senegal

(var. *leiorhachis*)

Slender Three-hook Thorn • Slaploot

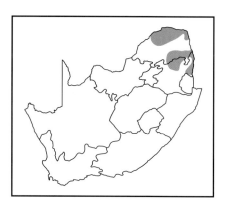

Outstanding features

- A single-stemmed, slender spindly tree with long, irregular straggling branches,
- The bark on the main stem is flaking, grey and corky, distinctly yellowish underneath,
- Young shoots are greenish-brown and sparsely hairy, older shoots are light-grey, smooth and hairless,
- Prickles are located at the nodes in threes, the central prickle is hooked downwards, the lateral prickles are straight or curved upwards,
- Leaves with 3–8 pinna pairs, 7–15 leaflet pairs per pinna and the petiole and rachis are hairy,
- Flowering spikes are compact with a light yellow to yellowish-white colour, peduncles are short and slightly hairy,
- The dehiscent pods are hairless, flat and straight, tapered at the base and rounded to acute at the apex.

194

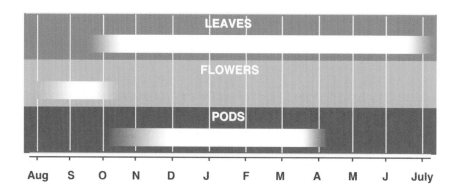

	Aug	S	O	N	D	J	F	M	A	M	J	July
LEAVES												
FLOWERS												
PODS												

Habitat

Occurs in savanna, often in low rainfall areas where it shows some preference for shallow gravelly soils.

General description

Usually a single-stemmed, slender spindly tree with long, irregular straggling branches. It has a sparse, open appearance and may reach a height of 17 m, though in most cases it will not exceed 6–10 m.

Main stem

Viewed from a distance the bark has a distinctly yellowish colour. The main stems of mature trees are usually partially covered with grey corky bark. This corky bark may be mainly transversely cracked, with occasional longitudinal fissures and is flaking. Underneath the corky bark a distinctive yellowish to orange colour is visible. Thin papery bark with a yellowish to orange colour is also present. The main branches are relatively smooth.

Shoots

Very young new season's shoots are greenish-brown and sparsely covered with short whitish hairs. They are also covered with light-coloured lenticels. Older, previous seasons' shoots are smooth and hairless and light grey in colour with some inconspicuous, transversely-elongated lenticels of the same colour. A darker brown colour may be visible underneath the grey colour. Much older shoots take on a yellowish colour with some flaking of the bark.

Thorns

The stipules are unmodified, not spinescent and do not persist. Prickles are located at the nodes in threes. The central prickle is hooked downwards and the two lateral prickles are curved upwards and arranged relative to each other at an angle of about 180°. The central prickle is usually better developed with a pronounced basal buttress. It is also more strongly recurved than the lateral prickles, which can in some cases be almost straight. They vary in length from 4–7 mm. Young prickles on new season's shoots are sparingly hairy with a reddish-brown colour, becoming darker towards the tips. Older prickles are hairless and vary in colour from grey-black to grey. The prickle bases are usually of the same colour than the shoots on which they are borne.

Leaves

The leaves are borne at the nodes, singly or up to 4 per node. The petiole and rachis are light green to yellowish-green and hairy. The petiole has a length of 2–20 mm, and the combined length of the petiole and rachis varies from 10–70 mm (30–55 mm typical). The ventral side of the rachis is occasionally armed with a number of small recurved prickles. The number of pinna pairs varies from 3–8 and the number of leaflet pairs per pinna from 7–15. The leaflets have a mean length of 4–7 mm and a mean width of 1.4–1.7 mm. The leaflets are the same colour above and below and the main vein is only readily discernible on the underside. The petiole has a basal swelling and immediately above it a small, inconspicuous green or dark coloured petiolar gland. A small, inconspicuous raised gland may occur on the rachis at some or all of the pinna junctions.

Inflorescence

Flowering spikes are borne at the nodes, singly or 2 per node on previous seasons' shoots. The colour of the developing buds is yellowish-green prior to full bloom. The open, fully developed flowering spikes are light yellow to yellowish-white and scented. The spike rachis is hairless. The spikes are compact with a length of 35–80 mm and a diameter of 15–22 mm. The peduncles are slightly hairy with a length of 1.5–8 mm.

Pods and seeds

The pods are flat and straight, occasionally with minor constrictions between seeds. The valves are thin and leathery with narrow, raised margins and distinct transverse venation radiating inwards from the margins. The pods are tapered at the base and rounded to acute at the apex. They are dehiscent and hairless, the young pods are green and they dry to a light brown or khaki colour. They attain a length up to 90 mm and a width of 15–20 mm. The pods contain up to 6 light brown-seeds. The seeds are flattened, circular, 10 mm in diameter, or roughly quadrate with a size of 10–14 x 7–11 mm. The areole with a size of 2.5–6 x 2.5–5 mm is visible as a central U - or horseshoe-shaped marking that is recessed. With quadrate seeds the axis of this marking is diagonally orientated.

Similar species

With the combination of a slender, spindly growth form and prickles that are located in threes at the nodes, it is unlikely to be confused with any other South African *Acacia* species. Specific differences between the two varieties of *A. senegal* are discussed in the text.

General

Name derivation: *senegal* = from Senegal in West Africa, and *leiorhachis* = smooth rachis, referring to the hairless rachis of the flowering spikes. There are four varieties of this species of which two are found in South Africa. Elsewhere in Africa, *A. senegal* var. *leiorhachis* also occurs in Ethiopia, Kenya, Tanzania, Zambia, Botswana, Zimbabwe and Mozambique. The wood is hard and heavy (air-dry 930 kg/m^3) with a light brown colour. No heartwood is present. The wood is susceptible to damage from woodborers and is not used.

196

ALPHABETICAL GLOSSARY

Alluvial - soils formed by the depositing of particles carried by a river.

Apex (plural apices) - the terminal point of a spine or a pod.

Areole - the area on either side of a seed.

Armed - bearing thorns (spines or prickles).

Axil - the upper angle between the leaf petiole and the stem or shoot on which it is carried.

Cilia - hairs, usually on the margins of leaflets.

Deciduous - the seasonal senescens and shedding of leaves.

Dehiscent - the splitting open of ripe pods to release the seeds (compare indehiscent).

Distal - furthest from the point of attachment.

Ellipsoid - a solid body elliptic in long section and circular in cross section.

Elliptic - oval and narrowed to rounded ends, widest at or about the middle.

Epidermis - outer covering of leaves and young shoots, usually consisting of a single cell layer.

Flaking - peeling off in small portions (bark in this case).

Flower - the structure concerned with the sexual reproduction in flowering plants.

Fissure - long narrow opening made by cracking or splitting.

Funiculus - the cord attaching the seed to the pod.

Gland - an appendage, protuberance or other structure which secretes sticky, oily or sugary liquid.

Globose - spherical or rounded.

Heartwood - the innermost, generally harder and somewhat darker wood of a woody stem (compare sapwood).

Hilum - the scar on the testa of a seed at which point it was joined to the funiculus.

Inflorescence - any arrangement of more than one flower.

Involucel - a whorl of bracts.

Leaflet - the individual division of a compound leaf, which is usually leaf-like and has a stalk of its own.

Lenticel - a pore on the surface of shoots and stems which facilitate gaseous exchange between plant tissues and the atmosphere.

Linear - resembling a line, long and narrow, with more or less parallel sides.

Node - the area of a stem or shoot from which a leaf or cluster of leaves emerges.

Oblong - an elongated but relatively wide shape, two or four times longer than broader with nearly parallel sides.

Ovate - egg-shaped in outline and attached at the broad end.

Panicle - an inflorescens with an axis that can continue to grow and does not end in a flower. It has many branches, each of which bears two or more flowers.

Peduncle - the common stalk of a flower.

Persistent - remaining attached and not falling off.

Petiole - the stalk of a leaf.

Pinna (plural pinnae) - the secondary division of a compound leaf.

Prickle - a small, sharp-pointed outgrowth of the epidermis or bark.

Rachilla - the axis of a pinna of a compound leaf.

Rachis -(plural rachides) - the axis of a compound leaf or the stalk of a spicate inflorescens.

Sapwood - the outer, newer, usually softer and somewhat lighter wood of a woody stem; the wood is alive and actively transports water (compare heartwood)

Savanna - describing vegetation with a herbaceous layer, usually dominated by graminoids, with an upper layer of woody plants which can vary from widely spaced to a 75 % canopy cover.

Scandent - climbing.

Sessile - attached directly without a supporting stalk.

Shrub - a perennial woody plant with two or more stems arising from or near ground level.

Sodic soil - soil with a high concentration of sodium (Na).

Spine - a hardened, modified stipule with a sharp point.

Spreading - extending outwards in all directions.

Stamen - the male reproductive organ, comprising a filament which bears an anther in which pollen grains are produced.

Stipules - basal appendages of a leaf petiole.

Stoloniferous - with stems which creeps along or above the surface of the ground.

Striations - parallel markings stretching longitudinally along the length of shoots and stems.

Spinescent - spiny (with a sharp point).

Valves - the two separable walls of a pod.

Venation - an arrangement of veins.

Tendril - modified branchlet which aids a scandent plant in attaching it to supporting vegetation.

KEY TO THE IDENTIFICATION OF THE
SOUTH AFRICAN ACACIA SPECIES

A common limitation of many identification keys is that they are either highly technical and/or require a comprehensive sample of both vegetative and reproductive plant parts in order to make a positive identification. The problems faced when compiling a simple, yet accurate identification key without complicating it with highly technical detail are many. At its best even the most sophisticated key will not be perfect. Not only do we all see and interpret features differently, but some species may show considerable variation in one or several characters, making it difficult to find characters that are consistent with all plants over the entire distribution range of that particular species. While it was inevitable that some technical aspects be included in this key, an attempt was made to limit the inclusion of technical aspects to the absolute minimum.

For the use of this key it is assumed that a complete tree is observed in the field. The key is primarily based on vegetative plant characters (growth form, thorns, shoots, bark and leaves). Reproductive plant characters (flowers, pods and seeds) are taxonomically very important, but may only be present on the tree for a limited period of time. A key that requires information on the flowers for example will render it useless when no flowers are present. For this reason only characters of a vegetative nature were included in the key, but reproductive characters are presented for purposes of verification.

How to use the key: The key is based on numbered options detailing differences in one or more plant characters. In each case evaluate the options/criteria presented and choose the most appropriate option. That option will either direct you to a next numbered option, or key out to a specific species. An extended keynote description is presented with each species. Should, for example, reproductive parts be present on the tree the identification of the species can be verify by comparing it with the description of the reproductive parts. The page number where the detailed description of that species can be found is also provided. Here additional information on its typical habitat and geographical distribution, which can assist in identification, is supplied. Should there be doubt as to the correct selection of a criterion, make a note of the number and go back to that point should the previous option prove to be incorrect.

1 (Begin here)

a   Thorns (spines) **straight, paired, located at the nodes** (bases
   may be inflated or not) _____ 2

b   Thorns (spines) **straight and recurved, paired, located at nodes**
   (recurved and straight spines usually occur separately in pairs at
   the nodes, but mixed pairs do also occur, bases of straight spines
   may be inflated or not, tips of straight spines may be recurved) _____ 18

c   Thorns (prickles) **recurved, paired, located at the nodes** _____ 20

d   Thorns (prickles) **recurved, unpaired and scattered irregularly**
   along the internodes _____ 30

e   Thorns (prickles) **recurved, in threes at the nodes** _____ 33

2 (from 1a)

a **Young shoots** and **to a lesser extend young thorns (spines) are
   covered with long, very conspicuous golden yellow or whitish hairs** _____ 3

b **Young shoots** are hairy, but unlike those above the hairs are either
   sparse or very short and densely packed (felt-like) _____ 5

c **Young shoots are hairless** _____ 8

— —

3 (from 1a, 2a)

a A **low, spreading, multi-stemmed bush,** the main stems are **green,
   smooth and shiny** _____ _A. stuhlmannii_ (page 48)

Extended keynote description of _A. stuhlmannii_
• A low, spreading bush up to 4 m with a horizontal spread that can exceed its height,
• Main stem is green, smooth and shiny,
• Young shoots are covered with long bright golden-yellow hairs,
• Paired spines are straight to slightly recurved, covered with long golden-yellow hairs when young,
• The petiole and rachis have a light green colour and are covered with numerous white hairs,
• Globose flowering heads are large and borne on short, hairy peduncles on previous seasons' shoots,
• Young pods are covered with long spreading greyish-white hairs, seeds are almost circular with little or
  no flattening.

b A **slender shrub or small tree with sparse, straggling branches,**
   the main stems are **reddish-brown or yellowish-brown** and covered
   with **thin layers of peeling papery bark,** young shoots are **dotted
   with small, black glands** _____ _A. permixta_ (page 32)

Extended keynote description of _A. permixta_
• Slender shrub or small tree with sparse, straggling branches, often bending downwards,
• The main stems are covered with thin layers of peeling papery bark,
• Young shoots are densely covered with whitish hairs and dotted with small, black glands,
• Paired, spinescent spines are slender and hairy when young,
• Pinna pairs range from 1-6 and the leaf petiole and rachis are hairy and dotted with small, black
  glands,
• Globose flowering heads are bright yellow, peduncles glandular and hairy, involucel conspicuous,
• The pods are small, with numerous reddish-brown to black glands and are moderately sticky.

c A **tree, mostly single-stemmed, with a spreading, flattened crown,**
   the **bark on the main stem is not smooth and shiny,** young shoots
   are **not dotted with small, black glands** _____ 4

201

— —

4 (from 1a, 2a, 3c)

a The **petiole and rachis are densely hairy** and the **pinnae are
   closely arranged** _____ _A. rehmanniana_ (page 74)

Extended keynote description of _A. rehmanniana_
• Small to medium sized tree, mostly single-stemmed, with a flattened, spreading crown,
• The bark on main stem is rough and dark grey, young branches are smoother with a red-brown to bright
  orange colour,

- Young shoots are densely covered with long hairs, golden-yellow on growing tips to whitish on slightly older parts,
- Paired spines are covered with golden-yellow to whitish hairs when young,
- The petiole and rachis are densely hairy, the leaflets are small and occur densely packed on hairy rachillae,
- Light coloured globose flowering heads with hairy peduncles are borne in panicles at terminals of new season's shoots,
- The dehiscent pods are hairless and straight without any constrictions between seeds.

b The **petiole and rachis are moderately hairy** and the **pinnae are not as closely arranged** as above _____ *A. sieberiana* var. *woodii* (page 78)

Extended keynote description of *A. sieberiana* var. *woodii*
- Beautiful tree, mostly single-stemmed, with a spreading, flattened crown,
- The bark on main stem is coarse, greyish to yellowish-brown and the outer layers peeling away in thin papery flakes,
- Young shoots, densely covered with long hairs, are golden-yellow on growing tips to whitish on slightly older parts,
- Paired spines are covered with whitish hairs when young,
- Leaves are fairly large, the petiole and rachis are moderately hairy and the leaflets are closely spaced,
- Globose flowering heads are cream coloured and the peduncles are hairy, involucel is located in the upper half of the peduncle,
- The indehiscent pods are large, straight to slightly curved, valves are woody, thick and hard.

— —

5 (from 1a, 2b)

a All parts of the leaves **densely covered with fine grey hairs** _____ 6

b All parts of the leaves **not densely covered with fine grey hairs** _____ 7

— —

6 (from 1a, 2b, 5a)

a Leaflets are **very small and laterally compressed, superficially resembling a single leaflet** _____ *A. haematoxylon* (page 82)

Extended keynote description of *A. haematoxylon*
- A shrub or medium sized tree with distinctive sparse, grey foliage,
- The bark is light grey, coarse with deep, longitudinal fissures and has a tendency to flake,
- Young shoots have a characteristic reddish-brown colour underneath an initial thin layer of whitish hairs,
- The spines are straight, moderately hairy when young, exceptionally slender and are raked forward,
- The leaflets are very small and laterally compressed, superficially resembling a single leaflet, all parts of the leaves are densely covered with fine grey hairs,
- Globose flowering heads are golden-yellow with slender, hairy peduncles,
- Pods are sickle-shaped, circular or contorted with a dense covering of short velvety grey hairs.

b Leaflets are **small but not laterally compressed** _____ *A. erioloba* x *A. haematoxylon* (page 90)

Extended keynote description of *A. erioloba* x *A. haematoxylon*
- A small tree, either single- or multi-stemmed with distinctly greyish foliage,
- Bark of mature trees is light grey, grey-brown to blackish, coarse with deep, longitudinal fissures,
- Young shoots with a reddish-brown colour underneath an initial thin layer of whitish hairs,

- The spines are straight, hairless to moderately hairy when young, and are raked forward,
- The leaflets are small and all parts of the leaves are densely covered with fine grey hairs,
- Globose flowering heads are golden-yellow, involucel located at the apex of hairy peduncles,
- Pods are sickle-shaped or circular with a dense covering of short velvety grey hairs.

—— —— —— —— —— —— —— —— —— —— —— —— —— —— —— —— ——

7 (from 1a, 2b, 5b)

a   Young shoots are **sparsely covered with whitish hairs**, shoots
    appreciably thickened and the **nodes pronounced**, thorns
    (spines) on **older shoots are stout and very short, on new
    growth they can be immense** _____ *A. robusta* subsp. *clavigera* (page 98)

Extended keynote description of *A. robusta* subsp. *clavigera*
- A medium to large sized tree, upright, single-stemmed with dark green foliage and thickened branches,
- Bark of mature trees is rough, dark grey with longitudinal fissures,
- Young shoots are sparsely covered with whitish hairs, appreciably thickened and the nodes pronounced,
- The paired spines on older shoots are stout and very short, on new growth they can be immense,
- Leaves with 2-7 pinna pairs, petiole and rachis are covered with hairs and the leaflets are large and dark green,
- Globose flowering heads are light yellow to cream with mostly hairless peduncles,
- The dehiscent pods are narrow, linear and straight to slightly curved, sub-woody, smooth and hairless.

b   Young shoots are **sparsely covered with whitish hairs**, but they
    are not **thickened** and the **nodes not pronounced**, thorns
    (spines) are **often distinctly raked backwards** _____ *A. nilotica* subsp. *kraussiana* (page 56)

Extended keynote description of *A. nilotica* subsp. *kraussiana*
- Small to medium sized single-stemmed tree of 5-6 m with a compact rounded to flattened crown,
- The bark of mature trees is rough, blackish-grey to black, with longitudinal fissures,
- Young new season's shoots are homogeneously green and covered with a thin layer of short whitish hairs,
- The paired spines are straight to slightly recurved and are often raked backwards,
- The leaflets are small and the leaflet pairs per pinna increase distally,
- Globose flowering heads are bright yellow with moderately hairy peduncles,
- Pods, with marked constrictions between seeds, have a beaded appearance and a characteristically sweet smell.

203

c   The bark on main stem is **rough and dark grey**, young branches are
    light grey, red-brown or bright orange with transverse wrinkling,
    young shoots are covered with **short whitish hairs and have a
    velvety feel** _____ *A. gerrardii* var. *gerrardii* (page 70)

Extended keynote description of *Acacia gerrardii* var. *gerrardii*
- A small to medium sized tree, mostly single-stemmed with a sparse, flattish crown,
- The bark on main stem is rough and dark grey, young branches light grey, red-brown or bright orange with transverse wrinkling,
- Young shoots are covered with short whitish hairs and have a velvety feel to the touch,
- The paired spines are straight to slightly recurved and may have thick bases,
- Leaves with 5-10 pinna pairs, petiole and rachis are hairy and leaflets are of an intermediate size,
- Globose flowering heads are cream coloured to almost white with moderately hairy peduncles,
- Pods are sickle-shaped and covered with short velvety grey hairs.

—— —— —— —— —— —— —— —— —— —— —— —— —— —— —— —— ——

8 (from 1a, 2c)

a **Low growing multi-stemmed shrub or small tree**, young shoots
are covered with **protruding glands and are sticky** (stickiness of the
shoots may vary from slight to distinct and is only discernible on young,
new season's shoots; the stickiness is often not limited to the shoots
and young leaves and young pods may also be sticky; pods often
covered with numerous black glands) _____ 9

b Growth form and shoots not as above _____ 13

— —

9 (from 1a, 2c, 8a)

a Main stems is **covered with thin segments of peeling papery bark**,
especially in the case of younger plants _____ 10

b Main stems **not covered with thin segments of peeling papery bark** _____ 11

— —

10 (from 1a, 2c, 8a, 9a)

a Main stems is characteristically **transversely wrinkled**, thorns
(spines) are **exceptionally slender, venation on the underside
of the leaflets is distinct** _____ *A. swazica* (page 36)

Extended keynote description of *A. swazica*
• A slender shrub or small tree that prefers rocky habitats,
• Main stem is characteristically transversely wrinkled, covered with thin segments of peeling papery
  bark,
• Young shoots are hairless and less sticky than other small glandular podded species,
• Paired, spinescent spines are hairless and exceptionally slender,
• Pinna pairs range from 1-5, leaflet size tends to increase towards the tips of pinnae, venation on the
  underside of the leaflets is distinct,
• Globose flowering heads are bright yellow, peduncles are long and involucel large,
• The pods are small, dehiscent with numerous black glands, moderately sticky to the touch.

b Main stems is **not transversely wrinkled**, thorns (spines) often
with **thickened bases** _____ *A. exuvialis* (page 40)

Extended keynote description of *A. exuvialis*
• An upright shrub or small tree, single- or multi-stemmed,
• The main stem is smooth underneath thin segments of yellowish to grey peeling papery bark,
• Young shoots are initially slightly sticky with a green colour, changing to reddish or reddish-brown,
• Paired, spinescent spines are straight to slightly recurved, often with thickened bases,
• Larger primary leaves and smaller secondary leaves occur and the leaflet size increases
  progressively from the base to the tip of each pinna,
• Globose flowering heads are bright yellow, peduncles long and involucel conspicuous,
• Pods are sickle-shaped, flat, tapered at both ends and have marked constrictions between seeds.

— —

11 (from 1a, 2c, 8a, 9b)

a   Leaves usually with **only a single pinna pair, occasionally two** _____ A. nebrownii (page 28)

Extended keynote description of *A. nebrownii*
• Erect multi-stemmed shrub or slender tree, often associated with banks of dry water courses,
• The bark is smooth with a bluish-grey colour and with some reddish tinges,
• Shoots, when very young, are covered with protruding glands and are moderately sticky,
• Paired, spinescent spines are slender and hairless,
• There is usually only a single pinna pair, occasionally two,
• Globose flowering heads are golden-yellow, peduncles glandular and basal involucel inconspicuous,
• The pods are small, dehiscent with numerous, protruding black glands, sticky to the touch.

b   Some leaves may only have a single pinna pair, but the **majority of leaves with more than 2 pinna pairs** _____ 12

— —

12 (from 1a, 2c, 8a, 9b, 11b)

a   Low growing **multi-stemmed shrub**, surfaces and margins of the **leaflets do not possess glands** _____ A. tenuispina (page 24)

Extended keynote description of *A. tenuispina*
• Low growing multi-stemmed shrub, associated with black turf soil,
• The bark surface is rough to the touch, dark grey to brownish, occasionally revealing a reddish-brown base colour,
• Young shoots are covered with numerous protruding glands and are very sticky,
• Paired, spinescent spines are slender and hairless,
• Leaves with 1-6 pinna pairs and sticky when young, leaflets comparatively large and hairless,
• Globose flowering heads are bright yellow with long, sticky peduncles covered with glands,
• The pods are small, dehiscent with numerous, protruding black glands, sticky to the touch.

b   **Multi-stemmed shrub or a slender, single-stemmed tree**, surfaces and margins of the **leaflets possesses glands** _____ A. borleae (page 44)

Extended keynote description of *A. borleae*
• Low growing multi-stemmed shrub, normally associated with clayed soil,
• The bark on the main stems of young plants is relatively smooth and dark coloured,
• Young shoots are covered with numerous protruding glands and are very sticky,
• Paired, spinescent spines are slender and hairless,
• The leaves, with 2-10 pinna pairs, are dark green, shiny and very sticky,
• Globose flowering heads are bright yellow with long, sticky peduncles covered with glands,
• The pods are small, dehiscent with numerous, protruding black glands, sticky to the touch.

— —

13 (from 1a, 2c, 8b)

a   Leaves with **more than 10 pinna pairs**, bark on the main stem is **thick, corky and relatively soft with deep longitudinal fissures** _____ A. davyi (page 52)

Extended keynote description of *A. davyi*
• Small single-stemmed tree with a rounded crown up 5 m high or a multi-stemmed shrub of about 2 m,
• The bark on the main stem is thick, corky and relatively soft with deep longitudinal fissures,

- Young shoots are hairless and smooth with a homogeneous bright green colour, while older shoots become covered with light coloured corky bark,
- Paired stipular spines are slender and relatively short,
- The leaves, typically with 16-24 pinna pairs, are fairly large, bright green to yellowish-green when young,
- Deep yellow globose flowering heads are borne in large panicles at terminals of new season's shoots,
- Pods straight or slightly curved, linear with marked to minor constrictions between seeds.

b Leaves and bark not as above _____ 14

— —

14 (from 1a, 2c, 8b, 13b)

a   The **bark is smooth, powdery** with a characteristically **lime-green
    to greenish-yellow colour** _____ *A. xanthophloea* (page 102)

Extended keynote description of *A. xanthophloea*
- A tall, single-stemmed, upright tree with a sparse rounded or flattened crown,
- The bark is smooth, powdery with a characteristically lime-green to greenish-yellow colour,
- Young shoots are smooth, hairless with a homogeneous bright green colour,
- The paired spines are hairless, white with darkened tips and raked forward,
- Leaves with 2-9 pinna pairs, petiole and rachis are largely hairless and grooved on top,
- Globose flowering heads are bright yellow with slender, hairy peduncles and prominent involucels,
- The indehiscent pods are straight, hairless with constrictions between seeds and slight swellings that mark the positions of the seeds.

b Bark not as above _____ 15

— —

15 (from 1a, 2c, 8b, 13b, 14b)

a Bases of paired thorns (spines) are **massively inflated and
   fused together at the base** ("ant-galls") (normal non-inflated
   spines may also be present), it is usually a **single-stemmed
   tree** _____ *A. erioloba* (page 86)

Extended keynote description of *A. erioloba*
- A single-stemmed tree up to 22 m, with main branches often considerably contorted,
- Bark of mature trees is grey, grey-brown to blackish, coarse with deep, longitudinal fissures,
- Young shoots are smooth, hairless, initially green but soon attain a dark red colour,
- Bases of paired stipular spines are often massively inflated and fused together at the base ("ant-galls"),
- Leaves with 1-5 pinna pairs, petiole and rachis are hairless and leaflets are comparatively large with prominent venation,
- Globose flowering heads are deep golden-yellow; involucel located at the apex of hairless peduncles,
- Pods are indehiscent, large and woody, sickle-shaped, greyish-green with a dense covering of velvety hairs.

b Thorns (spines) **not as massively inflated** as above _____ 16

— —

16 (from 1a, 2c, 8b, 13b, 14b, 15b)

a The shoots are **often appreciably thickened** and the **nodes pronounced,**
   thorns (spines) on **older shoots are stout and very short, on new growth**
   they can be immense, the leaves are borne at the nodes, **usually on**
   distinct "cushions" _____ *A. robusta* subsp. *robusta* (page 94)

Extended keynote description of *A. robusta* subsp. *robusta*
• A medium to large sized tree, single-stemmed with dark green foliage and thickened branches,
• Bark of mature trees is rough, dark grey with deep, longitudinal fissures,
• Shoots are smooth, hairless, appreciably thickened and the nodes pronounced,
• The paired spines on older shoots are stout and very short, on new growth they can be immense,
• Leaves with 2-7 pinna pairs, petiole and rachis are hairless and the leaflets are large and dark green,
• Globose flowering heads are light yellow to cream with mostly hairless peduncles,
• The dehiscent pods are fairly large, linear and straight to slightly curved, sub-woody, smooth and hairless.

b Either (or both) the shoots and the thorns (spines) not as above _____ 17

— —

17 (from 1a, 2c, 8b, 13b, 14b, 15b, 16b)

a Young shoots **grow in a marked zig-zag pattern from node to node,**
   thorns (spines) are **stout and often swollen,** especially at the base,
   on the leaflets **the main vein is sometimes indistinctly visible on**
   the upper surface but is not apparent underneath _____ *A. grandicornuta* (page 60)

Extended keynote description of *A. grandicornuta*
• Small to medium sized tree, usually single-stemmed with a rounded to irregular crown,
• Bark of mature trees is coarse with deep, longitudinal fissures,
• Young shoots are smooth, hairless and grow in a marked zig-zag pattern from node to node,
• The paired spines are stout and often swollen, especially at the base,
• Leaves with 1-5 pinna pairs, petiole and rachis are hairless to slight hairy and leaflets are comparatively large,
• Globose flowering heads are light cream to almost white with slender, hairless peduncles,
• Pods are sickle-shaped, green and hairless; dry pods with thin, brittle valves, dangling seeds are often hanging from the dehiscent pods.

207

b **Zig-zag growth pattern of shoots not a notable feature,** thorns (spines)
   not as stout and swollen as above, on the leaflets the **main vein is**
   clearly visible on the underside but indistinct above _____ *A. karroo* (page 64)

[Note: Only plants of the so called "typical" form, which occurs in the Karoo, Free State, interior regions of KwaZulu-Natal and over most of the northern parts of the country will key out here. Since this species is extremely variable some forms of *A. karroo* may be difficult to identify using this key. Please refer to page 68 for a discussion of the most notable variations of *A. karroo*.]

Extended keynote description of *A. karroo*
• Small to medium sized tree, usually single-stemmed with a rounded and somewhat spreading crown,
• Bark of mature trees is coarse, blackish-grey to black, longitudinally fissured with some horizontal cracking,
• Young shoots are smooth and mostly hairless and become progressively covered with a thin layer of bark,
• The paired spines are straight and mostly hairless,

- Leaves with 2-6 pinna pairs and 8-16 leaflet pairs per pinna, petiole and rachis are usually hairless,
- Globose flowering heads are bright yellow with hairless peduncles and a prominent involucel,
- Pods are sickle-shaped, green and mostly hairless; dry pods with thin, brittle valves, dangling seeds are often hanging from the dehiscent pods.

---

18 (from1b)

a Young shoots **appear hairless** but may be **sparingly covered with whitish hairs** _____ *A. tortilis* subsp. *heteracantha* (page 120)

Extended keynote description of *A. tortilis* subsp. *heteracantha*
- A small to medium sized tree, mostly single-stemmed with a conspicuously flattened crown,
- The bark on main stem is rough, dark grey and longitudinally fissured, stems of young trees is fairly smooth with marked transverse wrinkling,
- Young shoots are reddish-green to reddish-brown and sparingly covered with whitish hairs,
- Both long straight spines and smaller strongly recurved spines are present and occur in pairs,
- Leaves typically with 4-8 pinna pairs; petiole and rachis are hairy and leaflets are small,
- Globose flowering heads are small, light yellow to cream coloured with slender, hairy peduncles,
- Pods are twisted into a tight circle or into a helix of three to four turns, indehiscent and hairless.

b Young shoots are **densely covered with short whitish hairs and have a velvety feel to the touch** _____ 19

---

19 (from 1b, 18b)

a The long spines are **not massively inflated**, but their **tips are slightly recurved** _____ *A. hebeclada* subsp. *hebeclada* (page 108)

Extended keynote description of *A. hebeclada* subsp. *hebeclada*
- Growth form varies from a prostrate multi-stemmed shrub to a more upright shrub or small tree,
- The bark of the tree form is thickened, dark coloured and longitudinally fissured, in the prostrate form it is fairly smooth,
- Young shoots are covered with short whitish hairs and have a velvety feel to the touch,
- The paired spines are straight with only the tips slightly recurved, some shorter spines are strongly recurved,
- Leaves with 2-12 pinna pairs, petiole and rachis and to some extend the leaflets are hairy,
- Globose flowering heads are pale yellow to cream coloured with hairy peduncles,
- Pods are straight and stand erect, the valves are thick, woody and densely hairy with a felt-like appearance.

b The long straight spines are **not massively inflated** and their **tips are not recurved** _____ *A. luederitzii* var. *luederitzii* (page 112)

Extended keynote description of *A. luederitzii* var. *luederitzii*
- A small to medium sized tree, mostly single-stemmed with a rather open appearance,
- The bark on main stem is rough, dark coloured and longitudinally fissured, stems of young trees is fairly smooth with a red-brown colour,
- Young shoots are covered with short whitish hairs and have a velvety feel to the touch,
- Both long straight spines and smaller strongly recurved spines are present and occur in pairs,
- Leaves typically with 5-8 pinna pairs, petiole and rachis are hairy and leaflets are small,
- Globose flowering heads are cream coloured to almost white with light green, hairy peduncles,
- Pods are flat and straight, dehiscent and the valves are thin and brittle.

c The long straight spines are often **massively inflated ('ant-galls')**
_____ *A. luederitzii* var. *retinens* (page 116)

Extended keynote description of *A. luederitzii* var. *retinens*

- A small, multi-stemmed shrub or a small to medium sized, single-stemmed tree,
- The bark on main stem is rough, dark coloured and longitudinally fissured; stems of young trees is fairly smooth with a grey colour,
- Young shoots are covered with short whitish hairs and have a velvety feel to the touch,
- Both long straight spines and smaller strongly recurved spines are present and occur in pairs; the straight spines are often massively inflated ('ant-galls'),
- Leaves typically with 4-6 pinna pairs, petiole and rachis are hairy and leaflets are small to intermediate in size,
- Globose flowering heads are cream coloured to almost white with hairy peduncles,
- Pods are flat and straight to slightly curved, dehiscent and the valves are thin and brittle.

---

20 (from 1c)

a Leaves with **1-5 pinna pairs** and usually with **less than 10 leaflet pairs per pinna**, the **leaflets are relatively large** in comparison to the overall size of the leaf _____ 21

b Leaves with **3-60 pinna pairs**, some pinnae may have less than 10 pairs of leaflets, but in most cases there are **10 or more leaflet pairs per pinna**, the **leaflets are relatively small** in comparison to the overall size of the leaf _____ 24

---

21 (from 1c, 20a)

a A **upright, single-stemmed tree**, usually only **1-2 pairs of large leaflets** per pinna, some thorns (prickles) on the main stem and side branches **occur on conical knobs** _____ *A. nigrescens* (page 158)

Extended keynote description of *A. nigrescens*

- A tall, upright, single-stemmed tree with an irregular, rounded crown,
- The bark on the main stem of young trees is yellowish and papery, on older trees it is dark grey, coarse and longitudinally fissured,
- New season's shoots are smooth, hairless and green or reddish-brown, older shoots are partially covered with papery bark,
- The paired prickles are recurved, hairless and on older stems occur on conical knobs,
- Leaves with 1-4 pinna pairs and usually only 1-2 pairs of large leaflets per pinna, the petiole and rachis are hairless,
- Light yellow to cream coloured flowering spikes are borne in clusters towards the tips of previous seasons' shoots,
- The dehiscent pods are flat and straight, hairless, prominently venose, leathery with a green to reddish colour.

b Differ in one or all of the above criteria _____ 22

---

22 (from 1c, 20a, 21b)

a   A **medium sized, single-stemmed tree** with lateral branches often
down to ground level, the leaf **petiole and rachis are hairless**
_____ _A. welwitschii_ subsp. _delagoensis_ (page 150)

Extended keynote description of _A. welwitschii_ subsp. _delagoensis_
• A medium sized, single-stemmed tree with lateral branches often down to ground level,
• The bark on the main stem is fairly smooth, longitudinally fissured with a light grey to dark grey colour,
• New season's shoots are smooth, predominantly hairless and green with occasional reddish tinges,
• The paired prickles are strongly recurved, sharp pointed and hairless,
• Leaves with 2-5 pinna pairs, the petiole and rachis are usually hairless and the leaflets are fairly large,
• Light yellow to cream coloured flowering spikes are borne singly or in pairs at or between nodes of new season's shoots,
• The dehiscent pods have a reddish colour and are hairless, flat and straight with occasional constrictions between seeds.

b   The **leaf petiole and rachis are sparsely hairy** _____ 32

— —

23 (from 1c, 20a, 21b, 22b)

a   A **upright, single-stemmed tree,** usually with **more than 2 pairs
of leaflets** per pinna _____ _A. burkei_ (page 154)

Extended keynote description of _A. burkei_
• A medium sized, upright, single-stemmed tree with branching fairly high above the ground, a "small-leaflet" and a "large-leaflet" form has been described,
•The bark on the main stem of young trees is yellowish and papery; on older trees it is grey and fairly smooth to coarse,
• New season's shoots are sparsely hairy and green with reddish tinges,
• The paired prickles are strongly recurved, sparsely hairy when young and often occur on knobs on old stems,
• Leaves with 3-14 pinna pairs, the petiole and rachis are moderately hairy and the leaflet size extremely variable,
• Yellowish-white flowering spikes are borne at the nodes on both new season's and previous seasons' shoots,
• The dehiscent pods are hairless, prominently venose, flat and straight with occasional constrictions between seeds.

b   A **multi-stemmed shrub or small tree** of which the crown may
reach down to ground level, usually with **1-4 pairs of large leaflets**
per pinna _____ _A. mellifera_ subsp. _detinens_ (page 126)

Extended keynote description of _A. mellifera_ subsp. _detinens_
• A multi-stemmed shrub or small tree of which the crown may reach down to ground level,
• The bark is roughish with longitudinal fissures or fairly smooth,
• Young shoots are green and hairless, older shoots are reddish-brown, greyish-green or light grey,
• The paired prickles are well developed, strongly recurved, sharply pointed and hairless,
• Leaves with 2-3 pinna pairs and 1-4 leaflet pairs per pinna, leaflets are large, petiole and rachis are sparsely hairy,
• Flowering spikes are short with a light cream to white colour, buds are green to reddish-purple prior to full bloom,
• Pods are straight with minor constrictions between seeds, dehiscent and papery.

— —

24 (from 1c, 20b)

a **Young shoots** are **hairless** _____ 25

b **Young shoots** are **sparsely covered with hairs** _____ 28

─ ─

25 (from 1c, 20b, 24a)

a The **bark on the main stem** (or part of it) is **yellowish** and **covered
  with thickened, corky or papery, peeling bark** _____ 26

b Bark on the main stem not as above _____ 27

─ ─

26 (from 1c, 20b, 24a, 25a)

a A **small to medium sized, low branching, multi-stemmed shrub** or
  single-stemmed tree, leaves with **3-7 pinna pairs, petiole and rachis**
  are **moderately hairy** _____ *A. erubescens* (page 134)

Extended keynote description of *A. erubescens*
• A small to medium sized, low branching, multi-stemmed shrub or single-stemmed tree,
• The bark on the main stem is yellowish and covered with thickened or papery, peeling bark,
• Young shoots are smooth and hairless with a dark reddish-purple colour that changes to light brown or greyish-white,
• Prickles are strongly recurved, sharply pointed, paired and located at the nodes,
• Leaves with 3-7 pinna pairs, petiole and rachis are moderately hairy and edges of leaflets reddish when young,
• Flowering spikes have a light yellow to cream colour, sometimes with a pink tinge; peduncles are densely hairy,
• Pods are flat, hairless, predominantly straight with occasional constrictions between seeds and are dehiscent.

211

b A **large and distinctive tree, usually single-stemmed** with a
  rounded crown, leaves with **5-14 pinna pairs, petiole and
  rachis** are **hairless** _____ *A. galpinii* (page 166)

Extended keynote description of *A. galpinii*
• A large and distinctive tree, usually single-stemmed with a rounded crown,
• The bark on the main stem is grey to yellowish, coarse, corky, longitudinally fissured with the outer layers peeling away,
• Young shoots are green, smooth and hairless, while older shoots become covered with a thin layer of light brown bark,
• The paired prickles are hairless and recurved to almost straight,
• Leaves with 5-14 pinna pairs, petiole and rachis are hairless and the petiole is slender,
• Light yellow to cream coloured flowering spikes are grouped in clusters towards the tips of previous seasons' shoots; developing buds are purplish-red,
• The large dehiscent pods are flat, straight and hairless with distinct venation.

─ ─

27 (from 1c, 20b, 24a, 25b)

a   The leaves are **fairly large with 10-18 pinna pairs** and the leaves
    tend to droop _____ *A. caffra* (page 138)

Extended keynote description of *A. caffra*

- Small to medium sized, single-stemmed tree with a rounded or irregular shaped crown or a small multi-stemmed shrub,
- The bark on the main stem is light grey to dark grey-brown, rough, longitudinally fissured with some horizontal cracking,
- New season's shoots are mostly hairless and green to reddish-brown,
- The paired prickles are recurved, hairless and often small and poorly developed on older shoots,
- The leaves are highly variable, but typically with 10-18 pinna pairs and are fairly large,
- Light yellow to cream coloured flowering spikes are grouped in clusters towards the tips of predominantly previous seasons' shoots,
- The dehiscent pods are flat and straight with occasional constrictions between seeds.

b   The leaves with **3-10 pinna pairs** and the leaves tend to be **held
    erect** _____ *A. goetzei* subsp. *microphylla* (page 146)

Extended keynote description of *A. goetzei* subsp. *microphylla*

- A medium sized, single-stemmed tree with a rounded or somewhat spreading crown,
- The bark on the main stem is light grey to dark grey, moderately rough with irregular longitudinal fissures and some horizontal cracking,
- Young shoots are mostly hairless and green to reddish-brown while older shoots are grey with reddish-brown striations,
- The paired prickles are recurved, hairless and often small and poorly developed on older shoots,
- Leaves with 3-10 pinna pairs, the petiole and rachis are mostly hairless and the leaflet size variable,
- Light yellow to cream coloured flowering spikes are borne at the nodes, singly or grouped in clusters,
- The dehiscent pods are flat and straight with occasional constrictions between seeds, prominently veined and hairless.

--- --- --- --- --- --- --- --- --- --- --- --- --- --- --- --- --- --- ---

212

28 (from 1c, 20b, 24b)

a   A **tall, upright, single-stemmed tree**, the leaves are **large with
    14-60 pinna pairs** _____ *A. polyacantha* subsp. *campylacantha* (page 162)

Extended keynote description of *A. polyacantha* subsp. *campylacantha*

- A tall, upright, single-stemmed tree with a sparse, flattish crown which often exhibits stratification,
- The bark on the main stem is smooth and greyish-white or rough and peeling, on young trees it is yellowish and papery,
- New season's shoots are smooth, moderately hairy and green,
- The paired prickles are recurved, well developed on new growth, mature trees are almost without prickles, on older stems and main stems of young plants they often occur on knobs,
- The leaves are large with 14-60 pinna pairs, the petiole and rachis are moderately hairy,
- Light yellow to cream coloured flowering spikes are borne at the nodes towards the tips of new season's shoots,
- The dehiscent pods are hairless, flat and straight with prominent venation.

b   A **multi-stemmed shrub or small, single-stemmed tree**, leaves with
    less than 18 pinna pairs _____ 29

--- --- --- --- --- --- --- --- --- --- --- --- --- --- --- --- --- --- ---

29 (from 1c, 20b, 24b, 28b)

a The **bases of the prickles are elongated** and of the same **reddish-brown colour** as the prickles, **no glands are present on the rachis**
_____ *A. fleckii* (page 130)

Extended keynote description of *A. fleckii*
- A multi-stemmed shrub or small, single-stemmed tree with a rounded to flattened crown,
- The bark on the main stem is light grey, peeling longitudinally to reveal a yellowish ground colour,
- Young shoots are homogeneously green and sparsely covered with whitish hairs, older shoots have a whitish or greyish covering with a green under-colour,
- Prickles are strongly recurved, sharply pointed, paired and located at the nodes,
- Leaves with 8-16 pinna pairs, petiole and rachis are hairy, leaflets are small and the petiolar gland is conspicuous,
- Flowering spikes have a yellow-white to cream colour, peduncles are green and moderately hairy,
- Pods are flat, hairless, predominantly straight with occasional constrictions between seeds and are dehiscent.

b The **bases of prickles are not elongated**, there are **glands on the rachis** at the **junction of 1-3 of the distal pinna pairs** and **occasionally at the lowest 1-3 pairs** _____ *A. hereroensis* (page 142)

Extended keynote description of *A. hereroensis*
- Small to medium sized, single-stemmed tree with an irregular rounded crown or a small multi-stemmed shrub,
- The bark on the main stem is dark grey to greyish-brown and longitudinally fissured,
- New season's shoots are sparsely hairy and green to reddish-brown,
- The paired prickles are slightly recurved and sparsely covered with hairs when young,
- The leaves typically with 10-18 pinna pairs, the petiole and rachis are sparsely hairy and the leaflets are small and compact,
- Light yellow to cream coloured flowering spikes are borne singly or paired at the nodes on hairy peduncles,
- The dehiscent pods are flat and straight with occasional constrictions between seeds.

213

30 (from 1d)

a A **scandent shrub** with long trailing branches, often only visible on the crowns of surrounding vegetation, **main stems and older shoots are characteristically angular (5-sided), some shoots are modified into tendrils** _____ *A. kraussiana* (page 176)

Extended keynote description of *A. kraussiana*
- A scandent shrub with long trailing branches, often only visible on the crowns of surrounding vegetation,
- Main stems are characteristically angular (5-sided), fairly smooth with occasional minor longitudinal fissures,
- Shoots are angular and slightly hairy and dark-green when young, some shoots are modified into tendrils,
- Small, unpaired recurved prickles arise from the angular edges of shoots and stems,
- Leaves with 3-6 pinna pairs, the leaflets are large and the petiole and rachis are slightly hairy with a large petiolar gland near the petiole base,
- Yellowish-white globose flowering heads are borne in panicles at terminals of new season's shoots,
- The pods are hairless, flat and straight, tardily dehiscent to indehiscent with swellings over the seeds.

b Often **grows densely entangled with other vegetation**, forming thick
   impenetrable thickets, **occasionally a small free standing tree, main
   stems not angular, tendrils absent** _____ 31

— —

31 (from 1d, 30b)

a Young new season's shoots are **covered with short, densely
   packed orange hairs** _____ *A. ataxacantha* (page 172)

Extended keynote description of *A. ataxacantha*
• Often grows densely entangled with other vegetation, forming thick impenetrable thickets,
• Bark on the main stem of young trees is fairly smooth with longitudinal striations on which prickles are
  born,
• Very young new season's shoots are covered with short, densely packed orange hairs,
• Unpaired recurved prickles are scattered along dark-grey or brown striations on shoots and stems,
• Leaves are large, the petiole and rachis are hairy and the stalked petiolar gland is distinctive,
• Creamy-yellow flowering spikes are grouped in clusters towards the tips of new season's shoots,
• Ripe pods have a striking deep red to purple-red colour.

b Young new season's shoots are **hairless or only sparsely hairy** _____ 32

— —

32 (from 1d, 30b, 31b)

a A large, elongated yellow or dark-coloured **petiolar gland occurs
   immediately above the swelling at the base of the petiole**,
   mature leaves is dark green, undersides of the leaflets are
   hairless _____ *A. schweinfurthii* var. *schweinfurthii* (page 184)

Extended keynote description of *A. schweinfurthii* var. *schweinfurthii*
• A scandent shrub with long trailing branches, often growing densely entangled with other vegetation,
  forming thick impenetrable thickets,
• Bark on the main stems is fairly smooth, light brown with dark coloured, longitudinal striations on
  which prickles are borne,
• Young shoots are hairless and green, while older shoots are light yellowish-grey with light grey striations,
• Unpaired recurved prickles arise from raised striations on shoots and stems,
• Leaves are large with 6-17 pinna pairs, the petiole and rachis are hairless with a large petiolar gland
  near the petiole base,
• Yellowish-white globose flowering heads are borne in panicles at terminals of new season's shoots,
• The pods are leathery, hairless, flat and straight, tardily dehiscent to indehiscent.

b **Petiolar glands**, if present, **varies in position, shape and size**,
   mature leaves is yellowish-green, undersides of the leaflets are
   often densely hairy _____ *A. brevispica* subsp. *dregeana* (page 180)

Extended keynote description of *A. brevispica* subsp. *dregeana*
• A scandent shrub, often growing densely entangled with other vegetation, forming thick impenetrable
  thickets,
• Bark on the main stems is fairly smooth, light grey with light coloured, longitudinal striations on which
  prickles are borne,
• Young shoots are sparsely hairy, homogeneously green, while older shoots are light grey with darker,
  slightly raised, striations,
• Unpaired recurved prickles arise from raised striations on shoots and stems,

- Leaves are large with 6-20 pinna pairs, the petiole and rachis are hairless and the undersides of the leaflets are often densely hairy,
- Yellowish-white globose flowering heads are borne in panicles at terminals of new season's shoots,
- The dehiscent pods are leathery, flat and straight with distinct transverse venation.

— —

33 (from 1e)

a   **A low growing, multi-stemmed shrub with a compact, flattened crown**, bark on the main stem is dark grey and fairly smooth or light grey and corky _____ *A. senegal* var. *rostrata* (page 190)

Extended keynote description of *A. senegal* var. *rostrata*
- Usually a low growing, multi-stemmed shrub with a compact, flattened crown,
- The bark on the main stem is dark grey and fairly smooth or light grey and corky,
- Young shoots are greenish-white and covered with whitish hairs, older shoots are light grey, smooth and hairless,
- Prickles are located at the nodes in trees, the central prickle is hooked downwards, the lateral prickles are curved upwards,
- Leaves with 3-8 pinna pairs, 10-22 leaflet pairs per pinna and the petiole and rachis are hairy,
- Flowering spikes are yellowish-white and the peduncles are short and hairy,
- The dehiscent pods are slightly hairy when young, flat and straight, tapered at both ends and their apices strongly beaked.

b   **A single-stemmed, slender spindly tree with long, irregular straggling branches**, bark on the main stem is **flaking**, grey and corky, distinctly **yellowish** underneath _____ *A. senegal* var. *leiorhachis* (page 194)

Extended keynote description of *A. senegal* var. *leiorhachis*
- A single-stemmed, slender spindly tree with long, irregular straggling branches,
- The bark on the main stem is flaking, grey and corky, distinctly yellowish underneath,
- Young shoots are greenish-brown and sparsely hairy, older shoots are light grey, smooth and hairless,
- Prickles are located at the nodes in trees, the central prickle is hooked downwards, the lateral prickles are straight or curved upwards,
- Leaves with 3-8 pinna pairs, 7-15 leaflet pairs per pinna and the petiole and rachis are hairy,
- Flowering spikes are compact with a light yellow to yellowish-white colour, peduncles are short and slightly hairy,
- The dehiscent pods are hairless, flat and straight, tapered at the base and rounded to acute at the apex.

— —

REFERENCES

Arnold, T.H. & De Wet, B.C. 1993. Plants of Southern Africa: names and distribution. *Memoirs of the Botanical Survey of South Africa* No 62. National Botanical Institute, Pretoria.

Barnes, D.L. 1976. A review of plant-based methods of estimating food consumption, percentage utilisation, species preferences and feeding patterns of grazing and browsing animals. *Proceedings of the Grassland Society of Southern Africa* 11: 65-71.

Barnes, R.D., Filer, D.L. & Milton, S.J. 1996. Acacia karroo – *monograph and annotated bibliography.* Oxford Forestry Institute, University of Oxford.

Belsky, A.J., Amundson, R.G. & Duxbury, J.M. 1989. The effects of trees on their physical, chemical and biological environments in a semi-arid savanna in Kenya. *Journal of Applied Ecology* 26: 1 005-1 024.

Ben-Shahar, R. 1991. Successional patterns of woody plants in catchment areas in a semi-arid region. *Vegetatio* 93:19-27.

Bosch, O.J.H. & Van Wyk, J.J.P. 1970. Die invloed van bosveldbome op die produktiwiteit van *Panicum maximum*: 'n voorlopige verslag. *Proceedings of the Grassland Society of Southern Africa* 5: 69-74.

Brooks, R. & Owen-Smith, N. 1994. Plant defences against mammalian herbivores: are juvenile *Acacia* more heavily defended than mature trees? *Bothalia* 24: 211-215.

Brown, N.A.C. & Booysen, P. de V. 1969. Seed coat impermeability in several *Acacia* species. *Agroplantae* 1: 51-60.

Carr, J.D. 1976. *The South African Acacias.* Conservation Press, Johannesburg.

Coates Palgrave, K. 1993. *Trees of southern Africa.* Struik Publishers, Cape Town.

Coe, M. & Coe, C. 1987. Large herbivores, *Acacia* trees and bruchid beetles. *South African Journal of Science* 83: 624-635.

Cooper, S.M. 1982. The comparative feeding behaviour of goats and impalas. *Proceedings of the Grassland Society of Southern Africa* 17: 117-121.

Cooper, S.M., Owen-Smith, N. & Bryant, J.P. 1988. Foliage acceptability to browsing ruminants in relation to seasonal changes in leaf chemistry of woody plants in a South African savanna. *Oecologia (Berlin)* 75: 336-342.

Coughenour, M.B. & Detling, J.K. 1986. *Acacia tortilis* seed germination responses to water potential and nutrients. *African Journal of Ecology* 24: 203-205.

Davidson, L. & Jeppe, B. 1981. *Acacias – a field guide to the Acacias of Southern Africa.* Centaur, Johannesburg.

Donaldson, C.H. 1966. Control of Blackthorn in the Molopo area with special reference to fire. *Proceedings of the Grassland Society of Southern Africa* 1: 57-62.

Donaldson, C.H. & Kelk, D.M. 1970. An investigation of the veld problems of the Molopo area: I. Early findings. *Proceedings of the Grassland Society of Southern Africa* 5: 50-57.

Du Toit, J.T., Bryant, J.P. & Frisby, K. 1990. Regrowth and palatability of *Acacia* shoots following pruning by African savanna browsers. *Ecology* 71: 149-154.

Du Toit, P.F. 1968. A preliminary report on the effect of *Acacia karroo* competition on the composition and yield of sweet grassveld. *Proceedings of the Grassland Society of Southern Africa* 3: 147-149.

Dye, P.J. & Spear, P.T. 1982. The effects of bush clearing and rainfall variability on grass yield and composition in south-west Zimbabwe. *Zimbabwe Journal of Agricultural Research.* 20: 103-118.

Fagg, C.W. & Stewart, J.L. 1994. The value of *Acacia* and *Prosopis* in arid and semi-arid environments. *Journal of Arid Environments* 27: 3-25.

Furstenburg, D. 1991. *Die invloed van tanniene in plante op die voedingsekologie van Kameelperde (*Giraffa camelopardalis*)*. M.Sc.-thesis, University of Pretoria, Pretoria.

Garner, R.D. & Witkowski, E.T.F. 1997. Variations in seed size and shape in relation to depth of burial in the soil and predispersal predation in *Acacia nilotica*, *A. tortilis* and *Dichrostachys cinerea*. *South African Journal of Botany* 63: 371-377.

Grunow, J.O. 1980. Feed and habitat preferences among some large herbivores on African veld. *Proceedings of the Grassland Society of Southern Africa* 15: 141-146.

Guy, P.R., Mahlangu, Z. & Charidza, H. 1979. Phenology of some trees and shrubs in Sengwa Wildlife Research area, Zimbabwe-Rhodesia. *South African Journal of Wildlife Research* 9: 47-54.

Gwynne, M.D. 1969. The nutritive values of *Acacia* pods in relation to *Acacia* seed distribution by ungulates. *East African Wildlife Journal* 7: 176-178.

Hall-Martin, A.J. & Basson, W.D. 1975. Seasonal chemical composition of the diet of Transvaal Lowveld giraffe. *Journal of the South African Wildlife Management Association* 5:19-21.

Haro, G.O. & Oba, G. 1993. Dynamics of *Acacia tortilis* litter in the Turkwel river floodplain woodlands, Kenya. *African Journal of Ecology* 31: 200-209.

Hoffman, M.T., Cowling, R.M., Douie, C. & Pierce, S.M. 1989. Seed predation and germination of *Acacia erioloba* in the Kuised River Valley, Namib desert. *South African Journal of Botany* 55: 103-106.

Högberg, P. 1986. Nitrogen-fixation and nutrient relations in savanna woodland trees (Tanzania). *Journal of Applied Ecology* 23: 675-688.

Holz, G., Morley, M. & Schreuder, W. 1989. Pathogenicity of *Phoma glomerata, P. cava, P. eupyrena* and *Cytospora chrysosperma* on Blackthorn (*Acacia mellifera* subsp. *detinens*). *Agricola* 7: 37-42.

Holz, G. & Schreuder, W. 1989. Dieback of Blackthorn (*Acacia mellifera* subsp. *detinens*) in South West Africa. *Agricola* 7: 32-36.

Kalemera, M.C. 1989. Observations on feeding preference of elephants in the *Acacia tortilis* woodland of Lake Manyara National Park, Tanzania. *African Journal of Ecology* 27: 325-333.

Kennard, D.G. & Walker, B.H. 1973. Relationship between tree canopy cover and *Panicum maximum* in the vicinity of Fort Victoria. *Rhodesia Journal of Agricicultural Research* 11: 145-153.

Knoop, W.T. & Walker, B.H. 1985. Interactions of woody and herbaceous vegetation in a southern African savanna. *Journal of Ecology* 73: 235-253.

Miller, M.F. 1995. *Acacia* seed survival, seed germination and seedling growth following pod consumption by large herbivores and seed chewing rodents. *African Journal of Ecology* 33: 194-210.

Milton, S.J. 1987. Phenology of seven *Acacia* species in South Africa. *South African Journal of Wildlife Research* 17: 1-6.

Milton, S.J. 1988. The effect of pruning on shoot production and basal increments of *Acacia tortilis. South African Journal of Botany* 54: 109-117.

Novellie, P. 1989. Tree size as a factor influencing leaf emergence and leaf fall in *Acacia nigrescens* and *Combretum apiculatum* in the Kruger National Park. *Koedoe* 32: 95-99.

Moore, A., Van Niekerk, J.P., Knight, I.W. & Wessels, H. 1985. The effect of Tebuthiuron on the vegetation of the thorn bushveld of the northern Cape – a preliminary report. *Journal of the Grassland Society of Southern Africa* 2: 7-10.

Mucunguzi, P. 1995. Effects of bruchid beetles on germination and establishment of *Acacia* species. *African Journal of Ecology* 33:64-70.

O'Connor, T.G. 1995. *Acacia karroo* invasion of grassland: environmental and biotic effects influencing seedling emergence and establishment. *Oecologia* 103:214-223.

Owen-Smith, N. 1989. *Megaherbivores: The influence of very large body size on ecology.* Cambridge University Press, Cambridge.

Owen-Smith, N. & Cooper, S.M. 1987. Palatability of woody plants to browsing ruminants in a southern African savanna. *Ecology* 68: 319-331.

Owen-Smith, N. & Cooper, S.M. 1988. Plant palatability and its implications for plant-herbivore relations. *Journal of the Grassland Society of Southern Africa* 5: 72-75.

Pellew, R.A.P. 1983. The impacts of elephant, giraffe and fire upon the *Acacia tortilis* woodlands of the Serengeti. *African Journal of Ecology* 21: 41-74.

Pellew, R.A.P. & Southgate, B.J. 1984. The parasitism of *Acacia tortilis* seeds in the Serengeti. *African Journal of Ecology* 22: 73-75.

Pooly, E. 1993. *The complete guide to trees of Natal, Zululand and Transkei.* Natal Flora Publication Trust, Durban.

Ross, J.H. 1979. A conspectus of the African *Acacia* species. *Memoirs of the Botanical Survey of South Africa* No 44. National Botanical Institute, Pretoria.

Roux, D.G. 1972. Recent advances in the chemistry and chemical utilization of the natural condensed tannins. *Phytochemistry* 11: 1 219-1 230.

Rutherford, M.C. 1979. Plant-based techniques for determining available browse and browse utilization: a review. *Botanical Review* 45: 203-228.

Rutherford, M.C. 1980. Field identification of roots of woody plants of the savanna ecosystem study area, Nylsvley. *Bothalia* 13: 171-184.

Rutherford, M.C. & Westfall, R.H. 1994. Biomes of Southern Africa - an objective categorization. *Mcmoirs of thc Botanical Survey of South Africa* No. 63. National Botanical Institute, Pretoria.

Sabiiti, E.N. & Wein, R.W. 1988. Fire behaviour and the invasion of *Acacia sieberiana* into savanna grassland openings. *African Journal of Ecology* 26: 301-313.

Scholes, R.J. 1987. *Response of three semi-arid savannas on contrasting soils to the removal of the woody component.* Ph.D-thesis, University of the Witwatersrand, Johannesburg.

Smit, G.N. 1990. Cold damage of woody plants in the Sourish Mixed Bushveld. *Journal of the Grassland Society of Southern Africa* 7: 196-200.

Smit, G.N., Rethman, N.F.G. & Moore, A. 1996. Review article: Vegetative growth, reproduction, browse production and response to tree clearing of woody plants in African savanna. *African Journal of Range and Forage Science* 2: 78-88.

Smit, G.N. & Swart, J.S. 1994. The influence of leguminous and non-leguminous woody plants on the herbaceous layer and soil under varying competition regimes in Mixed Bushveld. *African Journal of Range and Forage Science* 11: 27-33.

Smit, G.N. & Van Romburgh, K.S.K. 1993. Relations between tree height and the associated occurrence of *Panicum maximum* Jacq. in Sourish Mixed Bushveld. *African Journal of Range and Forage Science* 10: 151-153.

Smith, T.M. & Goodman, P.S. 1986. The effect of competition on the structure and dynamics of *Acacia* savannas in southern Africa. *Journal of Ecology* 74: 1 031-1 044.

Smith, T.M. & Goodman, P.S. 1987. Successional dynamics in an *Acacia nilotica-Euclea divinorum* savannah in southern Africa. *Journal of Ecology* 75: 603-610.

Smith, T.M. & Shackleton, S.E. 1988. The effect of shading on the establishment and growth of *Acacia tortilis* seedlings. *South African Journal of Botany* 54: 375-379.

Steyn, M. 1994. *S.A. Acacias - identification guide*. Published by author.

Stuart-Hill, G.C., Tainton, N.N. & Barnard, H.J. 1987. The influence of an *Acacia karroo* tree on grass production in its vicinity. *Journal of the Grassland Society of Southern Africa* 4: 83-88.

Stuart-Hill, G.C. & Tainton, N.M. 1988. Browse and herbage production in the eastern Cape Thornveld in response to tree size and defoliation frequency. *Journal of the Grassland Society of Southern Africa* 5: 42-47.

Stuart-Hill, G.C. & Tainton, N.M. 1989. Water utilization patterns around isolated *Acacia karroo* trees in the False Thornveld of the eastern Cape. *Journal of the Grassland Society of Southern Africa* 6: 195-204.

Sweet, R.J. & Mphinyane, W. 1986. Preliminary observations on the ability of goats to control post-burning regrowth in *Acacia nigrescens/Combretum apiculatum* savanna in Botswana. *Journal of the Grassland Society of Southern Africa* 3: 79-84.

Teague, W.R. 1983. The expected response of *Acacia karroo* Hayne to moisture stress and defoliation. *Proceedings of the Grassland Society of Southern Africa* 18: 147-150.

Teague, W.R. 1989. Effect of intensity and frequency of defoliation on aerial growth and carbohydrate reserve levels of *Acacia karroo* plants. *Journal of the Grassland Society of Southern Africa* 6: 132-138.

Teague, W.R. 1989. The response of *Acacia karroo* plants to defoliation of the upper or lower canopy. *Journal of the Grassland Society of Southern Africa* 6: 225-229.

Teague, W.R. 1989. Patterns of selection of *Acacia karroo* by goats and changes in tannin levels and *in vitro* digestibility following defoliation. *Journal of the Grassland Society of Southern Africa*. 6: 230-235.

Teague, W.R. & Smit, G.N. 1992. Relations between woody and herbaceous components and the effect of bush-clearing in southern African savannas. *Journal of the Grassland Society of Southern Africa* 9: 60-71.

Teague, W.R. & Walker, B.H. 1988. Growth patterns and annual growth cycle of *Acacia karroo* Hayne in relation to water stress. 1. Leaf and shoot growth. *Journal of the Grassland Society of Southern Africa* 5: 85-95.

Teague, W.R. & Walker, B.H. 1988. Effect of intensity of defoliation by goats at different phenophases on leaf and shoot growth of *Acacia karroo* Hayne. *Journal of the Grassland Society of Southern Africa* 5: 197-206.

Timberlake, J. 1980. *Handbook of Botswana Acacias*. Ministry of Agriculture, Botswana.

Trollope, W.S.W. 1992. Control of bush encroachment with fire in the savanna areas of South Africa. Prestige farmers day proceedings 1991-1992. Special publication: Grassland Society of southern Africa. pp 8-11.

Van der Walt, P.T. & Le Riche, E.A.N. 1984. The influence of veld fire on an *Acacia erioloba* community in the Kalahari Gemsbok National Park. *Koedoe Supplement* 103-106.

Van Vegten, J.A. 1983. Thornbush invasion in a savanna ecosystem in eastern Botswana. *Vegetatio* 56: 3-7.

Van Wyk, B. & Van Wyk, P. 1997. *Field guide to the trees of southern Africa*. Struik Publishers, Cape Town.

Van Wyk, J.J.P., Bosch, O.J.H. & Kruger, J.A. 1969. Droogtebeskadiging van bosveldbome en groot struike. *Proceedings of the Grassland Society of Southern Africa* 4: 61-65.

Van Wyk, P. 1996. *Field guide to the trees of the Kruger National Park*. 3 rd edition. Struik Publishers, Cape Town.

Venter, F. & Venter, J. 1996. *Making the most of indigenous trees*. Briza Publications, Pretoria.

Von Breitenbach, F. 1990. *National List of Indiginous Trees*. Dendrological Foundation.

Wand, S.J.E., Midgley, G.F. & Musil, C.F. 1996. Physiological and growth responses of two African species, *Acacia karroo* and *Themeda triandra*, to combined increases in CO_2 and UV-B radiation. *Physiologia Plantarum* 98: 882-890.

Young, T.P. & Lindsay, W.K. 1988. Role of even-age population structure in the disappearance of *Acacia xanthophloea* woodlands. *African Journal of Ecology* 26: 69-72.

INDEX TO NAMES

Current names (both common names and scientific names) printed in bold type

221

223

Millimetres